# INTIMACY

JUNGIAN ODYSSEY SERIES • VOLUME I

# INTIMACY

## Venturing the Uncertainties of the Heart

*Published under the auspices of*
ISAPZURICH
(International School of
Analytical Psychology Zürich)
AGAP Post-Graduate Jungian Training

*Edited by*
Isabelle Meier, Stacy Wirth, & John Hill

*Preface by*
Nancy Cater

*Foreword by*
Murray Stein

Spring Journal Books
New Orleans, Louisiana

Published by
Spring Journal, Inc.
627 Ursulines Street #7
New Orleans, Louisiana 70116
Tel.: (504) 524-5117
Website: www.springjournalandbooks.com

Cover design:
Stacy Wirth

Cover layout:
Elsbeth Knaus, EKonText,
ekontext@bluewin.ch

Cover photograph:
*Bergfrühling im Flosch, Beatenberg, Switzerland*
by Fritz Bieri,
www.beatenbergbilder.ch

Printed in Canada
Text printed on acid-free paper

Library of Congress Cataloging-in-Publication Data Pending

Grateful acknowledgment is made to the respective publishers, institutions, and individuals for permission to reprint the following:

*Bergfrühling im Flosch, Beatenberg Switzerland*, cover photo, © 2008 by Fritz Bieri, reprinted by permission of Fritz Bieri.

"Zwei Berge gibt es," by Paul Klee in *Paul Klee, Gedichte*, Herausgeber Felix Klee, ©1960/2005, Arche Verlag AG, Zurich-Hamburg. English translation, "The Two Mountains," by Stacy Wirth, translated by permission of Arche Verlag.

"Chalet Heimat," photographer and location unknown, in Kurt Schmocker, *St. Beatenberg und wie sie früher war*, © 1988/1995, Verlag Schaefli AG, scanned and reproduced by permission of Alfred Stäheli, Schaefli & Maurer AG.

*The Artist at the Window* (1909, 70), Paul Klee, location and owner unknown, image provided by Zentrum Paul Klee, Bern, © 2008, Prolitteris, Zurich, reproduced by permission of Prolitteris, Zurich.

*St. Jerome in His Study*, (engraving, b/w photo), Albrecht Dürer (1471-1528), Bibliotheque Nationale, Paris, France, Giraudon, image license by the Bridgeman Art Library, Berlin, out of copyright, reproduced by permission of the Bridgeman Art Library, Berlin.

*St. Beatenberg 1909*, Paul Klee, Sammlung E. W. K. Bern, image provided by Stämpfli Verlag AG, © 2008, Prolitteris, Zurich, reproduced by permission of Prolitteris, Zurich.

*In the Quarry* (1913, 135), Paul Klee, Zentrum Paul Klee, Bern, image provided by Zentrum Paul Klee, © 2008, Prolitteris, Zurich, reproduced by permission of Prolitteris, Zurich.

*The Niesen* (1915, 250), Paul Klee, Kunstmuseum Bern, Hermann und Margrit Rupf-Stiftung, image provided by Zentrum Paul Klee, Bern, © 2008, Prolitteris, Zurich, reproduced by permission of Prolitteris, Zurich.

*Foehn Wind in Marc's Garden* (1915, 102), Paul Klee, Städtische Galerie im Lenbachhaus, Munich, image provided by Lenbachhaus Kunstbau, © 2008, Prolitteris, Zurich, reproduced by permission of Prolitteris, Zurich.

*Cacodaemonic* (1916, 73), Paul Klee, Zentrum Paul Klee, image provided by Zentrum Paul Klee, © 2008, Prolitteris, Zurich, reproduced by permission of Prolitteris, Zurich.

*Eros* (1923), Paul Klee, Museum Sammlung Rosengart Luzern, image provided by Stiftung Rosengart, © 2008, Prolitteris, Zurich, reproduced by permission of Prolitteris, Zurich.

*Carnival in the Mountains* (1924, 114), Paul Klee, Zentrum Paul Klee, image provided by Zentrum Paul Klee, © 2008, Prolitteris, Zurich, reproduced by permission of Prolitteris, Zurich.

# DEDICATION

*This book is dedicated*
*to all who undertake the epic voyage of soul,*
*and in particular to the students, analysts, and visitors of ISAPZURICH*
*who gathered from all over the world in Beatenberg*
*to explore the uncertainties*
*of the heart.*

# Contents

## PART III: EROTIC POWER AND THE HAPPILY-EVER-AFTER



## PART IV: UNCERTAIN HEART—UNBOUNDED HEART

# Acknowledgments

Our deepest gratitude goes to Nancy Cater and Michael Mendis of Spring Journal Books, who so confidently encouraged the idea of a Jungian Odyssey Series and guided us through the publication of this first book with untiring patience and good humor.

We are especially grateful to Penny Busetto (Cape Town), Nancy Krieger (France) and Katy Remark (Zürich) for working with the authors to edit the original manuscripts. Besides accomplishing this job within a very limited time frame, the three proceeded with great engagement and interest in the project. Special thanks are due to Stefan Boëthius (Zürich), Anna Bourgeois (Geneva), and again Katy Remark for their ongoing support as members of the Jungian Odyssey 2008 Committee.

Without the support of many ISAP students each year, our ship would be challenged to remain afloat. Among those—too many to mention here—we thank the ones who have remained from year to year: Nathalie de Béthune (Belgium), for her invaluable and continuing technical backing; Gérard Blum (Switzerland), who with great aplomb has always ensured that our guests find their way to ISAP and points beyond; and Mary Thomlinson (Canada), for her vigilant attention to the matter of course allocations and to making sure that the winds of change do not blow us off course.

Last, but certainly not least, we are indebted to the following individuals in Zürich who worked along with John Hill from 2004 to 2006 to create the first Jungian Odyssey, thereby preparing the ground for future Jungian Odysseys and the publication of this Jungian Odyssey Series: Cedrus Monte—who took on the responsibility of organizing the ship's launching in the dark and chill of February 2004—with his crew of Denise Blum, Suzanne Boëthius, Eileen Nemeth, and Constance Steiner-Blake.

John Hill, Isabelle Meier, Stacy Wirth
2008

# *List of Illusrations*

# *Preface*

Spring Journal Books is honored to publish for ISAPZURICH, the International School of Analytical Psychology in Zürich, Switzerland, the Jungian Odyssey Series, of which *Intimacy: Venturing the Uncertainties of the Heart* is the inaugural volume. The aim of this new Series is to publish annually a book composed of the papers presented at ISAPZURICH's Jungian Odyssey conferences, which are held each spring in a different and beautiful location in Switzerland and are based upon a theme that arises from the *genius loci*, the spirit of the place where the conference convenes.

Embarking on this collaborative publishing odyssey with ISAPZURICH seems particularly fortuitous, as it brings Spring into partnership with an institution with whom we feel a natural affinity. Strongly rooted in the history and traditional foundations of Jungian psychology, Spring and ISAPZURICH both share a spirit of adventure and the courage to chart and navigate new courses on their respective voyages.

The year 2004 was pivotal for both ISAPZURICH and Spring: it marked the founding of ISAPZURICH as well as Spring's move to its new home in New Orleans and the creation of the Spring Journal Books imprint. Both Spring and ISAPZURICH have continued on parallel creative and stimulating journeys since then. As ISAPZURICH developed its training program in Zürich and envisioned and initiated, in 2006, the innovative Jungian Odyssey conferences, Spring Journal Books developed its own new projects, launching two book series and publishing over 40 titles in Jungian psychology and related fields. Spring is delighted that our paths have now converged and that we can cast off on this new adventure together.

Spring's enthusiasm about publishing the Jungian Odyssey Series also arises from the imaginative way in which the Jungian Odysseys allow the theme of each year's program to emerge from the *genius loci*, the spirit of the place where the conference is to be held. Spring has a history of publishing works about the psychology of place, most recently a special 2-volume set of the journal on the theme of Psyche and Nature, and the books *Terrapsychology: Re-engaging the Soul of Place*, by ecopsychologist Craig Chalquist, and *Psyche and the City* (forthcoming 2009), a collection of essays looking at 20 great cities of the world through a depth-psychological lens, edited by Jungian analyst Tom Singer. Publishing the Jungian Odyssey Series provides Spring with a creative opportunity to further its commitment to this important topic and to offer to the Jungian community outstanding and cutting-edge work in the field.

Last but not least, publishing a book series that invokes the image of an odyssey has special resonance for Spring, since we recently had to confront the loss of home and deal with the longing to return home, both traditional "odyssean" themes. The oldest Jungian psychology journal in the world, Spring—like the Jungian Odyssey programs themselves, which change location each time—has followed a nomadic path. Spring has called a number of places home since its creation by the Analytical Psychology Club in New York in 1941: New York (1941-1969), Zürich (1970-1978), Dallas (1978-1988), Connecticut (1988-2003), and New Orleans (2004-present). Just one year after *Spring Journal*, with eagerness and energy, moved its offices to New Orleans and launched the Spring Journal Books imprint, Hurricane Katrina, a cataclysmic event of mythic proportions, struck the city on August 29, 2005 and left its mark indelibly on Spring. Since that event, even though Spring has maintained its New Orleans mailing address, the actual books and journals are stored outside the city so as to avoid damage from future storms, and Spring's editor and staff have found safe harbor in various other ports, working from offices in widespread locales, including New York City, Colorado, and Canada.

While the publishing output of Spring has, despite (or perhaps even because of) these challenges, greatly increased (no capsizing!) over this period, it has necessarily been a time of reviewing our navigational charts and plotting new courses. Luckily, Katrina did not leave Spring all washed up or beached, nor did we by any means abandon ship. Instead, through hard work and many serendipities, we managed to remain afloat and on an even keel, sighting more than one rainbow on the horizon. It is in this spirit of optimism and positive vision that Spring celebrates its collaboration with ISAPZURICH and the renewal of its earlier connection to the enchanting city of Zürich, the home of analytical psychology, where Spring made its home during a vital time in its history.

It has been a pleasure to work with Stacy Wirth, Isabelle Meier, and John Hill, the editors of the Jungian Odyssey Series, and we extend our thanks to Murray Stein, the current President of ISAPZURICH (who some years ago, as an analyst-in-training, worked at Spring when it was located in Zürich), for bringing Spring and ISAPZURICH together.

Nancy Cater
Publisher, Spring Journal Books

# Foreword

The Jungian Odyssey was launched in 2006 as an integral part of the post-graduate training program at the International School of Analytical Psychology, Zürich (ISAPZURICH). Since then, the Odyssey has continued as an annual, week-long retreat that wraps up each Spring Semester. Taking place each year in a different Swiss locale of extraordinary beauty, the Odyssey calls first for immersion in the *genius loci*, the spirit of the place. Indeed, this spirit inspires each year's theme, which is developed in the daily program of lectures, seminars, and experiential workshops led by members of ISAP's internationally renowned faculty and visiting guest scholars. The retreat's setting—with lodging, shared meals, excursions, meditation periods, and hikes in the surrounding landscapes—fosters intensive interpersonal exchange as well as quiet personal reflection.

The Odyssey as such is not just for ISAP students, but opens the week of study to anyone interested in learning more about Jungian psychology—making of this event a convening place for individuals from all around the world and many walks of life. For those exploring the option of full training at ISAP, the Odyssey offers a unique chance to evaluate the program and faculty, and to query ISAP students about their experiences. Immediately preceding the Odyssey, visitors may even opt to attend the Prelude, a week of lectures and seminars at ISAP's home campus in Zürich. Included are courses that introduce the newcomer to Jungian thought and some of the basic perspectives, ideas, and terminologies that characterize the field. Prelude participants also take in and enjoy the city of Zürich before moving on to the Odyssey proper and to a place of scenic beauty and wonder. Notably, many visitors return to ISAP for shorter or longer periods in order to take up personal work such as analysis or supervision and to study further the immense implications of Jungian psychology for themselves and for the world.

Great efforts are made by the planners of the program to bring the best possible speakers and teachers to the chosen locus and to make each Odyssey an experience to remember for all who attend and participate. In the course of time, the Odyssey has become an annual celebratory feast of the rich fare that ISAP offers at a more measured pace during the school year. The papers that follow in this volume testify, I believe, to the opulent diversity and wide range of opportunities offered by ISAPZURICH and the Jungian Odyssey for studying the many different aspects of C. G. Jung's analytical psychology.

Murray Stein
President, ISAPZURICH
Zürich
September 28, 2008

# Introduction: A Compass for the Journey

*Isabelle Meier, Stacy Wirth, John Hill*

It is our great pleasure to introduce this first publication of Jungian Odyssey lectures—those of Odyssey 2008, exploring "Intimacy: Venturing the Uncertainties of the Heart." Everyone who attends the Jungian Odyssey undertakes a personal odyssey, in a manner of speaking. At the very least, he or she makes the epic journey to the remote region of Switzerland in which the Odyssey takes place each year. Upon arrival, one enters the retreat setting, one begins to immerse oneself in the surrounding landscapes and the spirit of the place. Thus begins the week of intensive study, contemplation, and exchange with a highly diverse group of individuals from all over the world.

Odyssey 2008 took place in Beatenberg, a tiny Bernese village nestled on a plateau 3,937 feet (1,200 meters) above sea level, overlooking the glistening Lake Thun and across from the daunting peaks of the Eiger, Mönch, and Jungfrau. Beatenberg also features a network of dripstone caves, which penetrate deep beneath the earth's surface and extend into the belly of Mount Beatus. Here, as legend has it, a mighty dragon dwelt, threatening the whole area until, in the 6th century, the Irish monk Beatus expelled the beast and then made of the caves his lifelong retreat.

## Sounds and Symmetries of Belonging

The heights and depths of Beatenberg, with its dramatic views and inward mysteries, inspired Irish theologian, singer, and special Odyssey guest Nóirín Ní Riain to tune her ear and heart to the earth around her. From the three majestic mountain peaks, from within the erstwhile dragon's cave and monk's retreat, from the surrounding meadows, Ní Riain heard songs that cried out to be sung, that stirred her to bring their music to us, and which in turn drew us to sing with her. Her essay here is a humble tribute to that magical shared experience and to the other sources of her inspiration—not least to W. B. Yeats and Emma Jung.

Paul Brutsche, too, tunes into the spirit of the place, exploring its meaning for the artist Paul Klee. It happens that Beatenberg was the site of the young artist's first love—at the age of 12, he had here his first conscious experience of the uncertainties of the heart! Richly illustrated with images from Klee's life and work, Brutsche's discussion demonstrates Klee's lifelong connection to the area and his intimate rapport with the earth, which inspired his use of the image of the mountain to represent the uncertainties of life that divide the soul yet engender a yearning for transcendence.

John Hill—a native Irishman transplanted to Zürich—uses his own personal experience as a starting point to establish a link between landscape and the experience of home. Accordingly, he finds home in the intricately interwoven threads of place, the echoes of ancestors and kin, and the longing for paradise. Not forgotten is the painful experience of homesickness, which is often closely tied to the land—as is demonstrated in the experience of Swiss cattle herders and their plaintive songs, which were often repressed by the authorities because of the powerful feelings of nostalgia they evoked. Hill continues to consider home as a complex, feeling-toned phenomenon, which is recognized as such by scholars in philosophy, anthropology, and religion.

## Radical Body—Mother and Child

If locus and home arouse feelings of intimacy, such feelings arise just as much in the relationship between mother and child. Raffaella Ada Colombo explores this aspect by coupling neurobiology with analytical and developmental psychology. In particular, she focuses on affect attunement, especially as it evolves in the intimate vocal play between mother and infant. Colombo suggests that, "vocalizations and, later on, words as transitional phenomena, do not truly belong either to the self, or to the other." Rather, the spontaneous exchange of "ooohs" and "aaahs" belongs to a mutual domain, here identified as the mother archetype, which, in ideal circumstances, provides the vessel of intimacy required for the infant's emerging sense of self.

That the intimacy of the mother-infant dyad can harbor shadow is shown in the story of a child born with club feet. Kathrin Asper seeks to understand this through the myth of the crippled god, Hephaistos. In doing so, she sheds light on an archetypal relationship that is particularly colored by the child's bodily disfigurement and disability, and painfully wrought in cycles of maternal love and rejection. Medical procedures further disrupt natural bonding processes, contributing to the child's profound sense of being unworthy and unloved. Asper places such experiences in the realm of trauma, which "can be activated at any time later in life." Short of adequate psychotherapeutic intervention, she stakes hope in the archetypal idea that "there is always a place in heaven for Hephaistos."

## Erotic Power and the Happily-Ever-After

Without a doubt, the experience of intimacy can encompass love and hate, closeness and distance, belonging and yearning-to-belong. Ursula Wirtz takes up such shadowy nuances, amplifying George Berkeley's dictum, *esse est percipi*—to be is to be perceived. Even if intimacy has caused wounds or is entirely absent, the gleam in the eye of the other holds the potential to awaken healing eros, and thus also the capacity to experience previously unknown intimacy. The analytic encounter is no exception—and indeed Wirtz pleads the case for admitting the bitter-sweet power of Eros into the process of psychological growth and individuation.

The myth of Eros and Psyche is the lively point of departure for Mario Jacoby's reflections on the depth of eros's origin and its ambivalent creative-and-wounding power. Humorously noting that the index to Jung's *Collected Works* contains no reference to intimacy, Jacoby turns instead to Jung's comments on the "kinship libido," which focus on the yearning for mutuality in relationship. Jacoby proceeds to examine the infant's "innate sensual joy," as well as developmental processes that can, when disrupted, disturb the adult's capacity to experience intimate relationship. Finally, he underscores the value of intimate relatedness in the analytic transference/countertransference—but he also notes the obstacles and complexities involved, considering not least the impact of the analyst's own personal complexes.

Casting his dry wit on the subject, Allan Guggenbühl sees love as a force that not only puts us marvelously in touch with our bodies and the sparkle of life, but also "makes us crazy." Thus, we can also fall into the love complex, into tragic love, hysterical love, dual-narcissistic love—all of which sooner or later lead to dysfunction in everyday life, not to mention lost relationships. Is there a way of coping, or even a cure?

Guggenbühl provocatively submits that such relationships must fail—because when "transcendental qualities emerge, as in love, we are lost. The gods allow us to peek at other realities every now and then, but they do not want us to get too accustomed to them."

Drawing on history, biography, and the arts, Urs H. Mehlin devotes himself to the eternally recurring concerns of "intimacy and estrangement and the frightful proximity between love and hate." He carefully navigates the range of emotion arising in these straits, and goes on to develop a typology of lovers, thereby illuminating ideas and behaviors that in effect avoid or destroy the experience of intimacy. While we may hope and struggle for the "happily ever after," Mehlin cautions that intimacy "in relationships is not a permanent gluing together of the two partners, but rather a constant circling" around a mystery, which he calls the "Relational Self."

Deborah Egger-Biniores speaks of her own experience of being directly involved in the search for intimacy—in encounters with others, and with her own soul. Reflecting on these matters in the light of modern research on core gender identity, she challenges the terms typically employed among Jungians; in contrast to Jung's binary, "heterosexist" animus/anima, Egger prefers the unified *syzygy*. This image, she notes, not only resonates better with same-sex partners and transgendered, homosexual, and bisexual individuals, but it also more authentically mirrors the feeling of soul, with its comingling of feminine and masculine energies. The *syzygy* as such proclaims the imperative for both men *and* women to embody the divine marriage and to live and grow in accordance with its fluid dynamics—both as individuals and in relationship.

## Uncertain Heart—Unbounded Heart

Murray Stein creates a protected vessel for approaching the link between intimacy and transcendence when he asks, "Are we not breaching the walls of a sacred *temenos* when we talk with strangers in public about intimacy?" With due reverence, he lifts the veil on a number of relationships in which people become "deeply absorbed"—providing us a glimpse not only of relationships between intimates but also of relationships with nature, ideas, dreams, and religious symbols. Notably, these all contain the "silence and liminal space" that are needed for intimacy to intensify and assume the ineffable qualities of the uncanny, of mystery and magic, and of transformative power. Thus, Stein observes, relationship itself can be lived as the symbol and transcendent function that "breaches the boundary between inner and outer, psyche and world."

The American analyst Thomas J. Kapacinskas was another special guest at Odyssey 2008. He, too, tackles the subject of transcendence when he compares the initiation pathways of C. G. Jung and the philosopher and mystic Simone Weil. In a highly detailed, in-depth analysis, he sheds light on the different ways in which these two individuals sustained unconsoled suffering in order to realize "the necessity of the void and of affliction in bringing about ... wholeness-generating mystical experience."

Dariane Pictet orients our view to the east as she notes the rise of fundamentalism in Islam, counterbalanced by the worldwide surge in popularity of the Sufi mystic Mawlana Jalal-ad-Din Rumi. In this very moving contribution, Pictet describes Rumi as the "poet of longing," for whom "the heart is the center of all transformation, the seat of spirituality and compassion." Pictet follows Rumi's life and poetry, which point to suffering, longing, purification, and silencing, which Rumi calls the "polishing of the heart"—that labor that alone grounds and prepares the ego to open up to the "infinitely expanded dimensions" of Self and divine love.

In a similar vein, Bernard Sartorius introduces the mystic Ibn 'Arabi and his erotic, divinely inspired poems in *Tarjuman al-Ashwaq* (*The Interpreter of Desires*). With ardent passion of his own, Sartorius conveys the poet's wisdom, underlining the reality of the heart, which transcends reason and morality. The pathway to wholeness is constituted in the lived experience of erotic love, unfulfilled and opening to the unknown—which in itself marks the presence of the Divine. Sartorius suggests that our avoidance of uncertainty in relationships and in ourselves may amount to a fundamental error, for according to Ibn 'Arabi, as Sartorius puts it, "Those uncertainties are in themselves the answer to your quest for certainty. There is no firmer ground beyond the uncertainties than the uncertainties themselves."

---

In sum, the authors circumambulate the many guises of the heart and the many ways in which intimacy enters our lives—or seems to vanish from them, or remain absent altogether. None stakes a claim to ultimate definitions or conclusions. On the contrary, all maintain a deep respect for the mystery of intimacy, for the uncertain, the unknown, perhaps the unknowable. We hope that these essays will communicate the richness of Odyssey 2008 and, more importantly, inspire in the reader deeper musings on intimacy and the uncertainties of the heart.

# Part I

# Sounds and Symmetries of Belonging

Nóirín Ní Riain, D.Theol., is an internationally acclaimed Irish singer who has performed worldwide. A theologian and musicologist, she was awarded the first doctorate in theology from the University of Limerick in 2003. For her thesis, *Towards a Theology of Listening*, she coined a new term, "theosony"—from the Greek *theos* (God) and the Latin *sonans* (sounding). She is currently writing a book on the subject, which will be published shortly. The Irish National television station (RTE) recently broadcast a major documentary on her life and work. Author of books, articles, and CDs, she has entertained visiting diplomats on many occasions.

1

# The Ear of the Heart: Weaving a Tapestry of Transformative Listening in Song and Story

*Nóirín Ní Riain*

An "odyssey" today is any series of *wanderings*—and I wandered from Ireland to a spectacular Swiss mountain village at nearly four thousand feet high, Lake Thun at our feet, the triple mountain Goddesses, the Eiger, Monch, and Jungfrau, above our heads. This extravagant, breathtaking panorama, understandably, the love of Paul Klee's life, is called Beatenberg.

"Three" is a mystical number—a digit that embodies the mysterious in many world traditions. "One" thing alone symbolizes limitation; "two" bits and pieces make for balance and an exclusion of all else. But when three are grouped together, the realm of the imagination, of pure possibility, of intimacy is unveiled. The configuration of three kept recurring in many different guises on this expedition.

This was the third year of the ISAPZURICH Odyssey and it symbolized for me the power of a triennium of success and Spirit, where the unexpected, the surprising dwelt among us throughout.

The Irish-Swiss spiritual connection was already here before me. Beatenberg takes its name from a 3rd-century Irish hermit who, having been baptized in England by the Apostle Barnabas, was sent to Switzerland with St. Columba. No small wonder that he choose to live in solitude here in this transformative landscape that was later to shape Jung's perspectives. Beatus, who, legend has it, banished a mighty dragon from a local cave at the mouth of the lake of the Dragon, is now venerated as Switzerland's first apostle and his feast day is celebrated on May 9, yet another configuration of three. "Beatus" means "blessed" in Latin, and is the very first word of the Psalter (150 psalms, three times fifty), which he would have chanted daily. Indeed he was blessed to spend his days in such cosmic beauty of "hollow lands and hilly lands."

So, I was bringing it all back home. Glenstal Abbey, where I reside, has *three* patron saints: Joseph, Patrick, and Beatus's traveling companion, Columba. The day before I traveled to Beatenberg, a Greek icon to Saint Patrick (who banished snakes—i.e., miniature dragons—from Ireland) arrived at the monastery here to take its place in the monastic icon collection.

I presented and led a workshop at this conference on a feast day that is important for me—the Visitation of Mary to her cousin Elizabeth. The title of our conference here, taking place at the same time, perfectly fit the feast—*Intimacy: Venturing the Uncertainties of the Heart.* "Beatus" is Elizabeth's first word to Mary in their heart-to-heart meeting, during which the women and their two womb residents listened keenly to all around them.

My reason for being here, my role, was suddenly evident. We were simply to listen with the "ear of the heart"—as another monk, Benedict, advises in the first word of his 5th-century rule. Jung's four psychological functions, particularly intuition and sensation, are primarily, though not exclusively, the work of the aural senses. Thomas Aquinas had it right on this one. *Nihil est intellectus quod non prius fuerit in sensu.* (*Nothing is in the understanding that was not earlier in the senses*). Only that which is perceived through the senses is real. "Listen that you might live," Isaiah, the prophet of the Judeo-Christian tradition, puts it. We were to be in the here/hear and now for this week of the inmost sharings of heart-work. So during morning meditations, presentations, and workshops—all in earshot of the three silent giant mountains—we explored new ways of listening, experiencing sounds and silence together.

## *Modus Vivendi*—Odyssey Ways of Being in the Hear and Now

The uncertainties of the heart are the theme of a greater part of the repertoire of traditional Irish songs. G. K. Chesterton referred to this obliquely when he wrote that "all our wars are merry and all our songs are sad." There is truth in the song reference, although no one can really argue that wars can be merry.

Through the chronological day time at Beatenberg, I listened keenly to everyone, speakers and participants alike. Then in silent time, the *kronos* of day and night dreams, I tuned in to ancestral voices that subconsciously visited me through songs. These ancestors carefully selected and assembled voices/sounds (one word for both in Hebrew and Greek) through the following repertoire. Songs of unrequited love, lost youth, lamentation, fear, loneliness sounded in my heart and became theme songs to accompany the various moments. I sang them out whenever it seemed appropriate.

Four songs in particular wanted to be sung. These embody, reveal, and heal our ego-ideal, our archetypal inner selves, fears, needs, beliefs, and desires. Here are ancient myths, stories, and his/herstories that affect the rhythm of life—the creative expression of a people, which leads to transformation. These songs were intimately concerned with or connected to our conference on the poetics of intimacy and engaging the mysteries of love and the heart. There is an ancient Irish proverb: *Mo scéal féin, scéal gach duine—My story, everyone's story.* In these songs you can hear your own breath breathing into the song.

"Dónal óg" is the poignant four-phrased song from Connemara of a young girl whose lover has vanished into the mists without trace or sound:

> I whistled and called [for you] again and again, there was no answer, just one little lamb sadly bleating.

It is a tale of unrequited/unfulfilled love making contact with the spiritual. This young girl is re-echoing the ancient Christian cult of the Céili De, in which one's being is subconsciously wedded first and foremost to God. All other relationships are secondary and peripheral. Her final *crie de coeur*:

> You have taken east and west from me, you have taken my future and my past from me, you have taken the sun and moon from me, and my greatest fear is that you have taken my God from me.

The fear seems insurmountable, yet hope is in sight. The Erasmus saying that meant so much to C. G. and Emma Jung harmonizes with the heart of this song: *Vocatus atque non vocatus, Deus aderit* (Called or not called, God will be present).

"An Caoineadh" is the pre-Christian lamentation of a mother for her child who has died. Not only could it be named the oldest fragment of keening in Ireland, but it re-echoes and re-sounds some of the most ancient cosmic reverberations. The shattering silence out of which each phrase originates and has its destiny is woven into the power of this song, which has to do with deepest healing of horrific heartache that no parent should have to endure:

> Agus anuriadh, níl duine ar bith agam. Ochón is ochón ó!
> (And next year, there is no one at all here for me. Oh, alas and alas!)

"The Song of Wandering Aengus" is an enigmatic poem penned by William Butler Yeats on June 31, 1897:

> I went out to the hazel wood,
> Because a fire was in my head,
> And cut and peeled a hazel wand,
> And hooked a berry to a thread;
> And when white moths were on the wing,
> And moth-like stars were flickering out,
> I dropped the berry in a stream
> And caught a little silver trout.
>
> When I had laid it on the floor
> I went to blow the fire aflame,
> But something rustled on the floor,
> And someone called me by my name:
> It had become a glimmering girl
> With apple blossom in her hair
> Who called me by my name and ran
> And faded through the brightening air.
>
> Though I am old with wandering
> Through hollow lands and hilly lands,
> I will find out where she has gone,
> And kiss her lips and take her hands;
> And walk among long dappled grass,
> And pluck till time and times are done
> The silver apples of the moon,
> The golden apples of the sun.[1]

First published under the title "A Mad Song," it came as the perfect Coda to this conference/retreat, reiterating Jung's poetic claim that "... all the true things must change and ... only that which changes remains true."[2] The Jungian connection does not end here. Aengus is the god of all dreamers. Emma Jung was fascinated with this "dream-like character" as she called him. In her book on the elemental persons of the psyche, first published in English in 1955, *Animus and Anima,* she relates the colorful tale of the dreamful Aengus.[3]

A 9th-century Irish legend goes that every night for one year, a beautiful girl appeared to Aengus in dreamtime. In her hand, she held a lute upon which she played a haunting melody. He was so enchanted by the sound that he fell into a "wasting sickness." Eventually, the dreamtime girl is found by King Bodb Dearg. Three facts he discovers about her: her name is Caer; her father is the king of the Sí (the people of the underworld); and she changes into the form of a swan every other year.

Aengus must come to the lake of the dragon's mouth on an appointed day. When he arrives, he sees *three* times fifty (150—the same number of psalms in the Psalter mentioned above) swans on the water. There, he calls his loved one by name, and recognizing the sound of her name, she promises that she will come ashore if he returns to this lake of the Dragon again. When he renews his love, she comes and kisses him. Then, they fall asleep as two swans. Upon waking, they circle the dragon's lake on the wing *three* times to seal his promise to protect her. Finally, they fly away singing a magical duet. All who hear this will sleep for *three* days and *three* nights. The couple lived, and live, happily ever after.

Emma Jung situates this legend clearly in Jungian psychology. From the fact that Caer appears to Aengus in a dream, it is clear that she is destined for him and he cannot live without her, his anima. He submits to her conditions and indeed takes on her form, becoming a swan himself.

> He attempts to meet her in her own element, her *niveau*, in order to make her permanently his—conduct which should also prove of value psychologically, in relating to the anima. The magical song of the two swans is an expression of the fact that two beings of opposite nature, which yet belong together, have now in harmonious concord been united.[4]

Yet the relevance of this song, myth, and story is that the harmonious concord—the union of Aengus and Caer—continues to weave a tapestry of transformation in the lives of all who choose to listen with the Ear of the Heart.

---

## *NOTES*

[1] William Butler Yeats, "The Song of Wandering Aengus," in *W. B. Yeats: Collected Poems* (London: PaperMac, 1989 [1933]), pp. 66–67.

[2] C. G. Jung, "Rex and Regina," in *Mysterium Coniunctionis: An Inquiry into the Separation and Synthesis of Psychic Opposites in Alchemy, The Collected Works of C. G. Jung*, trans. R. F. C. Hull, vol. 14 (Princeton, NJ: Princeton University Press, 1970 [1963]), § 503.

[3] Emma Jung, "The Anima as Elemental Being," trans. Hildegard Nagel, in *Animus and Anima: Two Essays* (Dallas, TX: Spring Publications, Inc., 1985 [1957]), p. 50.

[4] *Ibid.*, pp. 50–51.

Paul Brutsche, Dr. phil., was born in 1943 in Basel. He studied philosophy and psychology, and received his doctoral degree from the University of Zürich. He trained at the C. G. Jung-Institut Zürich, and has been in private practice since 1975. He previously served as president of the Swiss Society for Analytical Psychology (SGAP) and the C. G. Jung-Institut Zurich. He was president of ISAPZURICH from its founding in 2004 until 2008, and continues to work at ISAP as a training analyst, supervisor, and instructor. His special areas of interest are art and picture interpretation. He has lectured in several countries.

# 2

# Paul Klee and the Symbol of the Mountain: On the Uncertainties of Human Existence

*Paul Brutsche*
*(translated by Stacy Wirth)*

## Introduction

The painter Paul Klee was born in 1879, here in the vicinity of Bern, and at early age developed a close relationship with Beatenberg. One translation of Klee's diaries reveals that Beatenberg was where he "fell in love" for the first time, in 1890, at the age of twelve. And in 1909 he executed an ink drawing to which he gave the title *St. Beatenberg*. In this talk I will address the motif of Beatenberg itself, "the mountain of the Holy Beatus." But I will go beyond this to deal with the mountain as a motif that runs powerfully throughout Paul Klee's work and becomes a major symbol in his artistic explorations of the uncertainties of human existence.

In 1903, at the age of 24, Paul Klee wrote an astonishing poem, "The Two Mountains." Let me begin by reading this to you:

> Two mountains there are,
> where all is bright and clear,
>
> the mountain of beasts, and
> the mountain of gods.
>
> Between them, lies the
> valley of humans in twilight.

> When one among them by chance lifts his head,
> he is gripped by a foreboding and
> unquenchable yearning;
> he who knows he knows not
> yearns for those who don't know they know not,
> and for those who know that they know.[1]

Reviewing the first verse, we note that the poem envisions two mountains, where light and clarity reign. On the one hand, there is the mountain of beasts, representing the laws of nature and instincts. On the other hand, there is the mountain of gods, which could stand for organizing, archetypal structures. Human existence, says Klee, plays out between these two orders: the order of nature and that of the spirit. Human existence unfolds within the shadowy valley of uncertainty, in the "betwixt and between." Human being is more conscious and questioning than animal being—and also more uncertain and doubting than godly being. This is the indefiniteness of the *condition humaine*.

From time to time, some seekers, like Klee, lift their heads and are overcome with yearning. Like Diogenes, they know that they *don't* know, and so they long for a pre-destined animal being that *doesn't* know that it doesn't know. Thus they can avoid confronting painful questions. Yet, at the same time, they yearn for the sovereign being of the creators, who *know* that they know, and are thus free of the plague of self-doubt.

The young Klee was apparently already attuning to what would become the guiding truth of his later life, namely, to be an unrelenting wanderer and explorer of artistic and spiritual life. Following this urge, he comes to *abide in uncertainty,* and *thereby* to become the recipient of increasingly deep and penetrating insights. As artist, he is repeatedly thrust into the chasm between unconscious nature and the divine creative spirit. Let us follow this existential tension as we view the artist through his works and in his person. We will look at a series of pictures in chronological order, covering nearly all of his various periods.

## *Chalet Heimat* (c. 1930)

Before introducing Klee's paintings, I want to share with you this photo of the artist himself. We see him here in Beatenberg, where he often spent his vacations, standing on the balcony of the Chalet "Heimat," or "Home" (Fig. 1). Long before the picture was taken, he had spent time at the chalet with his parents, thanks to relatives on his mother's side, who ran a hotel in the village. It is here that Klee is said to have fallen in love for the first time. More accurately, Beatenberg seems to be the place where he first experienced unrequited erotic passion. Writing in his journal in 1890 at the age of 12, he confesses:

> The first girl I approached with any carnal passion was little nine-year-old Helene from Neuchatel, a delicate beauty. I met her twice over a stretch of a few weeks during summer vacation, in my uncle's hotel in Beatenberg. A favorable moment came, and I drew her violently against me and would have covered her with kisses, if she had not fought me off madly.[2]

**Fig. 1**: Chalet Heimat

Here in Beatenberg, apparently as a somewhat fast-tracking prepubescent, Klee became acquainted with "the uncertainties of the heart," a topic to which we shall return many times in the course of this week.

In the photograph, Klee is much older, and had long been married to Lily Stumpf. Despite its poor quality, the image testifies to Klee's immediate link to Beatenberg. Not only that, but his position on the balcony could be said to symbolize the existential position that came increasingly to underpin his thought and art: he lingers at a threshold, supported from beneath by four sturdy columns rising from the earth, and sheltered from above by the triangular gabled roof that reaches out to the heavens.

Klee develops such oppositions in his journals and lectures as well as in his paintings. Moreover, as artist he moves between the appearances of material reality and its unseen spiritual dimensions, a movement that serves to usher the essences of people and things into the visible world.

## *The Artist at the Window* (1909)

A second introductory image, *The Artist at the Window* (Fig. 2), is obviously a self-portrait. Light filters through from the background, while the artist himself is veiled in darkness. His slightly hunched and twisted bearing and his down-turned mouth create the impression of worry, melancholy, and self-doubt. Here we have the person of the "Two Mountains" poem, the questioning man in the "valley of humans in twilight."

But perhaps in this seemingly lugubrious bearing we can discern as well a concentrated listening inward to something experienced as if it were light pouring in from an unseen source. This would be the realm of inner insight or illumination. From this realm the artist apprehends invisible truths and visions that direct themselves into the visible world through his hand and in his art. Out of this experience Klee felt compelled, as he wrote, "to render visible those impressions and conceptions not in themselves visual."[3] As we will soon see, Klee is in this sense a *translator*. He saw himself "as a creator directing the genesis of his works." Rather than *depicting* objective reality and its external appearances, he reaches beyond to discover inner essences, and reveals these by rendering their likeness in images. Instead of formally reproducing the merely visible, he illuminates life's depths and layers, which he discovers by "backward" movement to the primal source and formative power of nature. In his diary, Paul Klee writes:

> Creativity is characterized as a secret spark from somewhere, which kindles the spirit of man with its glow and ... moves through his hand and the movement is translated into matter ... the work.[4]

**Fig. 2**: *The Artist at the Window* (1909)

And elsewhere: "[The artist] neither serves nor rules, he transmits. His position is humble. And the beauty … is not his own. He is merely a channel."[5]

In a general sense, the image appears to say: Sitting here, in this place, the artist receives illumination, new revelations about the seen world. And in his artistic creation he translates the contents into the four-cornered, concrete reality of image. Spanning the world between

**Fig. 3**: Dürer, *St. Jerome in His Study* (1514)

foreground matter and background spirit, he is the bridge, the herald and mediator between this life and the other.

Experiencing a transcendent reality and becoming the instrument of numinous revelation is of course something that Paul Klee shares with other artists. This is sometimes so much so that the archetypal experience expresses itself with great imagistic similarity, even though centuries may lie between the works themselves. I have in mind, for instance, Albrecht Dürer and one of his three master engravings entitled *St. Jerome in His Study* (1514) (Fig. 3). Here we see Jerome, bent over and absorbed in translating the Bible into Latin, receiving light and illumination from an inner transcendental space—again with the source depicted as being located on the back and to the left. Pictures such as these, created in different eras by different artists, express the archetypal experience of the artist as a channel for the spiritual world.

## *St. Beatenberg* (1909)

This drawing, done in 1909, *St. Beatenberg* (Fig. 4), shows a landscape located in the immediate vicinity of our venue. Klee renders this steep-sided mountain cone with very fine pen lines. Broken, short, and rhythmic, his strokes bespeak motion—and also, ever-recurring beginnings. Here already Klee departs from the faithful reproduction of appearances. In doing so, he reveals the mountain as something that is essentially *in-the-making*—and something that *moves*. Similarly, the detail of the stepped pathway points to a mountain that invites exploration and penetration, that is, a mountain to be embraced with movement.

**Fig. 4**: *St. Beatenberg* (1909)

We could say of this picture in general that hard, weighty stone is broken up and dissolved to reveal an unfamiliar mountain reality—namely, the reality of an *inner* animation that invites dynamic interplay. Instead of depicting a static outer surface, the drawing discloses an interior vitality. (You will witness such inner life first-hand if you join Wednesday's excursion to the Beatus Caves). The mountain is now more than a thing, more than an inanimate material fact. It becomes a symbol of psychological striving, of progression from the here and now and the beyond to the realm of spirit.

Already in this relatively early work, which Klee executed at the age of 30, we discern certain accents that will characterize the later, well-known artist: his interest in what moves the world from the inside out, the spiritual treatment of nature, "movement" as the original source of creativity, and the creative process itself, which he saw as a "parable of Creation" in which the artist "imagine[s] himself God for a few moments," holding the primal spark and overseeing the genesis of a "cosmos" finely balanced in "parts that articulat[e] ... the whole" and are aglow with "mystery," "soul," and "impish laughter."[6]

## *In the Quarry* (1913)

*In the Quarry* (Fig. 5), a watercolor completed in 1913, portrays a stone quarry that lies in the general vicinity of Beatenberg. In this painting we are unavoidably confronted with nature. Our gaze is drawn to

**Fig. 5**: *In the Quarry* (1913)

the rose-colored mound surging up as the image's ground and center. The horizon rests high in the frame, appearing to be quite near. There is no way out—optically speaking, at least. Nature manifests herself as an immediate, all-embracing, and unalterable vessel and standpoint. She can be neither ignored nor denied. She is *here* in her complete fullness and breadth.

Paul Klee never did relinquish his recourse to nature. Over and over again, he sought the inspiring and animating contact with matter, with the body and instinct, with things natural. Indeed he untiringly searched within and outside of himself for life's primordial *origins*. This can well explain Klee's love of the quarry motif, which reveals the inwardness and sensuousness of earthly reality. He regarded himself as being "abstract with memories" (*"abstrakt mit Erinnerungen"*), that is, as an abstract artist oriented to life's archetypal dimensions, which resonate with the world's sensuous memories.

## *The Niesen* (1915)

*The Niesen* (Fig. 6) portrays the mountain that you see across from Beatenberg as you look toward the west. Klee painted this picture in 1915, following his trip to Tunisia with Louis Moilliet and August Macke, during which the three discovered the fascination of color, and Klee

Fig. 6: *The Niesen* (1915)

discovered his real calling as a painter. Certain elements lead us to conclude that this picture is meant to be more than a naturalistic portrayal of the mountain. As we have already seen, Klee wants not to reproduce the visible, but to "add more spirit to the seen … [and to] make secret visions visible."[7]

Consequently, Klee shows Mt. Niesen rising majestically towards the divine heights, where moon, sun, and stars all shine at the same time. With its triangular form and mysterious deep blue tone—symbolizing the spiritual beyond—the mountain stands in stark contrast to the earthy, material here and now. The latter takes form in the large variety of juxtaposed squares, while the mountain, in its singularity, reigns over all. Unity of the spirit and the diversity of matter stand in relation to each other both antithetically and in harmonious complementarity.

Ten years before Klee painted this watercolor, he wrote in his journal about the enormity of his evening experience of Mt. Niesen and the surrounding landscape:

> Around me the wonder of the spectacle. No strong emotions, no more intellect, no ethics! An observer above the world, or in the world a child. … One leaves the world of the here and now behind and builds a bridge to one beyond, where total affirmation is possible.[8]

In the painting, Klee seems to express the same experience in the oppositions of height and depth, blue and red, trinity and quaternity, unity and diversity, form and content, spirit and matter, transcendence and the here and now. We might think of the *unus mundus* with the corresponding world of material objects on the one hand and the inward spirit on the other.

Roughly midway between these two distinct worlds, we see a tree with five limbs. The tree may symbolize an individuation process that springs from the embodied life lived with the five senses and the five extremities. Human existence appears to be placed in a divide, where concrete, physical, and random conditions materialize in the foreground—while in the background there remains a yearning for an eternal and unalterable higher spirit. In other words, for Klee human existence unfolds *within the uncertainty* of the betwixt-and-between. This essentially uncertain existence harkens back to the "Two Mountains" poem and the "valley of humans in twilight"; and it is perhaps a meaning conveyed in this splendid painting of the Niesen.

## *Foehn Wind in Marc's Garden* (1915)

In *Foehn Wind in Marc's Garden*[9] (Fig. 7), the right edge of the painting is taken up entirely by the side of a house. Again, in the background, a Niesen-like mountain towers into the unreachable heights. In the center, between these two extremities, is a small hut surrounded by dark pines. In this hut we might see an image of the human condi-

**Fig. 7**: *Foehn Wind in Marc's Garden* (1915)

tion—being situated between the here and now and the beyond, surrounded and shadowed by dark uncertainties.

According to the scholar Jürgen Glaesemer, Klee's "complete artistic thought and works as worldview are determined by the tension between the polarities of the here and now and the beyond."[10] Already at the age of 23, Klee was preoccupied with such oppositions and noted them in his journal: antiquity and Christianity; physical reality and psyche; the objective and the subjective; the architectonic and the musical.

In *Marc's Garden* Klee uses the side of the house in the right foreground to convey a sense of the prevailing here and now. Being a humanly crafted architectonic structure, the house evokes our immediate and fundamental sense of belonging to the outer world of matter and objects. The distant beyond—the realm of "unquenchable yearning"—finds expression in a background infused with nature and the qualities of musicality, tonality, and rhythm—all of which resonate with inner subjective being and the spirit of transcendence.

Paul Klee made of his own questioning self the center that links the two realms—the material here and now and the otherworldly. As he wrote, "The *third* is a modest and unknowing self-apprentice, a tiny 'I'" (emphasis added).[11] This third, the "unknowing" and "tiny I," would seem to reside at the midpoint of *Marc's Garden*, in the shaded little hut with the vibrant red roof. Here Klee conveys the sense of an individual who gains meaning by *dwelling within* life's oppositions and *living with* its inevitable uncertainties.

## *Cacodaemonic* (1916)

*Cacodaemonic* (Fig. 8) was completed in 1916, when Paul Klee, as a German citizen, was drafted into the army and witnessed World War I—albeit at a distance. We shall return to the title, which obviously draws on the Greek word for a demonic spirit.[12] In this painting, a double mountain peak forms the background for a pair of eerie eyes. These belong to a rooster-like creature with a pointed comb. Yet, at the same time, they belong to a fish. The two animals are only vaguely distinguishable, seeming to flow into each other.

We could understand the image symbolically as a comingling of two opposing realms: the bird's upper world, or the sphere of the spirit, and the fish's lower world, or the sphere of the unconscious. That their comingling moreover amounts to a mutual contamination is suggested not only in the title, but also in the absence of harmonious difference: unlike

*The Niesen*, in which the shapes are so beautifully ordered, in *Cacodaemonic* the triangles and squares multiply themselves and converge in distorted, rhomboid shapes. Rather than appearing in coherent or complementary patterns, the colors are fragmented and scattered chaotically over the entire surface. Essential distinctions such as those of height and depth, spirit and matter, are lost.

Psychologically speaking, such a collapsing of differences points to demonic energies that are typically set loose when the spirit becomes concretized and expressed in enslaving ideologies. We see this in, among other places, war and the fanatical pursuit of dominance and ownership. What the process by its very nature entails is the elimination of a *necessary* uncertainty, the loss of a *needed* "humble and questioning I." It is not without reason that a dark, murky rhombus dominates the center of the painting, autonomously asserting itself, unrelated and in opposition to the whole. A sense of hyper-certainty emanates as the controlling force, fanatically and absolutely. Considering the year in which the painting was completed, 1916, we can reasonably assume that Paul Klee was working with the concept of likeness in an attempt to come to terms with the reality of the evil that had asserted itself collectively in World War I.

**Fig 8**: *Cacodaemonic* (1916)

## *Eros* (1923)

Despite its modest measurements (33 x 24 cm), this painting, *Eros* (1923) (Fig. 9), contains enormous meaning, demonstrating Klee's ability to communicate cosmic life and processes without relying on large formats. The steep lower pyramid conveys the sense of a world mountain or world axis, and serves as a symbol for spiritual transcendence.

**Fig. 9**: *Eros* (1923)

Belonging to this is a borderline phenomenon in its own right: the feeling of *translucence*, which is among the painting's essences, and which generally flows from the immaterial and yet real phenomenon of light. We all well know the fascination of stained glass windows in a cathedral. The *colors of the rainbow shimmer* through, suggesting a mystical experience that approaches the numinous, an encounter and merging with the divine.

In the interpenetrating triangles, the painting conceives Eros as a metaphysical union charged with archetypal energies. There is no reference to erotic passion, at least not on any obviously human plane. Yet Klee's conception is completely in line with Plato's, in which Eros holds together and enlivens *all* being.

Eros joins spirit (above) and matter (below), the sublime (yellow) and the elemental (green). It brings inside and outside into relationship, developing synchronistic correspondences between the subjective and objective worlds. Eros is at home between the brightness of daytime consciousness (left) and the twilight consciousness of sleep (right). Unlike the comingling that heralds contamination, confusion, and collapse of significant distinctions, Eros's joining brings the sublime experience of meaning and harmonious order. This dynamic is expressed in Klee's crystalline composition, and perhaps ultimately in the small, subtly glowing red triangle, which both recalls the "humble I" and also appears as the goal or climax of the union of opposites.

We note that the picture is completely *abstract* and is distilled to the essentials of the painter's art: color, line, contrast. Klee's particular mode of abstraction is held by the scholar Marcel Franciscono to be "responsible for the heightened sense of *intimacy* we feel [especially] in the late pictures" (emphasis added).[13] Abstraction in Klee's sense, we might say, evokes an intimate realization of Eros as such, illuminating its archetypal essences, its basic, deep, and infinite qualities.

If the intimate feeling of the painting is conceded, some of you may be puzzled about its seemingly dispassionate handling of Eros. Where is the warmth, the sensuousness, the concrete meaning for couples and others involved in relationship? Paul Klee was keenly aware of this problem. In a moving entry in his journal, referring to his passionate friend Franz Marc and to Marc's animal paintings, he wrote:

> My art lacks a passionate kind of humanity. I don't love animals and all kinds of creatures with earthly warmth. I neither bend towards them nor raise them to my own level. I dissolve myself in the whole and then stand on a brotherly

> level with my nearest, with all my earthly neighbours. … The idea of earth gives way to the idea of the universe. My love is devout; everything Faustian is alien to me. … My light glows too brightly to appear warm to many. I am therefore not loved by many. No sensuality, however noble, links me to them. I am a cosmic point of reference, not one of the species. … Art is ideal creation.[14]

You will no doubt devote much of the coming week to the question of the more human dimensions of passion, intimacy, and love. Klee as artist and thinker leaves us to speculate, hinting at an underlying archetype in the pair of upward pointing arrows. According to Klee's language of forms, these must express the yearning for something higher, something that far exceeds earthly limits. Klee reflects on such yearnings in his journal in a way that could read as a commentary to the painting:

> The father of every movement or projectile—therefore also the arrow was the thought: How do I extend my reach to that place? Across this stream, this lake, that mountain. Man's mental ability to traverse the realms of earth and the supernatural at will is, in its contrast to his physical weakness, the source of human tragedy. This conflict between strength and weakness is the dichotomy of human existence. Man is half winged, half captive. Thought as the medium between earth and universe. The further the journey, the more grievous the tragedy of needing to become movement and not yet being it![15]

## *CARNIVAL IN THE MOUNTAINS* (1924)

*Carnival in the Mountains* (Fig. 10) does not lend itself to an easy interpretation. In contrast to the foregoing images, this one seems to overflow with bizarre motifs. Four strange figures convene in some strange place, which appears to be far removed from civilization. Their meeting ground lies between two mountains, "in the valley of humans in twilight," to borrow from Klee's 1903 poem. These figures share neither the unconsciousness of the attending beasts, nor the omniscience of the gods. They seem tragicomic, wearing masks and performing a peculiar, contorted dance. Here we might see an image of the precarious human condition: the state of being banned from the paradise of natural law, and having become alien to oneself. But even more, the image brings to light the *artist's existence* as one of being driven out of the lowlands of ordinary life and into the highlands of the loneliness of the outsider. For Klee it is the crossing of this threshold that engenders transformation—for it contains the life of uncertainty, which gives rise to art that allows the emergence of "a changed, transmuted image of nature,"—a "rebirth of nature in art."[16]

The four masked figures gathered in the realm of uncertainty perhaps personify the functions that come into play in the artist's participation in "nature's rebirth in image." The woman in the hat on the left corresponds to the anima, which mediates insights from the unconscious. The small figure next to her suggests a child-like attitude, a readiness to play, to fantasize, to imagine. The bird with the antenna eye brings to mind the flight of the imagination *per se*, with special attunement to unusual insights from above. Finally, the large figure on the right points to labor, or the need to propel the alchemical *opus* towards the invention of new forms, techniques, methods—in short, the capacity for the artistic translation of inner creative impulses and ideas. In resonance with the universe, the artist engages these instruments to produce in "likeness to the Creation," as Klee says.

**Fig. 10**: *Carnival in the Mountains* (1924)

## *Bird Wandering Off* (1926)

The mysterious *Bird Wandering Off* (Fig. 11) was completed in 1926. Only a few objects emerge against the diffuse surface, challenging us to find a key idea that might help decode this enigmatic work. The painting as such bespeaks well Paul Klee's hermetic character. As he wrote in his journal (a statement later inscribed on his grave):

> I cannot be grasped in the here and now for I live just as well with the dead as with the unborn. Somewhat closer to the heart of creation than usual but far from close enough.[17]

This painting ranges from a light-washed chain of peaks in the upper middle to a dark mountain in the lower right. Here we have the treatment of a specifically human condition, namely, suspension between divine diffuseness and solid earth. This is a theme that Klee typically addresses with the mountain motif in both word and image. The mountain as such naturally evokes a transitional or middle realm, created by human ambivalence and uncertainty. Here the middle realm is furnished with sets of stairways, which recall the inevitably recurring cycles of psychological descent and ascent. The violet stairway on the left forms

**Fig. 11**: *Bird Wandering Off* (1926)

a sad-looking archway that leads to a black rectangle—a coffin-like symbol of endings, limits, and death. In the lower middle, the stairs form an ochre-toned arch, above which hovers a disc. Like a rising sun or full moon, this image in the painting is full of promise and new mornings. Klee understood himself to belong to both worlds, the world of the dead *and* the world of the unborn—to endings *and* beginnings.

Between these two realms flies the wandering bird of the painting's title, recalling Klee's idea that "[t]o wander about this way along the natural paths of creation is good training ...."[18] Here again, Klee seems to present a self-portrait: the artist as melancholy wanderer, pursuing an uncertain passage from one place or state to another—now descending to the depths and origins. Klee experienced the creative impulse arising from the archetypal chaos as a single act that widens and unfolds like a grain of sand expanding to become the universe. The motif of the greening maypole at the painting's center conveys something of this initial creative act that expands *ex nihilo*, or as Klee said, *ab ovo*—from the origin—to shape a cosmos of new meaning. The "valley of humans in twilight" thus not only constellates dire uncertainty; it also gives rise to the necessity to co-create the world.

## *Ad Parnassum* (1932)

I would like to close my talk on the motif of the mountain and Paul Klee with this painting entitled *Ad Parnassum* (Fig. 12, next page), one of his major works. In 1924 he wrote:

> Sometimes I dream of a work of vast scope, spanning all the way across element, object, content, and style. ... It must grow ... and if that work's time ever comes, then so much the better.[19]

Klee's dream was fulfilled with this splendid painting, completed in 1932, eight years before his death. Like the earlier Mt. Niesen, Parnassus rises into the heights of the firmament. For the Greeks, Parnassus, under the aegis of Apollo, the god of light, was the home of the muses, who brought art to life and inspired the creative process.

In Klee's conception, Mt. Parnassus reaches, beyond every terrestrial promontory, directly to the heavens of transcendence. But its upward thrust is countered by another pole: the reality of physical matter, expressed in earthy brown tones that run through the image's base and top and through its horizon and surface. Matter is presented as a foreground and all-encompassing reality, the immediate reality of everyday life. An arrow-like form, which seems to plunge directly into the earth, is the most obvious counterweight to the heavenward trajectory. The tendency to rise is diametrically opposed by the imperative to descend. *Ad Parnassum* appears to be Klee's gesture of yielding to *this* life—of *anchoring* in the immediacy of the here and now.

With this gesture, balance is achieved between spiritual strivings and material life, or, to mention other polar opposites in Paul Klee's conception of the world, the beyond and *this* life, the realm of the gods and that of the animals, those who know they know and those who don't know they don't know.

This painting presents a perfect balance, and not just in the painterly categories of form, color, and composition. From the standpoint of content, calm is finally achieved in the otherwise painful conflict between the urge to penetrate the beyond and the affirmation of everyday life, which so occupied Klee's work and thought. The mountain, once an image of melancholic, unfulfilled longing, now comes to symbolize mystical knowledge that is attainable in *this* life (the doorway) and that at the same time belongs to the vital reality of the spirit. In this sense, the mountain has been transformed to bring the previously distant and unobtainable goal into the immediacy of the here

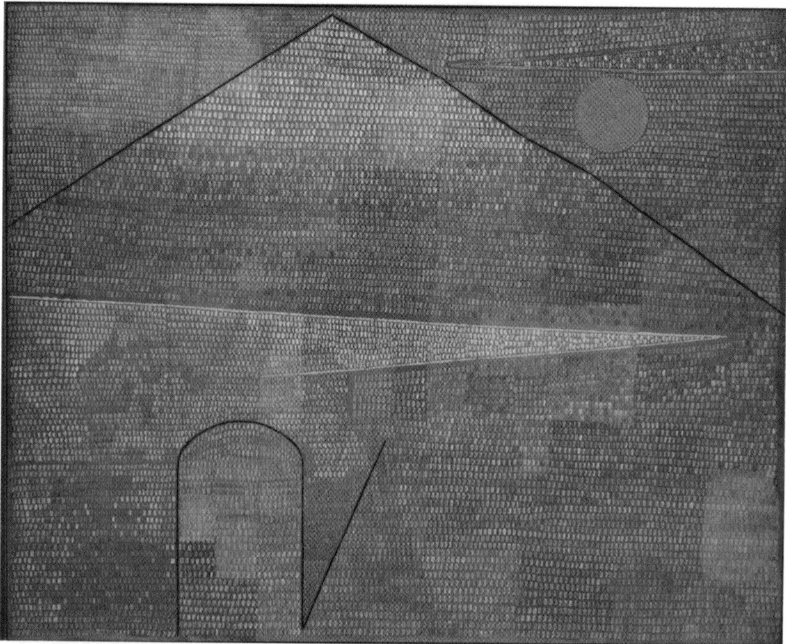

**Fig. 12**: *Ad Parnassum* (1932)

and now. It has become a happy and blessed mountain — a *mons beatus*, a "Beaten-berg."

---

## *NOTES*

[1] Paul Klee, "Zwei Berge gibt es [1903]," in *Paul Klee, Gedichte*, ed. Felix Klee (Zurich-Hamburg, Arche Verlag AG, 2005 [1960]), p. 55, trans. from the German by Stacy Wirth. The original German text appears below.

> Zwei Berge gibt es,
> Auf denen es hell ist und klar,
>
> den Berg der Tiere und
> den Berg der Götter.
>
> Dazwischen aber liegt das
> dämmerige Tal der Menschen.
>
> Wenn einer nach oben sieht,
> erfasst ihn ahnend
> eine unstillbare Sehnsucht,
> ihn, der weiss, dass er nicht weiss,
> nach ihnen, die nicht wissen, dass sie nicht wissen
> und nach ihnen, die wissen, dass sie wissen.

[2] Paul Klee, "Diary 1," in *The Diaries of Paul Klee 1898–1918*, ed. Felix Klee (Berkeley, Los Angeles: University of California Press, 1968), § 36.

[3] Paul Klee's "Creative Confession," (1919) in Carola Giedion-Welcker, *Paul Klee*, trans. Alexander Gode (New York: Viking Press, 1952), pp. 48 and 65.

[4] Paul Klee, in Stephen A. Martin, *The Spiritual Life of Paul Klee*, unpublished lecture, Bern, 1979.

[5] Paul Klee, *On Modern Art* (1924), trans. Paul Findlay (London: Faber and Faber Ltd., 1948), p. 15.

[6] Paul Klee, *Paul Klee, His Life and Work in Documents: Selected from Posthumous Writings and Unpublished Letters*, ed. Felix Klee, trans. Richard Winston and Clara Winston (New York: George Braziller, 1962), p. 155.

[7] Klee, *Modern Art*, p. 51.

[8] Paul Klee, "Diaries, no. 714, July 1905," in Jürgen Glaesemer, *Paul Klee: The Colored Works in the Kunstmuseum Bern* (Bern: Kornfeld and Cie., 1976), p. 34.

[9] The Foehn wind is a dry, warm wind that characteristically occurs on the down slopes of the Swiss mountains and is believed to give rise to uncontrolled emotions, among other things. The word "Foehn" is the German rendition of the Latin *Favonius,* one of the Roman wind gods, who corresponded to the Greek god Zephyrus.

[10] Jürgen Glaesemer, *Paul Klee: Leben und Werk—Katalog* (Teufen: Arthur Niggli AG, 1987), p. 24, trans. from the original German by Stacy Wirth.

[11] Klee, in Glaesemer*, Leben und Werk.*

[12] Etymologically, "Cacodaemonic" is derived from the Greek *kakos* (evil) + *daimon* (spirit). See "Cacodemon," Wikipedia, http://en.wikipedia.org/wiki/Cacodemon.

[13] Marcel Franciscono, *Paul Klee: His Work and Thought* (Chicago, IL: University of Chicago Press, 1991), pp. 199-200.

[14] Klee, in Glaesemer, *Colored Works*, p. 40.

[15] *Ibid.*, p. 44.

[16] Klee, in Giedion-Welcker, pp. 60-61.

[17] Paul Klee, *The Diaries*, in "Recollections," by Felix Klee, p. 419.

[18] Klee, in *Life and Work*, p. 177.

[19] Paul Klee, in *Paul Klee Notebooks, Volume I: The Thinking Eye*, ed. Jurg Spiller, trans. Ralph Manheim (London: Lord Humphries, 1961) p. 95.

John Hill, M.A., received his degrees in philosophy at the University of Dublin and the Catholic University of America. He trained at the C. G. Jung-Institut Zürich, has practiced as a Jungian analyst since 1973, and is a training analyst at ISAPZURICH. His publications include books and articles on the Association Experiment, Celtic myth, James Joyce, and the significance of home, dreams, and Christian mysticism.

# 3

# Home—The Making or Breaking of the Heart

*John Hill*

## My Own Home

Home structures the story of our lives. Mine began in Ireland, in a cloud of unknowing. I was told that I cried so much in the first few months of my life that I had to be operated on for a ruptured hernia. The transition from home in the womb to a non-holding environment damaged my attachment potential, damage that it has taken a lifetime to repair. Some of my nightmares have kept alive memories of early abandonment. In my fourth year, I contracted tuberculosis, discovered accidentally while I was staying with relatives. Unable to walk, I created an imaginary home, inhabited by imaginary parents, during the two years I spent in hospital. I believe those imaginary homescapes and the regular visits by a faithful aunt helped me survive an ordeal that my mind could barely acknowledge.

My father died when I was eleven. I believed my father had gone to heaven. Whenever I was under stress, I prayed to him for help. Later, whenever an aunt, uncle, or close family friend passed on, I felt something became added to my life. My mother belonged to a family that retained visible traces of its ancestry. Books, paintings, and a mausoleum were among the remaining vestiges of a long history. Perhaps those early experiences of loss, the visible signs of ancestry, and the continual exhortations of Catholic priests to believe in the existence of another world induced me to conclude that I was just one link in a long chain of generations. At an early age, I became aware that home was embedded in a much larger landscape, which contained my entire life story.

Surrounded by women in a fatherless household, I found home in my mother, my sister, and a housekeeper during my adolescent years. My mother loved fun and gaiety and she always advised me to be social and enjoy people, especially at parties and in sport. She hoped that I would become a banker or join the British army, and was unable to appreciate my decision to study philosophy. One day I tried to explain to her the meaning of "essence." She laughed and told her friends that the only essence she knew was the essence used in cakes. I knew my mother loved me, but she had no way of understanding who I was and especially what I was trying to be. Our housekeeper was different. She was a woman of the land, who had come to us before I was born and had devoted her whole life to our family. She provided the warmth and nurturance that my mother and sister could not. She communicated, in intimate ways, something of the ancient Irish heritage. She would tell us stories about the customs, superstitions, hardships, and dreams of times long ago, creating a world in which plant, animal, and human seemed to be woven in an invisible web of connections. Later, I came to understand this kind of relationship as an archetypal attachment to the Earth Mother, an attachment that heals the wounds of the heart. In boarding school I became conscious of homesickness as a painful and personal issue. I felt lost in the large, impersonal classrooms, refectories, and dormitories of that institution. My soul needed several weeks at the beginning of each term to befriend the new environment.

Having arrived in Switzerland, I began the next period of my life. These were good years. Home became marriage, children, and profession. Despite the relative poverty of the first ten years of family life, I don't think I ever felt more secure and fulfilled than I did in the shared home with a loving and loyal wife, partaking in the life and development of two wonderful boys. My family life was definitely matrilocal. My social life extended to my wife's family and friends only. Later, we lived in a beautiful wooden house in Einsiedeln, a small town with a massive basilica that houses the Black Madonna and is situated near a picturesque lake nestled in the majestic Alpine landscape. For many hours I worked in the garden, transforming our rather plain Swiss garden into a landscape of rocks and boulders, embellished with colorful shrubs and flowers—little Ireland!

There were, however, times when I became homesick for my native land and culture. Each year, I revisited Ireland to reassure myself that my homeland would not disappear but survive as part of my identity. Dreams of Ireland, Celtic myth, and modern Irish literature brought back the wealth of this background. They sustained my new life in Switzerland. As if to keep alive the memory of my original homeland, concrete sensory images would return again and again: the sound of the sea, the smell of turf, the lilt of Irish folk music. Conversely, today when I am away from Switzerland, I not only miss the music of the alphorn or the taste of Swiss pralines, but also the picturesque villages, the dark woods, and the majestic mountains of my adopted country. I must see, hear, or smell my home even when I am not physically in it. The French philosopher, Merleau-Ponty once wrote: "The body is not an object among objects but our way of belonging to the world."

After having experienced the trials of midlife, I am now entering the final stage of life. I feel more rooted and at home in myself than ever before. In the beginning, my life was invented by the expectations of an Anglo-Irish tradition at odds with my dormant inner self, which was connected with the unspoken ways of nature and nurtured by a housekeeper who embodied the mystery of Mother Ireland. Later, different selves were added through a series of temporary identifications with strong personalities. I can accept the house that I have built with its shine and its shadows. I have been able to translate, at least partially, the landscapes of Ireland into other homelands, particularly my adopted homelands, Switzerland and the Greek isle of Patmos, to which I return every year. My Irish soul delights in the sea, the barren rocks, and the little chapels of that holy island. I now have many loved ones, including my former wife, my children, dear friends, and professional colleagues, with whom I have shared the drama of life. It is only in these last years that I have learned to extend friendship in ways that are mutual and meaningful, and go beyond the confines of a matrilocal environment.

Home has become a function of consciousness, a consensual concept, and a way of constructing relationships to others and to the cosmos. Home is a work of art that takes a lifetime to create. It began with my parents and later included my own family, my children, a mystic, and close personal and professional friends. Part of its story is contained in attachment to houses, gardens, animals, landscapes, schools, churches, ideas, music, and works of art. Home can also be understood as attachment to major attitudes that change during the course of one's life. The theologian Jurgen Moltmann once described the powerful forces that mold the four stages of life as follows: trust, in childhood; longing, in youth; responsibility, in maturity; and wisdom, in old age. I have always been impressed by the Indian notion that a woman is never without a husband, imaged in the Gandharvas, supernatural lovers associated with nature and the stages of life.[1] One could apply the Gandharva legend to male psychology. My heart seems to be saying that I have had four marriages: to mother, wife, soul, and death. I have felt at home in these marriages. The final one is still in the process of being built. It began soon after I reached mid-life. It is the work of the spirit, a summing up, an acceptance of one's life narrative, for better or for worse, in order to face the final challenge. I hope that the shelters I have built for myself can in different ways provide shelter for others. I expect to take those shelters with me as I face the final question: Do we have a home that outlasts our short life on earth? Most of us will end our life on a mattress. That will be our final space on earth. I imagine the mattress could become a magic carpet that will carry me to unknown territory. Schopenhauer, in a remarkable statement, examined the fabric of that last space we call home:

> ... [L]ife may be compared to a piece of embroidery, of which, during the first half of his time, a man gets a sight of the right side, and during the second half, of the wrong. The wrong side is not so pretty as the right, but it is more instructive; it shows the way in which the threads have been worked together.[2]

## Home: An Archetypal Theme

Home and homelessness have been cherished themes for novelists, poets, musicians, and artists. The twin themes give rise to narratives about the continual making and breaking of the heart. The Biblical exile from the Garden of Eden, the search for the Promised Land, the Babylonian Captivity, and the lamentations of Jeremiah—all bear witness to joy or grief over homes gained or lost. The wanderings of the homesick Odysseus, exiled from his beloved homeland by the winds of Poseidon, his lamentations for Penelope on the rocks of Malta, and his final return home represent yet another great story of humanity's quest for home. Epic tales, whether conceived by one man or written over generations, are narratives of endurance. The vision of a cherished homeland, and the faith and courage of prophets, priests, and warriors in following this vision did much to shape the character of the Hebraic and Greek peoples, as Virgil's tale of the homeless Aeneas, the celebrated founder of Rome, later did for the Romans.

Home has also been an important theme in religion, philosophy, anthropology, politics, sociology, and psychology. Great religious leaders—Buddha, Christ, Saint Francis of Assisi, Mother Teresa—and their followers have left the comforts of a secure shelter and devoted their lives to alleviating the sufferings of their homeless brothers and sisters. Anthropologists have thrown into relief the significance of ritual and sacred space in defining the clan membership and cultural identity of various indigenous peoples throughout the world. The anthropologist Victor Turner, observing the ritual practices of people celebrating together, "was primarily excited by group life itself, life as expressed in lived-through experiences of the participants. Here lay all of those contradictory features that gave humans the ability to laugh and cry together."[3] Philosophers, especially existentialist philosophers, describe humanity as being thrown into existence. A sense of alienation from one's environment has motivated humans to pose those fundamental questions: Who am I? Where have I come from? Where am I going? Leaders of nations have waged wars in the name of "the homeland" and patriotism, not always in defense of their nation, but in pursuit of conquest, often ruthlessly destroying the homelands of those whom they subjugate. Politicians and sociologists have wrestled with the problems of population upheaval and mass migration. Today many millions are homeless and in search of a new home. Studies have shown that that process of finding home in a new cultural landscape involves a painful and complex passage of time, and is often transgenerational.

## The Broken Hearts of the Swiss

When I started to write about home, something happened that brought to mind the power of a nourishing environment in an intense way. I remembered an old woman who lived in a small house at the foot of the Alps. She was forced to leave her house because it did not measure up to the fire safety standards of Switzerland. The woman, who lived as people did in the Middle Ages, and whose identity was intimately bound to her house, her land, and her flock of sheep, was put into a psychiatric hospital by the health authorities. The nurses bathed and dressed her up for the first time in her life. Her heart was broken. She looked miserable, uprooted, homeless, and frightened of the alien environment in which she found herself, an environment with which she could in no way identify. The shock of the eviction did irreparable damage to her heart. When I visited her some weeks later, all she could say was, "Take me home." I could see that she had begun to withdraw from life, and within two months she was dead.

One is reminded of European descriptions of homesickness from the 18th and 19th centuries. There are many documents that read as tales of a broken heart, particularly among Swiss men, many of whom had left their Alpine homelands, which could no longer support ever-growing families, and become mercenaries in foreign armies. An abbreviated description taken from an encyclopedia published in the 19th century describes the effects of homesickness as follows:

> It is a form of grief at separation from the native soil and may become in men of great sensibility a real disease. It shows itself by a deep melancholy, difficult respiration, sighs, deadly paleness, immoderate heartbeats, and loss of appetite. Sleep flies away, or consists of dreams, which are filled with scenes left behind. Sudden death sometimes puts an end to this situation. A return home is the most effectual remedy.[4]

Johann Scheuchzer, writing in 1705, believed that homesickness was a special illness of the Swiss. In a well-read weekly journal he wrote:

> Why does it happen that the Swiss, who are such a free, strong, and courageous people, are overtaken by an illness that one would rather expect to find among the French, Italian, or other peoples whose bodies are tender and therefore more susceptible to homesickness?[5]

Scheuchzer was convinced that he had to resolve this matter so as to save the reputation of the Swiss nation. He believed that homesickness among the Swiss comes from taking in the denser air of the lowlands, which they, being used to the rarefied and subtle air of the Alps, are unable to adjust to. In the lowlands, the heavier, denser air exerts pressure on their blood circulation and thus slows down the whole system. They suffer from heart palpitations, insomnia, sadness, and a longing to return to the lighter air of the mountains. Scheuchzer recommended a cure for those Swiss who live in the lowlands and suffer from this illness. They are to be encouraged to return home or, if that is not possible, to climb a high mountain or tower. If mountains or towers fail to cure homesickness, the doctor can prescribe saltpeter, a substance containing compressed air, which is supposed to increase the air pressure in the arteries and thus counteract the pressure from the dense outside air, and if that is not available, a small dose of gunpowder![6] There seems to be no evidence that gunpowder was a successful cure.

In the 19th century, a psychological explanation for homesickness replaced the medical model. Johann Ebel, a medical doctor from Silesia, who settled in Switzerland, was convinced that the inhabitants of the Alps were the happiest and freest people of Europe. He believed that homesickness is more likely to occur in the simpler, non-intellectual person, whose feelings are the main source of satisfaction. This type of person is more focused on the inner than the outer. The soul of such a person finds more gratification in feelings of the heart than in intellectual development. The unsophisticated but happy inhabitants of the Alps are particularly prone to this illness when deprived of the world they love—their family, their goats, their cows, and the beautiful, towering mountains that surround them. It is no wonder, claimed Ebel, that they fall prey to homesickness when they are confined to a barracks and forced to serve as soldiers under the strict discipline of an authoritarian commander. Surrounded only by other men, who show no affection or tenderness, they feel alone, confused, and lost in a world unknown to them. They withdraw, become apathetic and bored. Their heart begins to live only on images of the past, and a longing for home overcomes them. Ebel cites one instance in which displaced Swiss workers were able to keep homesickness at bay:

> Some years ago men from Entlibuch were brought to Paris to work in a large Swiss Sennerie for the manufacturing of dairy products. They were content as long as they were working with cows and milk products, but as soon as the dairying ceased, they were troubled with homesickness.[7]

The Swiss *Kuhreihen*, a kind of folk melody used to call cattle, dating back to the 16th century, is well known in the history of folk music. Chronicles inform us that this music had the power to make the strongest men cry, lay down their arms, desert from the army, even die. Hofer reported that the mercenaries were strictly forbidden to whistle or play on the flute the *Kuhreihen* in case it awakened the "Delirium Melancholicum." Ebel claimed that this music derived its power to evoke extreme nostalgia less from its melody than from its capacity to awaken memories of herding cows and goats, which was part of the Swiss mercenaries' lives from childhood.

> This music enters the soul of the men of the Alps like a streak of lightning, creating images of the mountains, valleys, herds of cattle, family, and friends.[8]

Ebel went on to say that the *Kuhreihen* was so powerful that it could even affect Swiss cows:

> When the cows are parted from the country of their birth and hear this song, all the images of the past suddenly become alive in their brain. They become excited with a longing for home, toss up their tails, and start to stampede, break fences, and go completely mad. That is why near the town of St. Gall it was forbidden to sing or whistle the *Kuhreihen* in the presence of Appenzeller cows that have been separated from their homeland.[9]

During the 19th century the popularity of this music knew no bounds. There were several regional versions of the *Kuhreihen* (also known as *ranz des vaches*). In 1821, Joseph Bovet arranged the Gruyère version for men's chorus; it soon achieved great popularity in Switzerland. In 1829, Rossini incorporated the Appenzell version into the overture to his opera *Guillaume Tell*. Other versions appeared in the music of Beethoven, Berlioz, Schumann, Liszt, and Wagner.[10]

## Home: A Narrative Reality

So we must ask ourselves: Are we humans ever at home anywhere? What happens when we become estranged from others and ourselves? How many of us search for some person, place, or thing to which we can say: "You are mine and I am yours"? We are restless beings thrown into a world that can make or break the heart. Some of us have a golden start in life, having been brought up in a secure home created by loving parents. Others experience their early surroundings as a wasteland. Deprived of any look or gesture of recognition, their depleted heart and mind retreat into a world of silence. Life becomes a matter of mere survival, and sometimes a matter of living the life of others without even knowing it. We need the intimacy of a home, particularly at the beginning of life. Intimacy nourishes the heart and fosters trust in human relationships. Thus, intimate relationships bring with them great responsibility, especially the responsibility to protect those who are vulnerable. If that responsibility is not honored, the results can be devastating. Once trust is abused, the heart of the betrayed one is broken and his or her world falls apart. Imagine what now goes on in the minds of the wife and children of the Austrian, Josef Fritzl, who lived in the family intimacy of the upper levels of his house, while his daughter and three of her seven children (all fathered by him) were enslaved for 24 years in the cellar of the same house. Intimate relationships open the heart. With abuse, different forms of splitting can ensue, usually with devastating effect on the capacity to develop any further intimate relations.

Many are the narratives that bear testimony to the intimate significance of home. Some will tell frightening tales about never having had a home; others believe they are incapable of ever having one. Some will talk about traumatic experiences when leaving old homes; others express the unbearable pain of not being able to assimilate the new. Some narratives are not just about houses. The French philosopher, Gaston Bachelard, notes that any inhabited space, no matter how minimal, is seized upon by the creative imagination and transformed into home as a place of intimacy and protection.[11] As a poetic image and symbol prior to conscious thought, "home" transcends our memories of the actual houses we have inhabited. In moments when memory and imagination unite and the past and present interpenetrate, home becomes a multivariate symbol of the intimate values of inside space. "... [O]ur house is our corner of the world. As has often been said, it is our first universe, a real cosmos in every sense of the word."[12]

Home can be a particular landscape—an intimate memory of a mountain, sea, desert, or village. The following narrative describes the journey home of a young North American woman—a journey through a landscape imbued with archetypal myth and symbol, a journey that led her into a landscape of the heart in which self and other were scarcely distinguishable. She reconnected with her origins and the living universe responded.

> I went home recently and felt its significance for the first time. I never thought I would want to go back there, but as soon as I did and saw the landscape of my childhood home, I felt I never wanted to leave. As I drove through the open countryside, a moose blocked my way. She wouldn't move, and after some time it dawned on me that this could be the welcome of the Earth Mother. When I arrived at our house, I climbed up a hill to my favorite place. From there I could "see" the rolling prairies, the buffalo, and Indian teepees. This was my landscape and not the lush green woods and fields of Europe. I sat down and heard the wild geese flying south. I could have stayed there forever. When I was in Europe, and probably because of analysis, something changed in me. I have connected to the Earth Mother and am now capable of feeling at home—something I could never do before.

For some, home is static: the body, an inner experience, Planet Earth, a space in which to create, etc. Other home narratives are about being on the move. Home takes on the significance of a place of exile, a pilgrimage, or being a nomad—a frame of mind so aptly expressed in the words of a Native American: "I can pitch my teepee anywhere in the world because my soul is at one with the earth." Home, can, of course, also be a person. For some, home becomes alive through memories of attachments to parents or loved ones. They find home in the intimate atmosphere of a family, community, clan, or nation. There are narratives in which home is neither place nor person but the way something gets expressed. Home becomes a beautiful piece of music, a painting, an icon, a myth, a fairy tale, an embrace, a moment of deep emotional rapport. The well-known cabaret entertainer, Georg Kreisler, once claimed he could live well without having a home. Kreisler lived in several countries, but did not belong to any one of them. Home for Kreisler is the German language, music, and friends.[13] Some will say that home is not of this earth. Home is a connection with the ancestors or with those loved ones who have gone on before us. Home is heaven; home is God.

The extent of the theme is overwhelming. The origins of the longing for home are biological, as found in the animal instinct to mark territory. When faced with a predator, animals will react with fear or aggression in defense of their lairs, dens, or burrows. The emergence of this longing in humans can be traced to attachment and affiliation instincts, which later determine our feelings toward home through the ways we bond with people, places, and objects, all consolidating a sense of narrative identity and continuity. Regardless of whether we find home in a cardboard box or in a palace, each home narrative reveals a unique human destiny. Memories of home release a life story. Some stories are less dramatic than others. Few take home for granted. These few are more likely to be found in an ever-shrinking segment of the population, consisting of people who have never moved, never changed their abode. There are those who have never seen beyond the confines of their accustomed home. When confronted with what they consider alien, their heart clams up. They become insecure and cannot explore the riches that lie beyond their traditional environment. Home becomes an ideology, a belief about keeping things the way they have always been. The devotion to fixed patterns prevents the heart from being open to new experiences. The stranger, the migrant, the refugee are perceived as a threat, and everything is done to keep such people, especially if they are from another race or culture, out of the home and out of the heart.

But this does not mean that people who have never left home cannot have a sense of security and belonging. They are like old trees that have never been uprooted. Their innermost being reflects their surroundings and their tales of the heart reveal the unfathomable richness of their environment. This way of being is beautifully illustrated in Robin Flower's description of Tomas O'Crohan, the poet who lived on the Great Blasket, a rocky island off the coast of Ireland. In his poem "Tomas," Flower speaks of the cultural importance of the island, describing it as Europe's last untouched egg of Neolithic civilization:

> He had lived on the Island sixty years
> And those years and the Island lived in him,
> Graved on his flesh, in his eye dwelling,
> And moulding all his speech,
> That speech witty and beautiful
> And charged with the memory of so many dead.
> Lighting his pipe he turned,
> Looked at the bay and bent to me and said:
> "If you went all the coasts of Ireland round,
> It would go hard to you to find
> Anything else so beautiful anywhere;
> And often I am lonely,
> Looking at the Island and the gannets falling
> And to hear the sea-tide lonely in the caves.
> But sure 'tis an odd heart that is never lonely."[14]

In today's world, most home narratives are not happy ones. We increasingly hear tales of loss, abandonment, estrangement, exile, homesickness, and mass migration. The English word "world" stems from the Anglo-Saxon *weorold*—from *wer* (man) and *eld* (an age)—the literal sense being "age of man" or "course of a man's life." Our experience of "the world" comes from our entire lifetime. The world envisioned as the course of a lifetime differs radically from the world that is emerging from the newly forming global society, in which "[s]pace matters less ... as time is shortened."[15] How can one be at home in the world if time is continually shortened and space matters less? The world becomes real in terms of one's narratives about the times during which one has inhabited various spaces, as implied in the etymology of the word "world." The significance of the world becomes apparent when one looks at it in terms of a lived life. The world conceived of as a lived life implies that it is not a solitary "I" who perceives a world out there, but an "I" that is created from unconscious systems of deeper resonance with the environment formed over a lifetime. Humans create the world as a sphere of meaning by bonding with their surroundings in a given context and at a given time, selecting aspects of it that sustain, nourish, and bring to blossom their very being. These are the moments when our being becomes housed, to use an expression from Bachelard.

The stories of the uprooted peoples of our fast-moving times have made home a key issue and force us to reflect anew on human destiny. Today one is likely to encounter dramatic tales among those who have suffered loss of home and are continually on the move. When one is deprived of home, the search for home and its significance becomes a lifelong quest. Home is not just a specific place or person, but the search for home itself reveals that home is closely bound to the quest for identity. Those intimate emotional experiences surrounding the loss or gain of a particular home throw us back upon ourselves, compelling us to reflect on the purpose and meaning of our lives.

Why is the search for home so compelling? Some believe we cannot gain a sense of home without first having lost our home. It is in loss that we experience those memories of home that bring to consciousness the specific, concrete, and intimate events of a lifetime. They hit us on the sensory level: an image, a smell, a sound, or the taste of a favorite food. These are not just fleeting images, sounds, or tastes, but are embedded in special circumstances, which constantly repeated themselves and caused us to grow accustomed to them, thus binding us to our personal, family, and social history. We remember a world that we trusted and in which we felt secure. Christian von Krockow feels we never forget our childhood home because it is a world that remains always the same.[16] Frederick Buechner recalls that there was one childhood home he could never forget.[17] For him, the place and the people maintained a sense of permanence, as sense that they would keep going on into the future while others came and went. Eva Hoffman describes the lost home of her childhood in Poland.[18] She remembers the hum of the trams in Cracow, and the feeling that home was a world in which everything is unchanging and predictable. She knows that her home in Poland was no paradise, but in exile it would have become one for her if she had not succeeded in her struggle to find home in the New World. Yet she refers back to those early experiences as expressing the very core of herself—experiences of a whole world that preserved continuity and protected from fragmentation:

> How absurd our childish attachments are, how small and without significance. Why did that one, particular, willow tree arouse in me a sense of beauty almost too acute for pleasure, why did I want to throw myself on the grassy hill with an upwelling of joy that seemed overwhelming, oceanic, absolute? Because they were the first things, the incomparable things, the only things. It's by adhering to the contours of a few childhood objects that the substance of our selves—the molten force we're made of—molds and shapes itself. We are not yet divided.[19]

Memories of home and homesickness are by no means innate intimations of a paradise lost. They originate in experiences of the external world that were personal but imbued with cultural and symbolic significance. Presumably, at some point these experiences become internalized. They draw our attention to the history of our deeper self as recorded through the narrative power of memory. They are experiences of wholeness—when our internal feeling of wholeness was matched by an external world that was whole.

The need to be at home in the world is certainly influenced by those early childhood memories that make up the substance of home and homesickness. In some cases, the natural ability to attach oneself to some place, person, or thing may have become so impaired that the person is incapable of bonding in any way whatsoever, as is observed in instances of early abandonment. On the other hand, with the new freedom of our times, the attachment instinct can be manifested in an unlimited number of ways—not just in attachment to one family, one school, one village or one church, but to many different kinds of relationships, schools, professions, dwelling places, cultures, and religions, so much so that there is hardly enough time to feel at home in any one of them. Despite these unlimited possibilities, attachment does not develop as a matter of course to anything and everything. According to Bowlby, attachment is selective. As an inner disposition to form inner, enduring attachments, it manifests in children as a "clear hierarchy of preferences ... with a number of highly specific features, which include representational models of the self and attachment figures."[20]

Attachment is a living phenomenon. It is an expression of the life force within each individual that is striving unconsciously for containment, connectedness, and continuity. In deep attachments we may reexperience the disappointments and expectations of earlier relationships, which mirror a history of how we felt or how we wanted to feel. Attachment unleashes archetypal energies, energies that sometimes attract and engage, and sometimes even repel. It makes people and things come alive with tremendous intensity, and this gives unique meaning and purpose to the relationship. Here self-knowledge and knowledge of one's intimate history are essential to contain the energy and potential of relationship, see through projections, and recognize who we truly are.

It has become increasingly clear that it is easier for the adult person to become aware of the significance of these archetypal patterns if he or she has experienced in infancy a holding environment that matched an emerging awareness of self-continuity, which Daniel Stern identifies as one of the four "invariants" (or fundamental elements) of the core self.[21] And it is easier to maintain a sense of containment and continuity (not as a permanent state but as one of dynamic equilibrium) if one can protect oneself from the shallow influences of a lifestyle that prevents one from distinguishing superficial or pathogenic forms of attachment behavior from those enduring attachments that mirror who one truly feels oneself to be. With this foundation secured, memories of the time one experienced the world as whole become part of one's identity and history, and home may be understood as representing the possibility of a return to the core self—a dynamic process grasped through symbolic experiences that evoke hope, security, and continuity in a person's life so that he or she can survive those transitional processes by which we make new landscapes our very own.[22]

## Narratives from the Consulting Room

Psychotherapists encounter deeply moving home narratives in the symptoms, sufferings, hopes, and aspirations of their clients. Lack of empathy from parents and early abandonment by them can severely damage a child's ability to form attachments to anybody or anything. On the other hand, the compulsion to stick with the familiar at all costs can be a defense against coming to terms with the changing circumstances of one's life. Dreams and transferences can help people find roots, create new meaningful relationships, and initiate authentic understanding of what it means to be at home in one's self and the world. Home is a foundational experience. The therapist cannot provide home as a material substitute for what was missing in the client's childhood, but he or she can provide a context in which the meaning of childhood experiences, or lack thereof, can be re-appraised.

Often in the deep constellations of transference and counter-transference, the client finds opportunities to relive much of the past. Those of us who have experienced loss of home and abandonment have the possibility of repairing and restoring what has been lost when we enter into the deep mutual bonding of transference. Conflicts that arise in such analyses revolve around the issue of the analyst's accepting or rejecting the abandoned child in the adult client. This inner child rarely measures up to the rules and regulations of the adult world, particularly those norms that might resemble the ones he or she encountered in childhood that were destructive. Having once been abandoned, the inner child feels doubly let down when the analyst goes away on holiday, or when a process that has just got going is suddenly interrupted because the hour is over, or when the analyst gives more attention to his or her "other" family than to the "adopted" child in analysis. The analyst must realize that he or she cannot indulge in the fantasy of providing a home for all those who need one. But he or she must also recognize that the anger and rage that the client feels at the analyst's incapacity to meet all his or her needs has its place as well. The analyst must remain tolerant, for behind such rage, the earlier disappointments are being relived. Once the connection between the analytic constellation and the pain of the past reaches consciousness, the client can relive the despair of abandonment, this time aware that his or her analytic partner, as witness, serves to provide a context of containment, connectedness, and continuity, so that what takes place is not a mere repetition of earlier traumatic events.

The work of psychotherapy is to provide a setting in which the tales of hidden tragedies of the heart may be heard. The new therapeutic relationship can create a context in which the significance of home can be re-evaluated. Many people in therapy recount early scenes of unacknowledged violence and abuse, which have devastated their lives. They remember hardly anything else about their childhood and might articulate it only in terms of fear, anger, despair, guilt, or shame. Often the narrative does not hang together and is told in a confused or fragmented way. If the analyst attempts to intervene, he or she may find himself or herself shut out by a protective system that was erected to protect a core self that has long retreated into a world of silence. The damage done in childhood can have long-term effects. Images or dreams may reveal what it feels like to have had such a home. Some have experienced home as a dungeon, a dwelling place without windows or doors, a tower in an isolated or frozen landscape. Images of not having skin, of being turned to stone, or of being buried alive give visual form to the inner torment of those who fear their uncontained identity may be continually threatened from within and without. Sometimes these people feel so alone, they are afraid they will go mad. It is not easy for the analyst to enter into such an abode. But once the analyst accepts the invitation to enter, he or she can provide the sort of empathetic, patient, and understanding presence of an other that can be transformative.

As an invited guest, the analyst must learn to appreciate the hospitality of the host's inner home. He or she may not always be acquainted with the customs of that home. He or she may feel awkward or ill at ease and may even misunderstand the purpose of the visit. One analysand required that I always speak in a low voice. Another wanted to play games but insisted that he always had to win. The rules of this inner shelter might appear odd and irrational, but on careful analysis, one discovers that there are very serious reasons for their creation. The following narrative testifies to the child's incredible capacity to build up a protective system in order to maintain a sense of identity, belonging, and continuity, especially when the home environment fails to mirror the true self:

> My whole identity was caught up in winning or losing a game. As a child, I did not feel at home anywhere—not even in myself. But if I won a game, I felt I had a right to exist and I felt I belonged to some place or somebody. My identity was built on winning. I have never had a home; I have had to make it up myself. I would always measure each situation to see if I fitted in—if I had the right clothes or if I said the right thing. As I had no sense of inner belonging, I had to make it myself.

Some narratives about home are full of surprises. They can lift depression and bring healing to the momentary afflictions of a suffering soul. Ruggero, the renowned Italian film director, once told me about visits to his ancestral home in southern Italy:

> We lived in the town. When I was a child, we would often go back to the countryside and visit the ancestral home. My relatives were still living in the house. My grandmother was very powerful and strong. She never liked me climbing trees. She was afraid that the olive trees might be injured. I begged my father to buy a tree for me so that I could climb it. He bought a small plot of land with several olive trees. Now I could climb trees, our trees. I will never forget what my father did for me. We still own that plot

> of land. It is a little gold mine. Each year it provides several hundred liters of olive oil, more than enough for the whole family. Father was worried I might sell it one day. I would never do that. I could sell everything else, but not the field. My olive field—it is like a church. It never changes, like the surrounding landscape and the old people who live on the land. No matter what I do, they never change. They are reliable. When I go back to the village, meet my relatives, and see my olive field, I am at home.

Ruggero's narrative might appear to advocate a return home as the most effective remedy for homesickness. He has, however, lived in several different countries and has not suffered the profound sense of homelessness that causes confusion, disorientation, and loss of containment. He visits his beloved olive field only once in a while, and is under no compulsion to do so. Ruggero described his relationship with his parents as problematic. Outwardly, they were over-protective; inwardly, he felt misunderstood and neglected. Nevertheless, he remembered moments of vital exchange in which his whole being became reflected in their eyes. The purchase of the olive field was one such moment. It was highly significant that Ruggero's father supported him in defiance of his domineering grandmother, an act that strengthened Ruggero's identity as a man, so important in a culture in which females can be all-powerful in the family milieu. It created a connection to his ancestors and promised a future of wealth. His soul gained a sense of continuity and belonging, experienced as an inner resourcefulness to face the challenges of the future. Home was not the olive field, but that field represented an outer and inner reality that survived change and brought to Ruggero a sense of being in the world that was reliable.

The olive field narrative illustrates a foundational experience of soul kinship with self and the world—with family, culture, and the surrounding countryside. Home became an inner reality that Ruggero could take with him wherever he went. He could access the quality of those earlier attachments and affiliations to his original homeland so as to meet life's contingencies in appropriate and creative ways. The memory of the olive field was not stored as a fixed image but as a rich source of meaning that could be activated on registering cues from his environment. Like the fertile fields of his homeland, it remained an undefined potential that brought to memory again and again the promises of springtime, particularly at moments when the darkness of winter seemed overwhelming. It became a wellspring of hope and renewal that infused his being with a reliable narrative perspective on who he was and who he could be.

## Conclusion

This short essay is an elaboration of one I wrote in 1996.[23] Home has been a work of continual translation in both my personal and professional life. Memories of rivers, fields, seas, houses, villages, and people whom I loved or hated continue to act as a source of information and nourishment, bringing to consciousness narratives that have been lost or repressed in the course of a lifetime. Home is the collected stories of one's lives, regardless of whether those stories are "good" ones or "bad" ones. No individual or nation wants to be reminded of the darker side of life. But if we refuse to remember painful events, we are more likely to repeat them. Home narratives become far more interesting when they are analyzed for the ways people have deconstructed and reconstructed their personal and collective inheritance. François Bondy, a Swiss essayist, once said that modern humanity is broken humanity. Stories of home are often about the making or breaking of the heart. Great stories of the heart are about how to construct a shelter for that organ of longing that needs to be alone and yet needs to be connected to others.

I was not scheduled to give a talk (and hence write this paper) for the Jungian Odyssey. I did so in lieu of my dear friend, John O'Donohue, who was sadly torn away from us in January 2008. In honor of his life and work, I would like to end with his words.

> No one experiences your life as you do; yours is a totally unique story of experiences and feelings. Yet no individual is sealed off or hermetically self-enclosed. Although each soul is individual and unique, by its very nature the soul hungers for relationship. Consequently, it is your soul that longs to belong—and it is our soul that makes all belonging possible. No soul is private. No soul is merely mortal. As well as being the vital principle of your individual life, your soul is also ancient and eternal; it weaves you into the great tapestry of spirit which connects everything everywhere.[24]

---

## *NOTES*

[1] Alwyn Rees and Brinley Rees, *Celtic Heritage: Ancient Tradition in Ireland and Wales* (London: Thames and Hudson, 1961), p. 276.

[2] Arthur Schopenhauer, *Parerga and Paralipomena: A Collection of Philosophical Essays*, trans. T. Bailey Saunders (New York: Cosimo, 2007 [1894]), p. 102.

[3] Roger D. Abrahams, "Foreword," in *The Ritual Process: Structure and Anti-Structure*, by Victor Turner (New York: Aldine de Gruyter, 1969), p. vii.

[4] *The Popular Encyclopedia*, vol. 4 (London: Blackie and Son, 1859), p. 783.

[5] Johann Jakob Scheuchzer, "Von dem Heimwehe," in *Seltsamen Naturgeschichten des Schweizer-Lands wochentliche Erzehlung* (1705), quoted by Christian Schmid-Cadalbert, "Die unaussprechliche Begierde nach der Heimat: Als Heimweh noch krank machte," radio interview by Martin Heule, *Montagsstudio* DRS2, March 2, 1992, my translation.

[6] *Ibid.* See also, Johann Jakob Scheuchzer, *Natur-Historie des Schweitzerlandes* (Zürich: In der Bodmerischen Truckerey, 1716), p. 12.

[7] Johann Gottfried Ebel, *Schilderung der Gebirgsvölker der Schweiz* (Leipzig: Wolfischen Buchhandlung, 1798), p. 416, my translation.

[8] *Ibid.*, p. 419, my translation.

[9] *Ibid.*, p. 421, my translation.

[10] "Ranz des vaches," *The New Grove Dictionary of Music and Musicians*, Vol. 20, ed. Stanley Sadie, 2nd ed. (London: Macmillan, 2001), p. 826.

[11] Gaston Bachelard, *The Poetics of Space*, trans. Maria Jolas (Boston, MA: The Beacon Press, 1969), p. 5.

[12] *Ibid.*, p. 4.

[13] Christian Buckard, "Ich kann sehr gut ohne Heimat Leben," *Tages-Anzeiger*, December 5, 2005, p. 5699, http://www.tages anzeiger.ch/service/archiv/.

[14] Robin Flower, *The Western Island, or The Great Blasket* (Oxford: The Clarendon Press, 1973), p. 14.

[15] Gerard Delanty, *Citizenship in a Global Age: Society, Culture, Politics* (Buckingham, UK: Open University Press, 2002), p. 82.

[16] Christian Graf von Krockow, *Heimat* (Munich: DTV, 1992), pp. 8-10.

[17] Frederick Buechner, *The Longing for Home: Recollections and Reflections* (San Francisco, CA: HarperSanFrancisco, 1996), p. 11.

[18] Eva Hoffman, *Lost in Translation: A Life in a New Language* (New York: Penguin Books, 1990).

[19] *Ibid.,* p. 74.

[20] John Bowlby, *A Secure Base: Clinical Applications of Attachment Theory* (London: Routledge, 1988), p. 28-29.

[21] Daniel N. Stern, *The Interpersonal World of the Infant: A View from Psychoanalysis and Developmental Psychology* (New York: Basic Books, 1985), pp. 77ff, 199.

[22] John Hill, "At Home in the World," *Journal of Analytical Psychology* 14, no. 4 (1996): 585.

[23] *Ibid.*, pp. 575-598.

[24] John O'Donohue, *Eternal Echoes: Exploring our Hunger to Belong* (London: Bantam Books, 1998), p. xvii.

# Part II

# Radical Body—Mother and Child

Raffaella Ada Colombo, M.D., received her medical degree in 1988 and specialized in psychiatry in 1992. She graduated from the C. G. Jung-Institut Zurich in 2003. Since 1988, she has been working at a psychiatric hospital near Milan and maintaining a private practice as well. At the psychiatric hospital, she is involved in research on cognitive impairments of the prefrontal cortex and the limbic system. As a psychiatrist she has published articles on epidemiology, psychopathology, and psychopharmacology. She is interested specifically in the relationship of mind and brain and the interdisciplinary study of neuroscience and analytical psychology. She lectures on these subjects at ISAP.

# 4

# From Linguistic Intimacy to Sense of Self: Brain Interactions in Mother-Child Intersubjectivity

*Raffaella Ada Colombo*

## Introduction

The aim of this paper is to focus on the concept of intersubjectivity between mother and infant and on how a sense of self develops in the infant's brain and mind. In particular, intersubjectivity is investigated in the mother-child relatedness that emerges through the process of language learning. The earliest stages of this process involve vocalizations directed at the attunement of affects between mother and infant, such that a progressive organization of the mind occurs, culminating in the emergence of the sense of self in the infant. This is a dyadic phenomenon. The vocalizations between mother and infant create a mental space in which they share personal inner affects. In this sense, the vocalizations and, later on, words as transitional phenomena, do not truly belong either to the self, or to the other. We will examine how affective experiences can enter the intersubjective space, a phenomenon that we shall call *affect attunement*.

## The Mother Archetype and the Dyadic Mother-Child Space

The human experience of being held and contained in the warm embrace of the mother is a known vital feeling. To be cuddled and to feel dependent on warm maternal contact is to experience "mother" in its positive aspect. Fundamental features of mother are represented in the action of holding: protection, nurturance, looking after, helping, and reassurance. The dyadic experience of being touched and heard belongs to both inner and outer spaces experienced by the body and the mind, since it involves both emotional interactions and somatic perceptions.

The mother creates a new mental-psychic organization in order to deal with the requests to be held coming from the infant. A primary intersubjectivity is initiated with the opening up of the dyadic mind-body space. Mother and infant have to enter together into the realm of the mother archetype—the former, thanks to her previous experience of having been a child, the latter, thanks to the primal imperative to live and survive in an unknown territory. It may be that the mother, for the first time, begins to come to terms with the images, shapes, concepts, contents, aspects, and symbols of the personal unconscious experience of motherhood and the collective experience of the Mother. The mother archetype is activated by the dyadic experience as life-principle, the source of vital water, the unconscious, the cycle of creation. The space between mother and child is full of fantasies, expectations, and projections. The co-construction of patterns of behavior is realized in the dyadic relationship: infant and mother interact reciprocally and shape their intersubjective world together.

The sense of a subjective self gradually emerges as a result of the mother's ongoing sharing of emotions and feelings with the child. To experience positive states is to acquire positive patterns of learning, guaranteed by the presence of a flexible and safe mother. The transformation that occurs takes place within the distinctive realm of female biology. Biological processes reinforce the relation between mother and infant, transforming the experience of the "other" into the dyadic relation. The experience starts early on, at the beginning of pregnancy, in the womb, the symbol of fertility, containment, and protection, as well as of mysterious and hidden powers. The basic symbol for the feminine is the vase, and the womb as container is symbolized by cave, abyss, urn, gorge, water, night, and grave.

Through the mother we experience for the first time an inner and outer world; from this experience emerges an image, a reflection, an appearance not only of the outer motherly image, but of one that is older and much more primitive and abiding than the outer one.[1]

From the very beginning of the dyadic relationship, the issue is the connection between "me" and "you." The mother transforms the infant, but at the same time she, too, is unconsciously transformed, by the development of the infant. In fact, the infant plays a major role in the development of the attachment relationship. The interplay between object and subject occurs in both directions: from mother to child and vice versa, in a unity born out of their symbiotic dependence. "It is within this matrix of physiological and sociobiological dependency on the mother that the structural differentiation takes place which leads to the individual's organization for adaptation: the functioning ego."[2]

After an initial period in which the empathic process itself goes unnoticed, the infant gradually becomes aware that an empathic process bridging the two minds has begun. It is at this point that the process of distinguishing "me" from "you" is influenced by the mother's empathy. In fact, the mother's empathy now becomes a direct subject of the infant's experience.

At this stage, the visual modality is central. The mother's face is the most potent visual stimulus in the infant's world. The eyes play an important role in this specific social interaction. Bodily proximity and the visual modality interact to promote the development of coherent affect attunements. The mother's eye movements, gaze, body orientation, and locomotion in response to the infant provide the infant with information about the intentionality of the mother. "[F]or the first time, one can attribute to the infant the capacity for psychic intimacy—the openness to disclosure, the permeability or interpenetrability that occurs between two people ...."[3]

Inner sensations constitute the core of the self; they appear to be the central point around which the sense of the self crystallizes, the basis for the further construction of the sense of identity.[4] The subjective experience in both the infant and the mother stimulates a mind-brain development that is not reproducible in any other relationship, even if it is similar to the deep experience of being held. Under progressive stimulation from the infant's conscious experience, the infant brain undergoes differential development in various regions of the cerebral cortex. The shared exploration of the space between mother and child stimulates early maturation of specific cortical and subcortical areas of the brain such as the orbitofrontal cortex, the temporal and parietal hemispheres, and the amygdala.[5]

This dyadic process of brain development takes place under the influence of mother-infant interactions and results in the gradual integration of specific cerebral processes and functions. As Meissner states,

> ... [A]utonomous ego functions emerge in the course of complex transactions with the mother, the infant develops the capacity to delay responses, thus enabling modes of response based on stored information related to processes of self-regulation as mediated by maturation and reorganization of [the] orbitofrontal cortex. Thus secure attachment contributes to the development of cerebral structures supporting mentalization, especially in the right hemisphere ....[6]

The patterns of interaction in the dyadic relationship replicate the forms of specific emotional and bodily reactions. The repetition of non-stereotypic interactive exchanges gives rise to the co-construction of new patterns of behavior. The mother repeats the emotional attunement with the infant, transforming its experience into a dyadic intersubjectivity that constructs the deep experience of space and time. The maternal mirroring, attuning, and responsiveness induce the development of shared patterns of behavior and balanced affective experiences. Stern explains:

> Only when infants can sense that others distinct from themselves can hold or entertain a mental state that is similar to one they sense themselves to be holding is the sharing of subjective experience or intersubjectivity possible .... It is ... a working notion that says something like, what is going on in my mind may be similar enough to what is going on in your mind that we can somehow communicate this (without words) and thereby experience intersubjectivity.[7]

## The Evidence for Intersubjectivity Relatedness

It has been demonstrated that infants become aware that they can share their inner subjective experiences with a caregiver sometime between the ages of seven and nine months.[8] During this period, the ego of the infant is gradually emerging from the undifferentiated and fused dyadic experience. The infant's self begins to be separated from that of the other. The bodily boundaries undergo a perceptible change as a result of the experience of interpersonal contact. Prior to this, as Neumann has written,

> ... [the] *participation mystique* between mother and child is the original situation of container and contained. It is the beginning of the relation of the Archetypal Feminine to the child, and it likewise determines the relation of the mater-

> nal unconscious to the child's ego and consciousness as long as these two systems are not separated from one another.[9]

This relation remains fused until the two are separated from each other by the development of intersubjectivity. Between seven and nine months, the infant is still preverbal, and the sharing of its subjective experience cannot, therefore, involve linguistic interaction with the caregiver or the mother. The sharing is done, rather, through vocalizations and gestures.

There are three mental states that are of great relevance to the infant's interpersonal world: sharing joint attention, sharing intentions, and sharing affective states.[10] During the sharing of the focus of attention, mother and child are totally involved with the outer world. They discover the space around them by sharing emotional reactions. The main feature of the interaction at this stage is the gesture of pointing. This kind of gesture involves the experience of vision: both mother and child pay attention to visual stimuli directing their movements and attention toward objects.

> The gesture of pointing and the act of following another's line of vision are among the first overt acts that permit inferences about the sharing of attention, or the establishing of joint attention. Mothers point and infants point.[11]

It is interesting that the mother adds to the gesture a variety of complex vocalizations. These vocalizations indicate to the infant the modulation of the mother's emotions. Thus, the sharing of attention is augmented with gestures, postures, actions, and non-verbal vocalizations just prior (and presumably as a precursor) to the emergence of language.

The most common examples of intentional communication are protolinguistic forms of requesting. When the mother follows the infant's intention, the inter-intentionality becomes a real experience. Stern describes a typical interaction as follows: "The infant reaches out a hand, palm up towards mother, and while making grasping movements and looking back and forth between hand and mother's face intones, 'Eh! Eh!' with an imperative prosody ...."[12]

How does the infant learn to share its affective states with the mother? It would appear that the ability to interpret the emotional messages of facial expressions is at the heart of this process. At about nine months of age, the infant begins to notice a correspondence between its own affective states and the facial expressions it sees on the face of another person. This suggests that "[i]nteraffectivity may be the first, most pervasive, and most immediately important form of sharing subjective experiences."[13] Thus, non-verbal behavior, facial expressions, and vocalizations are the ABC of the infant's mechanism for communicating its inner experiences. According to Calkins and Hill, "To the extent that a caregiver can appropriately read infant signals and respond in ways that minimize distress or, alternatively, motivate positive interaction, the infant will integrate such experiences into the emerging behavioral repertoire."[14]

Tactile responses are a good example of how this works. When an infant experiences stress, the mother's soothing touch can lower its heart rate, and this, in turn, may evoke a more adaptive behavioral response on the part of the infant.[15] Visual cues are involved as well. When the infant encounters situations or objects that create uncertainty (e.g., a very strange-looking object or loud sounds and flashes), it looks, for reassurance, at the mother's face in an attempt to read her affective states. The act of checking the mother's reaction is fundamental to resolving the uncertainty. Thus, sharing reactions and intentions towards objects and events and exchanging proto-linguistic messages through vocalizations is the primary way in which infants learn how to modulate affective states.

It seems that the sharing of affective states precedes the sharing of mental states.[16] The specific cognitive ability to understand others as intentional agents implies the ability to interpret their behavior and to attribute mental states to them in order to form theories about their intentions, desires, and beliefs and to make predictions about their future behavior. The ability to posit the existence of other minds enables the infant, and later the child, to realize that two individuals can react with different emotions to the same event because their beliefs and desires are different.[17] It is primarily through affect attunement that the infant develops this ability.

Several processes go into operation during affect attunement.

> First, the parent [mother] must be able to read the infant's feeling state from the infant's overt behavior. Second, the parent [mother] must perform some behavior that is not a strict imitation but nonetheless corresponds in some way to the infant's overt behavior. Third, the infant must be able to read this corresponding parental [maternal] response as having to do with the infant's own original feeling experience ....[18]

When the infant is about nine months old, the mother begins to add a new dimension to her imitation-like behavior, a dimension that appears to be influenced by the infant's status as a potential intersubjective partner. The mother now expands her behavior repertoire beyond pure imitation into a new category of behavior called affect attunement.

A new dialogue starts between mother and infant. If the infant makes a face, the mother makes a face. However, this exchange of emotional reactions is not merely a mechanical repetition of acts of mimicking; rather, at each round in the "dialogue," the mother varies her imitation slightly, perhaps changing the pitch or intensity of her vocalization, using a "theme-and-variation format."[19]

To the casual observer, this interaction between mother and infant may appear to be straightforward imitation, but in fact what is really taking place is a sort of "matching" game in which the matching is largely "cross-modal." In other words, "the channel or modality of expression used by the mother to match the infant's behavior is different from the channel or modality used by the infant."[20] Stern provides a vivid example in the following description:

> A nine-month-old girl becomes very excited about a toy and reaches for it. As she grabs it, she lets out an exuberant "aaaah!" and looks at her mother. Her mother looks back, scrunches up her shoulders, and performs a terrific shimmy with her upper body, like a go-go dancer. The shimmy lasts only about as long as her daughter's "aaaah!" but is equally excited, joyful, and intense.[21]

It is important to note that in the matching that is going on here the mother and infant are not focusing on each other's external behavior, but rather on each other's inner states as revealed in some aspect of their observable behavior. As Stern points out, "The ultimate reference for the match appears to be the feeling state and not the external behavioral event."[22] By means of this cross-modal matching of inner states, the infant discovers its own subjectivity and its capacity for intersubjective relations, and it eventually learns to regulate its inner emotional states.

Why is attunement behavior so important? Because it re-casts the event and shifts the focus of attention to what is behind the behavior, to the quality of the feelings that are being shared between mother and infant. It is generally acknowledged that "imitation is the predominant way to teach external forms and attunement the predominant way to commune with or indicate sharing of internal states."[23]

The most common maternal responses to an infant's expression of affect are attunement, imitation, and verbal comments. To achieve the first of these, affect attunement, the mother has three dimensions at her command: intensity, timing, and shape.[24] The mother can match either the intensity, the timing, or the shape of the infant's expression of affect. Of these three, the one most commonly used is intensity. Through the mother's mirroring of the intensity of the infant's expressions, the infant receives an emotional stimulation that is vital for the development of specific cortical and subcortical areas, but particularly for the right brain.[25]

It is important to differentiate between *categorical affects*, such as sadness, joy, fear, and surprise, and what Daniel Stern has termed *vitality affects* or "forms of feeling."[26] Vitality affects are "dynamic, kinetic qualities of feeling that distinguish animate from inanimate and that correspond to the momentary changes in feeling states involved in the organic process of being alive."[27] We experience vitality affects "as dynamic shifts or patterned changes within ourselves"[28] or others. It seems that the infant first learns about vitality affects from its interactions with its own bodily stimuli. It also learns that there are transformational means for translating perceptions of external things into internal feelings besides those for categorical affects. The continual "negotiation" of interactions with the mother builds a specific pattern of learning and enactments that shape the child's behavior, his or her inner world, and the nature of his or her future relationships.

## Language, Emotions, and Brain Functions

We have long known that language has two distinct dimensions: the linguistic and the emotional. When a speaker speaks, the listener registers not just the message that the speaker is attempting to convey, but also the feelings in the speaker that underlie that message. These two dimensions of language are associated with specific regions of the cerebral cortex: the grammatical aspects of language are processed in the left hemisphere and the prosodic elements in the right hemisphere. However, the emotional aspect of communication is more "primitive" than the linguistic, and infants have access to it long before they have access to verbal language. Even before infants are able use words, they instinctively use vocalizations to express themselves, both to themselves and to those around them.

Through vocalizations and the innate pre-verbal language of the limbic system, mother and child conduct their affective and bodily interactions. Over the course of the infant's development, limbic emotional language and social-emotional intelligence become more complex and elaborate. Initially, the infant's emotional sound production appears to convey generalized meanings such as pleasure and displeasure.[29] Gradually, the vocalizations become modified, depending on the context, and are increasingly shaped by and tied to specific moods or events and social-emotional phenomena.[30]

A variety of sounds associated with specific emotions such as fear, sadness, caution, alarm, and pleasure convey information about inner emotional states. The expression of these states forms the basis of interpersonal relations, even if they are expressed differently in different cultures and traditions. Social-emotional and related contextual nuances—feelings of fear, love, anger, happiness, sadness, sarcasm, or empathy—are communicated vocally and non-linguistically. As Meissner states,

> ... [T]he mind registers information either verbally or nonverbally. The verbal system encodes for language and logic and serves shared communication with others. The nonverbal system encodes sensory imagery and motoric, autonomic, visceral, and somatic representations, for which emotions serve a major organizing function.[31]

It is prosody—the intonation, inflections, and rhythms of spoken language—that reveals the affective states of the speaker. Clues to the prosody of speech, such as the tone, inflection, stress contours, amplitude, timbre, pitch, rate, and melody of the voice, are detected by the right hemisphere.

Facial expressions, body postures, and gestures provide additional nuances, which enhance the understanding of the non-verbal messages. The right hemisphere has the ability to evaluate the states of mind of other individuals as well as their emotions and intentions.[32] According to Schore, the right hemisphere "... is specialized for the processing of socioemotional information and bodily states. The early maturing right cerebral cortex is dominant for attachment functions ... and stores an internal working model of the attachment relationship."[33]

In order to understand a spoken message in its totality, we need to interpret the tone of the speaker's voice, pay attention to the prosody, and follow the narrative. The interaction of language and narrative is central to the elaboration of emotional meanings. Language and narrative are powerful tools in the creation and maintenance of the self. In the bi-hemispheric language system, the social-emotional-vocal functions are associated with and mediated by the limbic system (the amygdala, the cingulate gyrus, the hypothalamus, and the septal nuclei) and are represented at the level of the neocortex in the right temporal and frontal lobes. Through the limbic system it is possible to communicate social-emotional nuances via multiple modalities, as is reflected in the evolution of emotional speech. The limbic system is responsible for our ability to laugh, cry, and express sympathy or compassion, as well as for our desire to form or maintain emotional attachments.[34] The amygdala is one of the most active components of the limbic system, especially in vocal production. It is actively involved in social-emotional limbic language, continually monitoring auditory, visual, and tactile events so as to detect those with emotional and motivational implications.[35] It is of primary importance with regard to all aspects of emotion, including the capacity to process love or anger and to form long-term emotional attachments.[36] When it is stimulated, a variety of complex vocalizations, emotions, behaviors, and moods are triggered, including those indicative of pleasure, sadness, happiness, fear, anxiety, anger, and rage.[37]

Another component of the limbic system involved in vocal production and activated by vocal stimuli is the septal nuclei, which lie in the medial portions of the hemispheres near the hypothalamus. The septal nuclei play a major role in emotional functioning and also produce emotional vocalizations, especially those associated with feelings of pleasure.[38]

The third component of the limbic system is the cingulate gyrus, which is located directly above the corpus callosum and consists of two segments, referred to as the anterior cingulate and the posterior cingulate. The anterior cingulate is involved in the generation of intimate maternal behaviors and the maintenance of an emotional attachment between mother and infant through infantile sounds such as laughing, crying, or howling.[39] It also plays a role in in the expression of emotional nuances, emotional learning, long-term attachments, and vocalizations.[40] The posterior segment, on the other hand, is involved in the integration of visual input, memory-cognitive activities, and visual-spatial activities.[41]

It is mainly through the amygdala and the anterior cingulate that emotional and motivational significance and nuances are extracted from or imparted to auditory and other perceptual input. Via the rich interconnections maintained with the neocortex, auditory information processed by the temporal lobe becomes infused with emotion. It is through the cingulate gyrus and its interconnections with the right frontal lobe that tonal variations and emotions, including feelings of maternal concern, can be imparted directly into the speech stream to convey more accurately what the speaker intends to say.[42] At birth, the amygdala is immature and the infant freely expresses feelings of aversion and rage, or pleasure and quiescence. As the amygdala and hippocampus begin to develop and mature, the infant becomes more reality-oriented and more social. Alongside this, the infant learns to attend selectively to externally occurring events and to store information in memory.[43]

Thus, the amygdala, the septal nuclei, and the cingulate gyrus are of primary importance in the development and maintenance of long-term social and emotional attachments.

## Mother-Infant Communication through Vocalizations

Vocalizations have played a vital role in the evolution of mammals, and especially of primates. A lost infant animal's cry of distress helps the mother animal to locate her infant, and conversely, vocalizations from the mother help the lost infant to orient itself and find its way back to its mother. This has led Rhawn Joseph to conclude that the complex social-emotional communication observed in humans very probably developed from early mother-infant interactions.[44] As we have already seen, the use of sounds to convey emotions is intimately connected with the limbic system, and as humans evolved, the maternal care of infants came to rely increasingly on this limbic form of communication, which Joseph has termed "limbic language."[45] Researchers have observed that adults generally, but mothers in particular, have a tendency to exaggerate the prosodic features of vocal communication, such as pitch and intonation, when interacting with infants. Research has also demonstrated that women in general are better at using this sort of limbic language than men. Joseph provides a broad overview of some recent findings in this area. He notes that women of all ages have been found to express their emotions more freely than men, as well as to feel and show empathy and recognize the emotional valence of facial expressions more easily. Their speech has greater tonal variation than that of men, who tend to use a monotone. Five or six tonal variations have been identified in female speech as opposed to two or three in male speech.

At the neurological level, the anterior commissure, the bundle of nerve fibers that connects the right and left amygdala and the right and left inferior temporal lobes is 28.4% larger in heterosexual females than in heterosexual males, according to one study.[46] This indicates that there is greater communication between the two brain hemispheres in women than there is in men, and this in turn suggests that the two dimensions of language mentioned earlier, the grammatical and the emotional, are better integrated in women. Furthermore, given that the anterior cingulate gyrus evolved, at least in part, in a maternal context and/or promoted the development of maternal feelings and long-term mother-infant attachment, the larger size of the female anterior commissure may also account for the greater desire on the part of females to nurture, hold, cuddle, and take care of infants in contrast to males.

The infant's attachment to its mother occurs in two stages, the amygdaloid stage and the septal stage. This is because the amygala matures before the septal nuclei. Up to the seventh month, the infant will smile at anyone's approach, even that of a complete stranger. This behavior corresponds to the amygdaloid stage, during which septal nuclei and the cingulate gyrus are still less well developed. However, around the seventh month, the infant begins to develop a distinct and almost exclusive attachment to a single caregiver (usually its mother) and this is accompanied by a corresponding decline in its indiscriminate interaction with everyone in its surroundings.[47] From this point on, the fear of strangers becomes increasingly pronounced. Studies show that 70% of nine-month-old infants respond negatively to strangers, and by one year of age, this proportion has reached 90%.[48] In this phase of development, long-term attachment to the mother becomes established under the influence of the cingulate gyrus and the septal nuclei, which tend to inhibit the kind of indiscriminate social contact promoted by the amygdala in the earlier stage. This shift of the infant's focus to the mother is crucial for survival, since it establishes for the infant the presence of a primary caregiver as the primary source of its emotional development.

While developments in the neural structure of the infant's brain affect its behavior, there is also a reverse influence. As Schore states, "... the maturation of the infant's brain is experience dependent, and ... these experiences are embedded in the attachment relationship ...."[49] If good, safe contact with the mother is minimal or absent, the neural architecture of the limbic regions is also likely to develop abnormally.[50] Under such circumstances, the infant's emotional development will be disrupted and he or she will have difficulty engaging in successful social interactions later in life. Thus, the maturation and regulation of emotions must be understood as occurring in the nurturing inner and outer space of the dyadic relationship, for it is via the interactions of limbic nuclei that emotions such as love, jealousy, rage, fear of abandonment, or possessiveness are generated.

Research[51] using functional MRI to determine the neural underpinnings of maternal love and romantic love has found that these two emotions are related in that they share certain regions of the reward circuitry in the brain. "Both deactivate a common set of regions associated with negative emotions, social judgment, and ... the assessment of other people's intentions and emotions."[52] Since the anterior cingulate gyrus is involved in attention, maternal behavior, and reward-based learning, the researchers were led to conclude that "human attachment employs a push-pull mechanism"[53] by which the forces that prompt us to maintain an appropriate social distance are overcome, and we are drawn to one another. This is a twofold process, in which the brain's critical faculties and its mechanisms for negative emotions are deactivated and, at the same time, the centers involved in reward and pleasure go into action. It turns out that the intimacy between mother and infant is not so different, after all, from the intimacy between two lovers. Perhaps this is because both forms of intimacy are essential for our survival as a species.

## *NOTES*

[1] C. G. Jung, "The Dual Mother," in *Symbols of Transformation, the Collected Works*, trans. R. F. C. Hull (Princeton, NJ: Princeton University Press, 1956/1967), vol. 5, § 500.

[2] Margaret S. Mahler, Fred Pine, and Anni Bergman, *The Psychological Birth of the Human Infant: Symbiosis and Individuation* (New York: Basic Books, 1975), p. 45.

[3] Daniel N. Stern, *The Interpersonal World of the Infant: A View from Psychoanalysis and Developmental Psychology* (London: Karnac, 1985), p. 126.

[4] Mahler *et al.*, p. 47.

[5] Rhawn Joseph, *Neuropsychiatry, Neuropsychology, and Clinical Neuroscience: Emotion, Evolution, Cognition, Language, Memory, Brain Damage, and Abnormal Behavior* (Baltimore, MD: Lippincott, Williams & Wilkins, 1996); Allan N. Schore, "The Effects of Early Relational Trauma on Right Brain Development, Affect Regulation, and Infant Mental Health," in *Infant Mental Health Journal* 22, no. 1-2 (2001): 201-269; Larry R. Squire and Barbara J. Knowlton, "The Medial Temporal Lobe, the Hippocampus, and the Memory Systems of the Brain," in *The New*

*Cognitive Neuroscience,* ed. Michael S. Gazzaniga (Cambridge, MA: MIT Press, 2000), pp. 765-779.

[6] William W. Meissner, "The Mind-Brain Relation and Neuroscientific Foundations: II. Neurobehavioral Integrations," in *Bulletin of the Menninger Clinic*, vol. 70, nr. 2 (2006): 106-107.

[7] Stern, p. 124.

[8] *Ibid.*

[9] Erich Neumann, *The Great Mother*, trans. Ralph Manheim (Princeton, NJ: Princeton University Press, 1991 [1955]), p. 29.

[10] Stern, p. 128.

[11] *Ibid.*, p. 129.

[12] *Ibid.*, p. 131.

[13] *Ibid.*, p. 132.

[14] Susan D. Calkins and Ashley Hill, "Caregiver Influences on Emerging Emotion Regulation: Biological and Environmental Transactions in Early Development," in *Handbook of Emotion Regulation*, ed. James J. Gross (New York: Guilford Press, 2007), p. 235.

[15] *Ibid.,* p. 240.

[16] Colwyn Trevarthen, Penelope Hubley, "Secondary Intersubjectivity: Confidence, Confiding and Acts of Meaning in the First Year," in *Action, Gesture and Symbol: The Emergence of Language*, ed. Andrew Lock (New York: Academic Press, 1978), pp. 183-230.

[17] Hedy Stegge, Mark Meerum Terwogt, "Awareness and Regulation of Emotion in Typical and Atypical Development," in *Handbook of Emotion Regulation*, ed. James G. Gross (New York: Guilford Press, 2007), p. 275.

[18] Stern, p. 139.

[19] *Ibid.*, p. 140.

[20] *Ibid.*, p. 141.

[21] *Ibid.*, p. 140.

[22] *Ibid.*, p. 142.

[23] *Ibid.*

[24] *Ibid.*, p. 148.

[25] Joseph, *Neuropsychiatry*; Schore, "The Effects of Early Relational Trauma;" Squire, Knowlton, "The Medial Temporal Lobe."

[26] Stern, pp. 53ff.

[27] *Ibid.*, p. 156.

[28] *Ibid*, p. 57.

[29] *Ibid.,* p. 236.

[30] Rhawn Joseph, "The Neuropsychology of Development: Hemispheric Laterality, Limbic Language, and the Origin of Thoughts," in *Journal of Clinical Psychology*, 38, no. 1 (1982): 4-33; Esther Milner, *Human Neural and Behavioural Development* (Springfield, Il: Charles C. Thomas, 1967); Jean Piaget, *The Origins of Intelligence in Children* (New York: Norton, 1952).

[31] Meissner, p. 105.

[32] Robert Ornstein, *The Right Mind* (San Diego, New York, London: Harcourt Brace & Company, 1997), p. 113.

[33] Schore, p. 209.

[34] Joseph, *Neuropsychiatry*.

[35] Edmund T. Rolls, "Neurophysiology and Functions of the Primate Amygdala," in *The Amygdala*, ed. John P. Aggleton (New York: Wiley-Liss, 1992); Kent M. Perryman, Arthur S. Kling, and Robert L. Lloyd, "Differential Effects of Inferior Temporal Cortex Lesions upon Visual and Auditory-Evoked Potentials in the Amygdala of the Squirrel Monkey (*Saimiri sciureus*)," *Behavioral and Neural Biology*, 47, no. 1 (1987): 73-79; Masaji Fukuda, Taketoshi Ono, and Kiyomi Nakamura, "Functional Relation Among Inferiotemporal Cortex, Amygdala, and Lateral Hypothalamus in Monkey Operant Feeding Behavior," *Journal of Neurophysiology* 57, no. 4 (1987): 1060-1077.

[36] Rhawn Joseph, *The Naked Neuron: Evolution and the Languages of the Body and Brain* (New York: Plenum, 1992).

[37] Paul D. MacLean, *The Triune Brain in Evolution: Role in Paleocerebral Functions* (New York: Plenum, 1990); Pierre Gloor, "Role of the Human Limbic System in Perception, Memory, and Affect: Lessons from Temporal Lobe Epilepsy," in *The Limbic System: Functional Organization and Clinical Disorder*, ed. Benjamin K. Doane and Kenneth E. Livingston (New York: Raven Press, 1986), pp. 159-169.

[38] Joseph, *Neuropsychiatry*.

[39] *Ibid.*

[40] See MacLean, pp. 394-410.

[41] Orrin Devinsky, Martha J. Morrell, and Brent A. Vogt, "Contributions of Anterior Cingulate Cortex to Behaviour," in *Brain* 118, no. 1 (1995): 279-306.

[42] Joseph, *Naked Neuron*; Anne Fernald, "Meaningful Melodies in Mothers' Speech to Infants," in *Origins and Development of Non-Verbal Communication: Evolutionary, Comparative, and Methodological Aspects*, ed. H. Papoušek, U. Jürgens, and M. Papoušek (Cambridge, UK: Cambridge University Press, 1992), pp. 262-282.

[43] Joseph, "Neuropsychology of Development."

[44] Joseph, *Neuropsychiatry*.

[45] *Ibid.*

[46] Laura S. Allen and Roger A. Gorski, "Sexual Orientation and the Size of the Anterior Commissure in the Human Brain," in *The Proceedings of the National Academy of Sciences* 89, no. 15 (1992): 7199-7202.

[47] Joseph, *Neuropsychiatry*.

[48] *Ibid.*

[49] Schore, p. 207.

[50] Joseph, *Neuropsychiatry*.

[51] Andreas Bartels and Semir Zeki, "The Neural Correlates of Maternal and Romantic Love," in *NeuroImage*, 21, no. 3 (2004): 1155-1166.

[52] *Ibid.*, p. 1155.

[53] *Ibid.*

Kathrin Asper, Dr. phil., was born in 1941 in Zürich. She studied literature and pedagogy, and received her doctorate in Literature, with a dissertation on Gustave Flaubert. She trained at the C. G. Jung-Institut Zürich, has been in private practice since 1975, and has given lectures worldwide. Besides many publications in German, her publications in English include *The Inner Child in Dreams* and *The Abandoned Child Within: On Losing and Regaining Self-Worth*. Her areas of special interest are narcissism and self-esteem, problems connected with physical disability, trauma, and psychotherapeutic approaches and perspectives on fairy tales, literature, and art.

5

# Hephaistos, Born with Club-Feet—Lame and Ugly: The Intimate Relationship between Hephaistos and His Mother in the Mirror of Our Time

*Kathrin Asper*

## Thomas's Story

A mother who had given birth to a boy, Thomas, shared her experiences with me and told the story of her little son in the first year of his life:

> The feet were crooked and turned inwards, the soles turned upwards. My first thought was: *My son will have to spend his life in a wheelchair!* On the first day of his life I had to rush with him to the nearby children's hospital. I was worried about going there in a taxi without a companion and no safe car-container for newborns. I just knew that I had *to function*. The diagnosis in the clinic was: congenital clubfeet of a major order. The pediatrician turned Thomas's little feet into a normal position. That must have hurt him terribly; *I shall never forget his crying.*
>
> Later—he was just 17 hours old—his feet and legs were put into plaster up to the hip. From then on we had to go twice a week to the clinic, where the plaster was cut open and replaced by a new one. This took place over a period

of 10 weeks, and from then on once a week because growth had slowed down. The plaster had no padding, as this would produce better results. The baby could be given a bath only in the short interval between two plasterings. Often the feet and legs swelled and hurt and ever so often the skin got a rash, which necessitated removal of the plaster, skin treatment, and the application of a new plaster.

Surgery of the feet was done in two operations. At 10:00 a.m. we had to be in the clinic; it was January and it had snowed heavily. Driving was difficult and we were worried we would not arrive on time. The surgery went well; we shared the small room with another mother whose son had to undergo surgery as well. Thomas suffered a lot of pain. He cried often, for long periods, and was restless in the waking state and enormously jumpy. After a few days, the boy regained his old self gradually.

I developed a high fever and must have contracted an infection. Because of that, I was a danger to Thomas and the other patients, and the doctors wanted to send me home. I protested, and Thomas was allowed to leave the hospital with me and to go home.

Three weeks later, the second operation took place. It went well. Again, the room was very small and packed, and again it was very difficult to breastfeed Thomas; after all, he and his plaster weighed 12 kilos and there was no appropriate chair to handle the procedure.

Soon he was his old self again. *Super how such a young child bounces back!*

After the healing process was complete, Thomas got splints, and was started on physiotherapy—5 times a day! The splints had to be removed each time he had physiotherapy and, after the treatment, put on again. In between and during physiotherapy, he bawled and screamed, because the interventions were painful. That also meant little freedom for his legs. Up until the operations, Thomas enjoyed practically no free movement of his legs, and could not kick. With the splints, he could kick and use his legs freely once the splints were removed. Most of the time Thomas hated the splints, and I had to use all the tricks I could think of to put them on again. Besides the splints, he needed special plastic containers for his feet; they had to be fixed and only when splints and containers were fixed could Thomas be dressed in his leggings.

At the age of 16 months Thomas learned to walk freely.

> Now Thomas has made it to normalcy. For me the greatest joy is that nobody notices "that" with the feet.

The relationship between Thomas and his mother highlights the many factors that can have an influence on the mother-child relationship:

- shock at birth
- worry, anxiety
- a sense of hopelessness about the future
- pain for the baby
- periods of hospitalization
- surgery
- physiotherapy
- stigmatization and other social issues
- difficulty in carrying the baby because of the plaster and its additional weight
- striving to make the baby "normal"

## Outline of the Myth

According to Kerényi,[1] Hephaistos, the Greek god, is said to be the son of Hera and Zeus, but of the many versions of the myth, the most popular one tells us that he was the son of Hera alone. At the beginning of the relationship between Hera and Zeus, the heavenly couple met only in secret, and it was during this period that Zeus gave birth to his daughter Athena without any involvement from Hera. Not to be outdone, Hera decided to have a child without the help of Zeus, and thus she gave birth to Hephaistos.

There are several stories about the birth of Hephaistos and the time thereafter. The most popular runs as follows: Hephaistos was born with crooked and bent feet, the soles and toes were bent backwards, and he was ugly. Hera threw him out of Olympus. After a long fall to the sea, the sea goddesses Thetis and Eurynome received him in their lap. He stayed with them for nine years and worked as a blacksmith in a grotto, producing buckles, earrings, and necklaces for them. No one knew about it, neither men nor gods—no one except his saviors. A lesser-known story says that Hephaistos wanted to help his mother against Zeus, but the father god took him by his heels and threw him from the sacred threshold of the Olympic palace. Again it was a long fall and Hephaistos arrived breathless at sunset on the island Lemnos. There he was found and cared for.

Yet another story tells us that Hera took her son to the island of Naxos, where Kedalion taught him the art of forging iron. Hephaistos was asked to create beautiful thrones for the gods. One of the thrones was for his mother Hera. When she sat on it, she felt tied to the throne by invisible strings and the throne rose into the air. No one could free her. Once the other gods realized that Hephaistos was behind this prank, they asked him to free his mother. Defiantly, he answered that he did not know of a mother. Ares then pitched in and tried to get a hold of Hephaistos, but to no avail; he had to flee from the flames of Hephaistos's smithy. Finally, Dionysus succeeded in bringing Hephaistos to Olympus by means of a ruse: he made him drink some wine. As Hephaistos was not accustomed to wine, he quickly got drunk. Dionysus placed him on a donkey and triumphantly led the drunken god to Olympus. Roars of laughter greeted them. Hephaistos released Hera, but not for nothing: he asked for Aphrodite and Pallas Athena to be his wives. That was granted, but neither marriage was happy.

Besides beautiful jewelry, armor, and thrones, Hephaistos also created Pandora, the first woman, who brought death, illness, defects, and suffering to humankind. He did this at the request of Zeus, who wanted to punish mankind for stealing fire from the gods. The story is well known: Pandora released from her box all the miseries into the world, but she was able to shut the box before hope could escape.

For himself Hephaistos crafted golden women, who helped him in the smithy (prototypes of modern-day robots), and stools that moved by themselves (prototypes of the wheelchair).

## Attachment and Medical Trauma

Traumatic events are always threatening, causing feelings of menace and helplessness beyond the processing ability of those affected. One's experience of oneself and the world is shaken.[2] Since the attachment phase is the primary period of structural growth, traumatic events during this period can cause a particularly serious disruption in the dyadic regulation of the emotions. During this phase, the individual's adaptive and non-adaptive systems are formed, and the way they are formed influences all subsequent relations with self, the world, and the transpersonal. Impairments at this stage have a negative effect on the regulation of emotions, and this interferes with the normal developmental process of the child.[3]

Recognition of the psychosocial implications of medical trauma has been slow in coming in trauma research. However, we now know that disease and disability can have traumatic psychological consequences. While studies have been done for cancer, heart disease, and AIDS patients,[4] we still have little precise knowledge as to how surgery in the bonding phase of an infant's development influences the quality of attachment to its primary caregiver or affects the formation of neural connections and their later development.[5] Our present knowledge of the factors that interfere with attachment formation,[6] as well as neurobiological research,[7] case studies,[8] and the practical work of psychotherapists, have all led to the conclusion that medical treatment of congenital disabilities in combination with other factors has a potentially traumatic effect on infants and may have serious negative consequences in the long term.[9]

Early relational experiences resulting in the formation of an attachment between mother (or other primary caregiver) and child play a decisive role in the child's later development. Ideally, the infant's relational range meshes with that of the mother, whereupon the mother seeks empathic solutions to physical, interpersonal, and intrapsychic problems. If the attachment formation is relatively unhindered, a foundation is laid for the development of feelings of security, trust, belonging, and continuity, and for the experience of consolation and acceptance. An "internal working model" is established, by which expectations of subsequent trustful encounters are embedded in the infant's developing mind.[10] Disruptions during this bonding phase may give rise to "insecure" or "disorganized" attachment. The result is an attitude to life characterized by uncertainty and lack of trust, and relational expectations that are shaped by anxiety, distrust, and ambivalence.

Impairment of the infant's motor apparatus, as in the case of Thomas, can affect the quality of its attachment to its mother. The obstructed movement requires special corrective measures, such as physiotherapy, and this necessitates periods of separation from the mother, which disrupt the infant's sense of continuity and inner presence of the mother.[11]

Once the attachment has been formed, it undergoes no essential changes over the course of the individual's life, though it is capable of being changed consciously through insight and new experiences. Thus, disturbances during the bonding phase may cause greater anxiety and depression in later life[12] and may lead to complex post-traumatic stress disorder (C-PTSD).[13]

## Co-Traumatic Processes

Having a child with a disability creates uncertainty in the parents and requires them to adapt to a situation that is completely unfamiliar to them.[14] The parents are traumatized by the stress and trauma of the child, who in turn absorbs the traumatic experience of the parents, so that we can speak of a co-traumatic process.[15]

The prospect of having a child gives rise to idealistic fantasies in the parents-to-be regarding the child and their family life in the future. Consequently, in the head and heart of the mother and father, an imaginary baby is "born" even before the actual birth of their child takes place. It will be a happy child because they want to give it everything! Into the imaginary child is incorporated the archetypal attributes of the divine child, whose role it is to make everything new. This natural process enables the parents-to-be to look forward to the happy event with joy and confidence. However, their positive fantasies are also accompanied by darker ones, which may be summarized as: "Will everything be all right? Will the baby really be healthy and develop normally?" Fortunate the parents whose faith in the future is unshaken! Usually, the positive fantasies prevail, and this has a positive effect on the parents' preparations for the child that is to come. Following the birth of the "real" baby, however, the parents must reconcile the discrepancy between the imaginary child and the real one. If there is a birth defect, this task is made all the more difficult.

On the surface, parents whose baby is born with a defect react primarily with joy at having the child, accompanied by a particular devotion to caring for the child and an overwhelming feeling of wanting to do everything to provide a normal life for it. Beneath the surface, however, fright, anxiety, fear, feelings of guilt and shame, and, occasionally, self-blame arise. Added to this are such practical concerns as how and where the defect should be treated and who will pay for the treatment.

Rarely acknowledged but with serious consequences for both mother and infant is the revival of memories of earlier injuries and trauma in the mother. Pregnancy and childbirth are vulnerable times, because they constitute a transition in life. Such stressful transitions can activate earlier unconscious attitudes that can add to the stress.[16] For example, a mother who herself experienced severe discrimination in childhood may cut herself off from the feelings associated with this experience and may thus become insensitive to the emotional needs of her child when it faces rejection on account of its disability.

A parent who dealt with his or her own personal medical trauma earlier in life by going emotionally numb may adopt the same strategy when the child with birth defects undergoes surgery or gets some other form of treatment and suffers pain. In that case, the child will feel emotionally abandoned,[17] because resonance and attunement to its needs are missing.

Birth defects involving impairment of movement, such as in Thomas's case, require constant, regular, and painstaking care on the part of the mother. The mother has, in fact, to become a co-therapist with the physiotherapist who is treating her child. She has to concentrate on the correct movement and position of the feet, for example. This means that over time a great deal of energy is devoted to the child's physical condition and less attention is paid to its emotional and intentional communication. This has serious consequences for the development of the child's communication and association faculties at the emotional and cognitive levels. The child's messages are interrupted or ignored, and this damages the child's trust in the communicative power of its own spontaneous movements, and also in its ability to initiate interaction with others through those movements. If insecure attachment in the initial, pre-verbal period continues, for the child this means, in the widest sense, that it is not being heard or seen. It may lose confidence in its ability to express itself and thus fall internally silent. For both mother and child, this means increased stress and an unconscious escalation of uncertainty. Obstructions in the body's kinetic apparatus, such as those caused by dysplasia, cerebral palsy, or clubfoot, require surgery and intensive and ongoing physiotherapy. This means persistent correction of spontaneous movement, which may well be accompanied by pain.

The body's natural limits are exceeded and the body is taken over from the outside by the intrusive, foreign interference in the child's movement.[18] For example, in the past, treatment for dysplasia involved wrapping the lower body and extremities in plaster, which had to be replaced every few weeks in line with growth, and this required periods of hospitalization. The procedure was continued up to the third year of the child's life. Not only was the child's freedom of movement thereby obstructed, but the child also lost visual and auditory contact with the mother, since the mother could not carry a child in plaster around the house, quite simply because of its weight. As a consequence of the treatment and the co-traumatic processes that begin during the bonding period, the attempts by both mother and infant to form a secure dyad are thwarted. For the child, this is an encroachment on its trust and its sense of security, but it also means a loss for the mother, who is unable to experience a stress-free dyadic relationship with the baby. Some mothers develop a "preoccupied attachment"[19] style or sink into depression.[20]

Congenital defects usually require early medical and physiological intervention, often involving measures that exceed the limits of the body and require extended separation from the mother. These potentially traumatic interventions often begin during the sensitive bonding stage and thus have a major influence on the preverbal formation of vital processes, since they mark the baby psychobiologically and form the basis for feelings of abandonment, anxiety, existential threat, and pain. In neurobiological terms, these early experiences create neural connections that are stored in implicit memory. They cannot be called up at will into consciousness and cannot be represented in speech, but they nevertheless influence how future events in the child's life are experienced and how these experiences are integrated.

Certain traumatic events—e.g., invasive medical treatment—may act as a trigger *later* in life, releasing the affect associated with these early experiences in the form of "acute post-traumatic stress disorder" (PTSD). In times of crisis, earlier experiences may be revived, causing psychic stress and necessitating a re-running of the developmental process. Long-term traumatic consequences may be manifested in the form of "complex post-traumatic stress disorder,"[21] which must be recognized and treated circumspectly. Early traumatic experiences hitherto silent for many years cross the threshold into consciousness with chaotic results. Basic convictions wobble, one's perspective of the future disappears. Those affected no longer comprehend themselves, develop psychic and somatic complaints, and are at risk of committing suicide. The disorientation and helplessness of those concerned, their families, and their caregivers is great because the thread of their own history has snapped. There is also the risk that the person going through the crisis may mistakenly attribute his or her problems to early parental rejection or neglect, an issue that we will return to later.

It is unfortunate that the delayed consequences of congenital physical disability and the medical trauma that usually accompanies it receive too little attention in education, research, and psychotherapy, not to mention the general neglect of physical disability in psychotherapy and theory-formulation.[22] In addition, the demand for psychotherapy for disabled individuals is low. This is so because, among other reasons, psychotherapy routinely applies theories and approaches derived from the treatment of "physically normal" individuals to those with physical disabilities. Psychotherapy's insensitivity to the special needs of people with physical disabilities may cause such individuals to feel rejected and misunderstood, and this in turn may frighten them off from seeking psychotherapeutic treatment. In the past, they were merely names in the files of various medical specialists, and their emotional experiences and concerns were largely ignored.[23] Today, however, thanks to the paradigm shift being promoted by "Disability Studies," the voice of individuals with disabilities is increasingly being heard.

Still, life is a constant struggle for the physically disabled, since their disability is a permanent stress factor. In developmental terms, separation and autonomy are often delayed on account of physical disability. The physically disabled are less likely to live independently or get married, and if they marry, they usually do so later than their non-disabled counterparts. They are still the object of discrimination and stigmatization in society at large[24]; they often encounter occupational restrictions and are generally excluded from military service.

## Hephaistos and Hera today

It is not uncommon for people to assume that a mother with a physically disabled child does not want the child and has a hard time accepting it. Hera, who threw her club-footed son from Olympus, seems to epitomize this kind of maternal attitude to a disabled child. But is the assumption really justified? Not to my knowledge, based on what I have seen working with mothers with children who "have something."

It has to be admitted, as we saw earlier in Thomas's mother's case, that there is an initial shock; in this moment of shock, some mothers might prefer that the baby not live, or they might be ashamed of it and leave it at the clinic longer than necessary for fear of the reaction of relatives, neighbors, and friends when they bring it home.[25] Usually, however, mothers adapt quickly to the new situation, and the sense of hopelessness gives way to a fierce determination that the baby should get all the medical and therapeutic care necessary to make it "normal," to find a place in society where it can belong. It is also important to bear in mind Winnicott's description of pregnancy and early motherhood: the mother complex takes the lead in the personality of a woman the moment she becomes a mother. Because of this, he compares this early period of motherhood to a "normal illness."[26] The point of similarity between the two is the fact that in both cases the individual is taken over by a complex. However, in the case of early motherhood, it is a healthy, needed "illness" because it results in growth-fostering energy, which becomes the safeguard of the young life.

And yet, as a counterpoint to this positive, life-affirming reaction from the mother, another phenomenon has been observed among our disabled clients, and the disabled in general: they are often convinced that their mother did not love them, that she rejected them. They feel anger towards their mother, even hate her, and hold her responsible for all the pain and hardship they have had to endure. Something else that we have observed is that if a disabled person has "normal" siblings, either the mother seems to give preferential treatment to the child with the disability and to be overprotective of him or her, or she distances herself from the disabled child and treats it with a certain coldness so that a kind of void develops between the child and the mother.

What has also come to my attention in seminars and in supervision and through the accounts of disabled people who have tried psychotherapy is the odd fact that therapists all too easily see the client's difficulties as stemming from the mother's inability to accept the child's disability. This mother-bashing, without the appropriate investigation into the disability and its medical underpinnings, without an analysis of the impact that the disability has on the quality of the attachment, and without an understanding of the way co-traumatic processes develop between child and mother, often has devastating effects. The therapist—usually being unaware of the special problems associated with disabilities—lays the blame on the mother much too easily, often as a defense against his or her own fear and helplessness in dealing with the situation, and thus damages the vital bond between mother and child. Unaware of the especially difficult issues that disabled young adults face over separation from their mother, some therapists encourage and even precipitate separation. In so doing, they cut off the life support system that the mother has been providing for her disabled child over the years. They prematurely, and with little instinct, rob the client of his or her safe place at a time when he or she needs it the most in order to be able gradually to take over responsibility for his or her life *as well as*—and this is what sets the disabled apart from "normal" young people—take over responsibility for the disability and its management and care.

As we have seen above, a congenital disability, with its many medical and therapeutic interventions, is potentially traumatic, causes stress in both child and mother, and is disruptive of the attunement that develops between mother and child through their interaction. This can result in insecure bonding and ambivalence between mother and child.

From an archetypal perspective, what ensues is the constellation of a negative mother complex, which affects the child as well as the mother. In this sense, the myth of Hera rejecting her son enacts the negative archetypal configuration between mother and disabled child and the ambivalence that develops between them. Hephaistos clearly developed an ambivalent relationship towards his mother, as is evident in his rejection of her, while at the same time wanting to protect her from Zeus. Furthermore, he creates a beautiful throne for her, but at the same time, he fastens her to it as the throne rises into the air. All this clearly points to his conflicted feelings towards her.

After his long fall from Olympus, Hephaistos was received by Thetis and Eurynome. They were sea goddesses, and their natural habitat was the sea, a symbol of the unconscious. We may say that they represent the positive archetypal mother in the unconscious. They symbolize the deep-seated archetypal instincts that rise in the mother of a disabled child to care for that child, to raise it and help it socialize and integrate into society.

According to the less well-known story of Hephaistos and his mother mentioned above, Hera took her son to the island Naxos, where Kedalion taught him the art of forging iron. What is split apart into Hera and the sea-goddesses in the better-known story appears in this story joined together as one single character, Hera. Hera throws the child out, but it is also Hera who takes him to Naxos and ensures that he is taken care of.

This version of the myth depicts the constellation of the archetypal bipolar mother, which in real life is often observed in the interaction between a mother and her disabled child. It must be remembered, however, that in many cases the rejection springs from the many medical and therapeutic interventions that are initiated and the stress and co-traumatic processes that develop between mother and child rather than from the mother's dislike of the child.

Both clients and therapists often make unwarranted associations in this regard. Since the client cannot recall his or her earliest times, which is usually when the most severe interventions took place and when the stress level was the highest, he or she tends to fall back upon assumptions about what happened, and from these sometimes faulty assumptions mistaken associations emerge. As mentioned before, the early experiences, up to the age of three, are stored in implicit memory, the contents of which cannot be reached consciously. However, these experiences leave their imprint and continue to evoke emotions and at times cause somatic sensations such as pain—experiences for which there are no symbolic representations, no words! They cause stress, anxiety, worry, upheaval. The child—and later the adult—is in dire need of organizing these experiences. In the absence of conscious memories of these events, however, mistaken connections are often made: my mother rejected me because she did not love me. And with this conclusion, an explanation and an orientation are found that therapists easily buy into, thus reinforcing the tragic story.

## Creativity

The mother of a disabled child serves as a life support system in the sense that she—in addition to fostering growth as mothers do in general—encourages and helps to achieve socialization for her disabled child in a way that mothers of "normal" children do not.

Not only is Hephaistos the only god who works, but he is also very talented and creative. The sea-goddesses—archetypally the positive mother aspect—lay the foundation for his creativity. As already mentioned, in the lesser-known story it is Hera herself who takes Hephaistos to Kedalion, who then teaches him the art of forging. Kedalion is related to the Kabeiroi, the phallic companions of Mother Earth. In yet another version of the myth, the home of Hephasitos is Lemnos, also an island associated with the Kabeiroi, where they were called Hephaistoi. These details of the myth, together with the care that Hephaistos receives from the sea-goddesses, clearly show Hephaistos's close relationship to the feminine and the dwarf-like companions of the Great Mother.

These smith-dwarfs—sometimes also called Daktyloi (fingers)—are the fingers of the Great Mother, her creativity. Murray Stein, in his article "Hephaistos: A Pattern of Introversion," shows Hephaistos's close relationship to the mother, to Mother Earth and her creativity. It is from the feminine, from within the *prima materia*, from the fire in the earth, that Hepahistos's creativity is born. He is not a father's child, has not been socialized and brought to manhood by a father, as is usually the case, but by the care, fire, promptings, and "fingers" of the Great Mother archetype. As Murray puts it, "The Hephaistian configuration remains deeply situated in the feminine mysteries of childbirth and fertility and has little to do with the labors of masculine heroism."[27]

Hephaistian art is amazingly life-like. To mention only one example, consider the female-like servants. Homer tells us: "They looked like real girls and could not only speak and use their limbs but were endowed with intelligence and trained in handwork by the immortal gods."[28]

## Summary

As promised in the phrase from the title "Hephaistos and His Mother in the Mirror of our Time," this paper has presented the many parallels between the ancient myth and our time. The relationship between a mother and her disabled child is fraught with many difficulties and tensions. This does not mean that there is no love, as the myth seems to suggest. Rather, the bipolar mother—represented by Hera and the sea-goddesses—forms the archetypal basis for the relationship. As we have seen, the dynamics between mother and disabled child are multidimensional. If the bonding period is marked by separation, stress, and medical and therapeutic interventions, this can, along with other factors, have long-term traumatic consequences, which may be manifested much later in life. Worry, anxiety, and guilt in the parents can influence the emotional life of the child, and this in turn may have repercussions upon the parents, triggering co-traumatic processes between child and parents.

If a child is born with a congenital disability, the disability marks the very first years of its life and has a significant influence on the neural connections forming in its developing brain. These in turn determine how future experiences get integrated. Early experiences, including traumatic ones, are stored in implicit memory, where they lie dormant and inaccessible to consciousness, but can be activated at any time later in life by subsequent traumatic events. When this happens, these early experiences appear without symbolic representation or any means of being articulated, and they flood ego-consciousness with overpowering emotions, leaving the person disoriented and in dire need of help. If the therapist does not take into account the fact that early childhood experiences are inaccessible to conscious memory, and in addition fails to probe into the client's medical history, there is a danger that incorrect associations will be formed and the client may conclude that he or she was unloved as a child, a conclusion that will do more harm than good. Let us never forget that there is always a place in heaven for Hephaistos.

---

## *NOTES*

[1] Karl Kerényi, *The Gods of the Greeks* (London: Thames and Hudson, 1951).

[2] Bessel A. van der Kolk, Alexander McFarlane, and Lars Weisaeth, eds., *Traumatic Stress: The Effects of Overwhelming Experience on Mind, Body, and Society* (New York and London: The Guilford Press, 1996).

[3] Allan N. Schore, *Affect Regulation and the Repair of the Self* (New York, London: W. W. Norton & Company, 2003). See Chapter 4.

[4] Elizabeth Mundy and Andrew Baum, "Medical Disorders as a Cause of Psychological Trauma and Posttraumatic Stress Disorder," in *Current Opinion in Psychiatry* 17, no. 2 (2004): 123f.

[5] Markus A. Landolt, *Psychotraumatologie des Kindesalter* (Göttingen: Hogrefe, 2004), p. 68.

[6] Karl Heinz Brisch, *Bindungsstörungen: Von der Bindungstheorie zur Therapie* (Stuttgart: Klett-Cotta, 2000), p. 77; Karl Heinz Brisch and Theodor Hellbrügge, eds. *Bindung und Trauma* (Stuttgart: Klett-Cotta, 2003).

[7] Schore, see especially Chapter 2.

[8] Barbara Diepold, "Zum Einfluss realer Traumatisierungen auf die Entwicklung von Kindern," in *Analytische Kinder- und Jugendlichen-Psychotherapie* 27, no. 1 (1996): 73-86.

[9] Dieter Bürgin, "Potenziell traumatogene Faktoren in der Intensivmedizin," in *Jahrbuch der Psychotraumatologie* (Kröning: Ansager-Verlag, 2007), pp. 43-50.

[10] Inge Bretherton and Kristine A. Munholland, "Internal Working Models in Attachment Relationships: A Construct Revisited," in *Handbook of Attachment: Theory, Research, and Clinical Applications*, ed. Jude Cassidy and Phillip R. Shaver (New York: Guilford Press, 1999), p. 89-111.

[11] Patrizia Egger, "Die Besetzung des Körpers," in *Die Welt als Barriere: Deutschsprachige Beiträge zu den Disability Studies*, ed. Erich Otto Graf, Cornelia Renggli and Jan Weisser (Rubigen/Bern: Edition Soziothek, 2006), pp. 75-82.

[12] Brisch, p. 234.

[13] Judith L. Herman, *Trauma and Recovery* (New York: Harper & Collins, 1992).

[14] Daniel N. Stern and Nadia Bruschweiler-Stern, *The Birth of a Mother: How the Motherhood Experience Changes You Forever* (New York: Basic Books, 1998). See Chapter 9.

[15] Karl-Heinz Pleyer, "Co-traumatische Prozesse in der Eltern-Kind-Beziehung," in *Systemata* 18, no. 2 (2004): 132-149.

[16] Selma Fraiberg, Edna Edelson and Vivian Shapiro, "Ghosts in the Nursery: A Psychoanalytic Approach to the Problems of Impaired Infant-Mother Relationships," in *Journal of the American Academy of Child Psychiatry* 14, no. 3 (1975): 387-421.

[17] Kathrin Asper, *The Abandoned Child Within: On Losing and Regaining Self-Worth* (New York: Fromm Publications, 1993), p. 147.

[18] Egger.

[19] Beate Gomille, "Unsicher-präokkupierte mentale Bindungsmodelle," in *Bindung im Erwachsenenalter*, ed. Gabriele Gloger-Tippelt (Bern: Verlag Hans Huber, 2001), p. 201.

[20] A. Riecher-Rössler and M. Steiner, eds., *Perinatal Stress, Mood and Anxiety Disorders*, (Basel: Karger Verlag, 2005).

[21] Herman.

[22] Rhoda Olkin, *What Psychotherapists Should Know About Disability* (New York: The Guilford Press, 1999).

[23] Arthur W. Frank, *The Wounded Storyteller: Body, Illness, and Ethics* (Chicago: The University of Chicago Press, 1997).

[24] Erving Goffman, *Stigma: Notes on the Management of Spoiled Identity* (Englewood Cliffs, N.J.: Prentice Hall, 1963).

[25] Mirjam Kalland, "Psychosocial Aspects of Cleft Lip and Palate: Implications for Parental Education," Doctoral dissertation, University of Helsinki, 1995, pp. 97ff; 102ff; 124ff.

[26] Donald W. Winnicott, *Through Pediatrics to Psychoanalysis* (New York: Basic Books, 1975), p. 302.

[27] Murray Stein, "Hephaistos: A Pattern of Introversion," in *Facing the Gods*, ed. James Hillman (Irving, TX: Spring Publications, 1980), p. 73.

[28] Homer, *The Iliad*, trans. Emil V. Rieu (Harmondsworth, UK: Penguin Books, 1966), pp. 417-420.

# Part III

# Erotic Power and the Happily-Ever-After

Ursula Wirtz, Dr. phil., is a Jungian training analyst with a diploma from the C. G. Jung-Institut Zürich (1982). She received a doctorate in philosophy from the University of Munich and a degree in clinical and anthropological psychology from the University of Zürich. She is currently on the faculty of ISAPZURICH, and works as an analyst in private practice in Zürich. She has taught at various European universities and is the author of numerous publications on trauma, ethics, and spirituality. She is also involved in the training of fledgling Jungian groups in Eastern Europe and is a member of the ethics committee of the IAAP.

6

# Yearning to Be Known: Individuation and the Broken Wings of Eros

*Ursula Wirtz*

Welcome to the Odyssey! I invite you to explore with me the erotics of encounter—to venture into the intimacies of the analytic dyad in search of insight, knowledge, and loving connectedness. My paper is guided by the image of a kaleidoscope; in it poetic, philosophical, psychological, and mythological elements emerge and ultimately merge with each other to form a whole.

Tuning in and paying homage to Eros, I will begin with a poem entitled "You Exist" by the Jewish German poet Hilde Domin:

> You are
> Wherever eyes look upon you.
> Wherever eyes meet your eyes,
> You are born.
>
> You are held up by a call;
> It's ever the same voice—
> There seems to be but one
> Wherewith everyone calls.
>
> You fell
> But have not fallen;
> Eyes hold you up.

You exist
Because eyes want you,
Eyes look upon you
And affirm that you exist.[1] (My translation.)

## Seeing and Recognition: Intersubjectivity and the Dialogical Principle

*Esse est percipi*—To be is to be perceived. This philosophical insight by George Berkeley has found a very touching expression in Hilde Domin's poem. We can find profound implications of this for the art of analysis in Winnicott's work: "When I look I am seen, so I exist. I can now afford to look and see."[2]

Perception brings everything into being; to be means to be visible. When I am not seen or mis-seen, I feel unreal. I doubt myself and all relationships, and consequently I do not develop a stable sense of who I am. Attachment theory has taught us that the bonding process between mother and child is nurtured through the non-intrusive loving acceptance of the gaze. The exchange of looks between mother and infant also points to the importance of both being mirrored: the mother in the smile of the baby, and the baby in the gleam in the mother's eye. One does not exist without the other; they form a dyad. Being seen and known confers factual existence on me as "I." This lays the foundation for a stable feeling of self-worth and also for the ability to love. The secret of the I's need of the Thou has been revealed to us by Feuerbach and Martin Buber: "In the beginning was relationship." Emmanuel Levinas, the great philosopher of alterity,[3] also stressed the healing power of relationship, which gives support when all other supports have given way: "We exist in the accusative," we are alive when we are spoken to, or breathed or looked upon.

The problem of the Other, the Thou or the otherness that we encounter in analysis, has also emerged as a fundamental problem in contemporary philosophy and ethics, as the work of Levinas has shown. But it was already rooted in the philosophical concepts of recognition and intersubjectivity found in Fichte and Hegel, where reciprocal or mutual recognition is understood as the capacity to allow the other to be. To be recognized is to count for something in the eyes of the other, to be acknowledged and respected by the other. Hegel identifies love as a form of mutual recognition. Reciprocity in the fundamental structures of recognition has also been acknowledged by Jung, who sees it as the transformative ingredient of the analytic encounter: "For two personalities to meet is like mixing two different chemical substances: if there is any combination at all, both are transformed."[4] For healing to take place, the psyche of the analyst must be involved to its full depth. Analyst and patient must be transparent to each other. Jung enlarged our understanding of what it means to relate to each other in the true sense; he taught us that relationship can help us to become aware that we share our humanity. He encouraged analysts to be moved by the analytic encounter and he stressed the value of responding authentically to our patients. Jung even encouraged his students not to hide behind a professional persona but to be natural, vulnerable, and open. Ferenczi went a step further with his idea of "mutual analysis" and enunciated the following principle in his clinical diaries: "Without sympathy there is no healing." I would say: Without Eros there is no analysis. Eros is an indispensable condition for our work of serving the life of the soul.

The African philosophical and spiritual concept of "Ubuntu" points in a similar direction, defining individuals in terms of their relationships with others. We need to be open and available to others because in some deeper sense all of us belong to a greater whole, we are interconnected. The Zulu maxim *"umuntu ngumuntu ngabantu"* ("a person is a person through [other] persons") corresponds to the Chinese saying: "I am because I belong."

Recognition is indispensable to healthy psychic development. Our sense of identity and of self-worth are the products of repeated acts of recognition. As patients, we want to see the gleam in our analyst's eye, we want to be known, welcomed, and recognized as we are in our "thusness." Being seen and known gives us insight into our essence and helps us to become authentic human beings. It can be a deeply healing and transformative experience to discover one's true self and expand one's whole being and awareness. In the loving, non-judgmental gaze of the analyst, the unique reality of the other is affirmed and the establishment of a coherent lovable self is enabled. Affirming the other's being, trusting in the other, nurturing the soul's often labyrinthine paths—these activities are part of the midwife function of the analyst, whose task it is to assist in the birthing of a new sense of self, which allows the client to be reconciled with who he or she is. Analysis involves an authentic connection in which clients can experience being seen and held empathically.

## The Art of Seeing and the *Wu-Wei* Attitude

Seeing lovingly is lucid seeing, in which an I meets a You in the *temenos* of the analytic space. Seeing is a transformative act, fueled by the power of the imagination, by which it becomes possible for something new to emerge. Analysis, which is a variation on the theme of the Other, makes the other visible again; it attempts to reveal the true face of the other. The midwife function of the analyst is seen in the analyst's empathic responsiveness in welcoming the emerging self. True analysis preserves the ontological distance and separation between subjects; yet a mediation of the self to itself by the other takes place.

Being seen with the eyes of love kindles the capacity to love. I am thinking of love in terms of the poetic view of the Russian writers Dostoevsky and Marina Zwetajewa: love is the capacity to see a person as God intended him or her to be, even if his or her parents stood in the way of his or her realizing this intention. To love means to recognize the deepest and best qualities in a person and to make it possible for these qualities to emerge and become effective. Love is what brings all things into being and sustains their existence. The wings of Eros help us to get a glimpse of the divine in the Other, because the eye "belongs to the self" and enables us to see things as they truly are, as Esther Harding[5] has written.

Analysis is, in my understanding, the art of seeing: seeing in terms of insight and self-knowledge, seeing intuitively. The eye in this context serves as a door of access between the inner and outer worlds. In an allusion to alchemical texts, Jung invites us "to keep the eyes of the mind and the soul well open" in order to gain "golden understanding."[6] Yearning to know and be known, gaining insight and knowledge, becoming conscious—these are eye-opening experiences, as Genesis 3:7 implies: "Then the eyes of both of them were opened and they realized that they were naked."

The potency of the look, the penetration of the persona-veil is masterfully portrayed in the work of the Surrealists, and in particular René Magritte. He understood perception as an intimate, erotic, fluid interpenetration. He was fascinated with the mirror, with what is clouded, multiple, and changeable, with the erotics of the gaze.

What we try to perceive is the thusness of the other, freed of all concepts of how the other is supposed to be so that the Tao, or self, can take its own course. Bion refers to this capacity as dwelling in a mode of being full of uncertainties, mysteries, and doubts, "without memory, desire and understanding."[7] This attitude of listening within, of lettings things be, of "thinking unconsciously," as Jung once said he did, creates an alert state of spiritual openness, of serenity and active receptivity. In the East it is referred to as the *wu-wei* attitude, the art of letting things happen—action through non-action, a kind of vigilant passivity. This Taoist wisdom describes a paradox in which being is doing, in which diverse modes of awareness come into play, including imagination, intuition, and sensory perception. When we keep our heart in a state of *wu-wei*, we are more finely tuned to the other person, relying on an unfocused sort of listening that goes beyond Freud's "evenly hovering attention." We need to cultivate a mind that is open and receptive, surrendered to the archetype of the sage within as an inner guide who helps us to be more receptive to intuitive insights about ourselves and the clients we work with.

As analysts, we need to let things happen in the psyche, trusting the process and its own time and pace instead of consciously interfering. The therapist's mind is the facilitating environment that Winnicott talks about. Our responsibility is to enhance our intuitive capabilities by building this inner creative play-space that Winnicott described, or through Bion's state of "*reverie*," in which an "unconscious symmetry" develops and self and other become interchangeable.

The precondition for this state is a level of self that is silent, empty of thought, and filled with longing, a zone in which we feel truly comfortable and at home in receptive stillness.[8] We need to empty our mind of preconceptions and prior notions of how things should go before we can enable others to achieve genuine change. The task of the analyst is to cultivate a "beginner's mind," as a Zen practitioner might say, so that he or she is able to stay in the present moment, engage in the here and now, conscientiously trying to hold the intimate tension of moment-to-moment awareness.

## Individuation and the Yearning to Be Known

A couple of years ago, I saw some graffiti at the Zürich art museum. It read: "Who am I and if yes how many?" This cryptic message touches on our desire to know and to be transformed by knowing. Who is this "I" that is thinking, feeling, analyzing? Is this "I" a separate, objective reality separate from other objective realities? Or is there an entanglement between I and you such that whenever we talk about an "I," we categorically presuppose the existence of a "you," and vice versa? Jung's dream of the meditating yogi who had his own face might be recalled in this context. The yogi is the other and yet himself; they share the same face.

Another perspective on the interdependence of identity and the relational self is expressed in Jung's comment:

> One cannot individuate without being with other human beings. … [T]he self is like a crowd, therefore being oneself, one is also like many. … [O]ne can only individuate with or against something or somebody. Being an individual is always a link in a chain ….[9]

The archetypal striving for knowledge, the unveiling of who we are beneath all the layers of our persona is the *opus* of the individuation process. Yearning to be known in my most intimate self, yearning for insight and knowledge about who I am at the core of my heart is a deep archetypal longing, as we see in the Scriptures: "For now we see through a glass, darkly, but then face to face: now I know in part, but then shall I know even as also I am known" (1 Cor. 13:12).

In order to straighten out the tangle of my existence, my own "golem," I need to have before me a human being who sees me, who unconditionally accepts my being as I am, someone who believes in me even though I may long since have stopped believing in myself, someone who carries for me the flame of hope long after my own may have gone out, someone who will accompany me on the search for my self when I have long since lost any trace of it.

It is important to be aware that the seat of knowledge is not the head but the heart. The Hebrew word for knowledge is *da'ath*, a term that refers to both sexual knowledge and knowledge about life. To know means to love, to take care of, to approve, guard, and protect. This is a holistic understanding of knowing: a knowing by the mind and the senses coupled with an understanding by the heart. According to the Book of Genesis, eating from the Tree of Knowledge awakens consciousness of our sexual being; we become aware of who we are. Biblical language indicates that sexual intimacy is a fleshly form of knowing, often referred to as "carnal knowledge."

Wishing to be known and understood, to be "met," is a striving for unity, a yearning for psychic growth. In this process we reveal our innermost vulnerabilities as clients, we allow the other to enter into our most intimate spaces, hoping to experience the emotional resonance that might heal our wounds, hoping to be truly received by the other and valued for what we are.

When I show myself to the other in this way, when I disclose my vulnerability, I reveal my true self and make contact with the very center of my being. I become real and this makes it possible for the other to relate to me authentically. This may lead to an intimacy in which the emerging self of the other is facilitated into life. But this may also be a very frightening experience, one that is utterly painful and to be avoided at all costs, because it puts me in touch with the pain of not having been seen by those whom I depended on to be seen, this is, my own parents.

The condition of being vulnerable, of being unguarded and exposed to one's neediness, can be experienced as a threat of death. Sometimes we work with clients who have a deep-seated fear of their need to be mirrored and will do anything to avoid getting in touch with this longing to be known and seen. Their wings of Eros may have been crippled by traumatic childhood experiences of helplessness and dependence. The growing awareness of an early narcissistic wound can be so overwhelming that some patients cannot bear it; they withdraw out of resistance and thus undermine any attempts on the part of the analyst to connect with them. Not only might they "decapitate" the analyst, that is, devalue him or her as being not good enough, as Mario Jacoby has pointed out in his book *Individuation and Narcissism,*[10] but they might even abort the analysis because they cannot forgive the analyst for having seen their deepest pain and need for redemption through love. The intimacy is so painful to bear, the longing to merge so threatening, that they prefer to flee. This happens particularly when the analyst gets under the analysand's skin and the image is mirrored so empathically that it calls for a level of intimacy and closeness that threatens the analysand's ego-boundaries. Patients with this kind of narcissistic wound defend themselves against intimacy and tend to break off the relationship, often with huge rage, because some sore spot has been touched.

We may consider the process of individuation as a process of development in which meaning is created—and whereby we transform and recreate ourselves and our own personal myth again and again with the help of the self-regulating powers of our psyche. Individuation is concerned with the synthesis of opposing forces in the psyche. This whole-making process implies the integration of all opposites, masculine and feminine, light and shadow, consciousness and unconsciousness, as we can see in the various individuation journeys of our culture, for example in alchemy, in the quest for the Holy Grail, in the *Oxherder Pictures* of the Zen tradition, or in Mozart's *Magic Flute*.

Embarking on an individuation quest, we encounter and embrace our soul's desire for wholeness, a more profound and effective personal integration, a rebalancing of inner and outer. In turning religiously to our dreams, our imaginings, our wounds and visions, we develop a comprehensive view of who we are, trying to embody the questions our soul poses to us.

A similar insight is expressed in the Buddhist teaching found in "The Threefold Refuge": "If we do not deliver ourselves in this present life, no hope is there ever to cross the sea of birth and death." Or in the Gospel of Thomas: "If you do not bring forth what is within you, what you do not bring forth will destroy you" (v. 70).

An analysand of mine shared with me her notes from a very labyrinthine individuation journey:

> I am shaken up, disoriented, terrified. This path is horrible. I am afraid of falling into a pit, of being sucked up into the wound, afraid of the descent. The wounds are calling out to me; they don't want to be put under the cement. I am a prisoner of myself; when I get out of one box, I find myself in the next box. There is no life in me. I do not know who I am. I am a body without a soul but with a big head. I have lost hope but not my determination. I have to go this path to the end; I have no choice, I am driven, seized, pushed by some power bigger than me. The energy on this path knocks everything down, but you have to keep going, you can't stop. It's so scary, this tremendous threat of being swallowed up when I get closer. Hope is absent; there's only darkness around me, and yet I am sure it is the right path. But do I ever get out of it?

Being known can ultimately be understood as an experience of wholeness, an awakening of creativity and imagination, a homecoming, a bringing forth of "the hidden treasure." For Jung, the analytic process is about discovering and unveiling this treasure by mirroring to each of our patients the sacred image of themselves, a process that moves us towards realizing our own wholeness.

It is our nature to be whole, claims Jung, and analysis facilitates this wholeness. Such an approach to analysis would include also the acceptance and loving embrace of inevitable human imperfections. Analysis is not an exercise in narcissistic inflation, but a protracted and painful striving to find a conscious attitude that allows an ongoing creative dialogue between the conscious and the unconscious. In a letter to Dr. Margaret Braband-Isaac he wrote:

> As a matter of fact we have actually known everything all along; for all these things are always there, only we are not there for them. The possibility of the deepest insight existed at all times, but we were always too far away from it.[11]

Jung considered it his foremost task to open people's eyes to the fact that humankind has a soul and that there is buried treasure in the field that needs to be unearthed. To Upton Sinclair he wrote:

> What we need is the development of the inner spiritual person, the unique individual whose treasure is hidden on the one hand in the symbols of our mythological tradition, and on the other hand in their unconscious psyche.[12]

But we humans, searching for an identity, are not the only ones yearning to be known. From Sufi mystics such as Ibn al-'Arabi we learn that even God sighs with longing to become known and to be delivered from his solitude by the people in whom he reveals himself. The mystics relied on an extra-Koranic revelation in which God attests: "I was a hidden treasure and I yearned to be known. Then I created creatures in order to be known by them."[13] A solitary God, sighing with longing to become known, yearning to be uncovered, points to our responsibility as human beings to mirror this hidden God. We are created with an intrinsic urge to turn to where we came from, to discover our true self. Our creation is intentional: we are intended to know and reflect our Creator, the supreme archetype according to Sufism. Eros is the force that stirs us to seek knowledge, to desire union. In the Christian tradition, we are called to incarnate God's love for humanity and join in a bond of love that infuses life into all that is.

Mystics teach us that the divine is always in a state of becoming: God is the spirit of becoming. This is in keeping with Jung's understanding of the ongoing evolution of the Self and the god-image in the human psyche. Jungian psychology enshrines this conviction that God dwells within us and that we as psychotherapists are empowered to work in and with the divine in us.

The transpersonal aspect of the psyche can make itself felt in the course of the quest for one's self. The knowledge gained on the path to individuation awakens us to an understanding of the true nature of reality, namely, that we and the outside world are not separate, that the self and the divine are not discrete entities but interpenetrate each other, and that consciousness and not matter is the ultimate basis of the universe. These insights of Jung's in regard to the non-dual nature of reality establish his kinship with mystics such as Meister Eckhart and the masters of Zen Buddhism.

Self-knowledge is the coming to awareness of the divine in us. This transcending of ego-consciousness and entering "the Self field"[14] is in keeping with the injunction of the mystics to look within, where the truth dwells. Jung claimed that unconsciousness is the greatest sin and that becoming conscious is a spiritual obligation. In his autobiography, written towards the end of a long and productive life, he wrote:

> The decisive question for man is, is he related to something infinite or not? That is the telling question of his life. Only if we know that the thing that truly matters is the infinite can we avoid fixing our attention upon futilities and upon all kinds of goals which are not of real importance .... In the final analysis we count for something only because of the essential we embody, and if we do not embody that, life is wasted.[15]

Individuation is not only an intrapsychic process of differentiation and integration but also a profound interpersonal and spiritual process. This process of growing in awareness is connected to Eros, the relational force that stimulates us to come to know ourselves and what lies beyond us.

## Eros and the Erotic

> We should regard the erotic force, whether divine, angelic, poetic, psychic, or physical, as a unifying and commingling power.
>
> —St. Dionysius the Areopagite

What is Eros and the Eros principle—or, speaking within the mythological paradigm, who was Eros?

Eros, in early Greek Orphic mythology, is described as a mystic divinity, the first of the gods in the universe. According to Hesiod, he was preceded only by Chaos and Earth. He hatched out of the World Egg and set the universe in motion. Driven by his desire to see the light of the world, he tears open the egg and becomes the god who shatters the harmony of the world, who emerges from darkness into light. He is the revealer of light, a symbol of our strongest drive to become conscious.

Eros-Phanes, the primeval god of procreation, the generator of life, appears as a cosmogonic elemental force, as the creative power that destroys the harmony of the universe, but also as the creative energy that binds together the fragmented parts and makes whole again the broken world. Eros mediates between the human and the divine, between heaven and earth, helping us to recognize our universal relatedness.

According to Hesiod, Eros, the fairest among the gods, the keeper of the keys of heaven and earth, was the uniting power of love that brought order and harmony among the conflicting constituents of Chaos. Only in the late classical Greek period does Eros, with his glittering golden wings, the charming source of sweet delight, become for poets and philosophers a metaphor for beauty and youth. In Greek lyric poetry, Sappho celebrates him as the limb-loosening, bittersweet, irresistible creature that makes her tremble. Socrates dwells on his spiritual attributes: his likeness to wisdom, his loving awareness of beauty, and his desire for goodness and truth. In Plato's view, the ascent of Eros is an ethical task. Eros in his highest development is seen as selfless, for he loves goodness for its own sake. In the *Symposium*, Plato notes, through the mouth of Aristophanes, that we humans are always in pursuit of the wholeness that we lost when we were cut in half by Zeus. Legend has it that humans were originally spherical beings with four arms, four legs, and two faces. One day, in a fit of hubris, they attempted to scale Mount Olympus and attack the gods. To teach them a lesson, Zeus cut them into two, producing a male half and a female half, and this is why we are destined to search forever for our other, missing half. Eros recognizes what has been forgotten and directs us to our lost object of knowledge. What we are striving for is the original unity, the restoration of our primary oneness. We desire because we are incomplete. Eros resides in the bittersweet yearning of ever-unfulfilled desire, the longing for self-completion and self-transcendence. Some myths tell us that Eros is the son of Expediency and Poverty, the one who pushes us to become what we were meant to be, to actualize our potential. Through Eros we are drawn to create and to come into being. Eros not only wounds us with desire but also provides us with wings to fly so that we can encounter the numinosity of transcendence. Eros, with his golden pinions and arrows as the highest love, is a personification of love of wisdom, knowledge, and truth. The archetypal significance of Eros as a daimon resides in his capacity to wound and to heal, to lift the soul up to the contemplation of goodness. For Plato, goodness, the divine, truth, and beauty are all identical, and to love means to bring forth beauty both in body and in soul.

Eros is also a dangerous god, chaotic, chthonic, with no regard for boundaries. We suffer when Eros reveals his origin in Chaos. We experience him as an overwhelming psychic force, powerful, dangerous, and unsettling. Eros attracts us and threatens our sense of stability, of law and order. He takes us out of our mind, and when we are hit by his darts we are confronted with our shadow, with jealousy, envy, hatred, with the darkest of our passions.

## The Eros Principle

Jung saw Eros as having a dual aspect, belonging both "to man's primordial animal nature" as well as "to the highest forms of the spirit."[16] He called Eros a principle of connection: "The concept of Eros could be expressed in modern terms as psychic relatedness, and that of Logos as objective interest .... Most men, though, are erotically blinded—they commit the unpardonable mistake of confusing Eros with sex."[17] In his view, women—being "far more psychological" than men—are much more capable of unifying with their Eros function what "Logos has sundered."

Eros is about the creative union of opposites within the psyche, the *coniunctio*, a central motif in the individuation process. The integration process is constellated when Eros is awakened and love is encountered in the meeting of body, spirit, and mind, when inner and outer worlds become one. Eros is the mediator: he helps us to encounter life as an organic whole and to overcome the fragmentation and alienation of our consciousness. We recognize Eros in our desire to live a meaningful life, to care and be compassionate, to merge and create.

Eros is libidinal energy and sacred creativity, a desire for wholeness, a deeply human urge to connect and reach beyond oneself. But Eros is also an intrapsychic mediator, a connection between the two souls living in my breast that help me to access my innermost centre. As a relational force, it works in two directions, towards self and away from self, deepening our capacity to relate and to make connections when we are attracted to something or someone. Eros binds together and creates oneness out of the many.

This potent, vital, dynamic capacity of Eros to attract separate entities to each other and set them in motion is beautifully expressed in a dream of one of my analysands, which I have permission to share with you. The analysand, an ISAP candidate, had been immersed the night before in alchemical and ancient Hellenic and Egyptian religious texts in preparation for a presentation at a seminar on alchemy the next day. She reported the following dream:

> All of the elements that make up the material of the world, the earth, the universe (like the elements of the Periodic Table in chemistry class) were moving with great energy among each other like a grand dance. And that which made them dance was Eros. It was as if someone said out loud to me in the dream that it was Eros.

She commented that she was present in the dream scene as a kind of witness. Even as a mere witness, she was so taken up by the humor, the playfulness, and the joyfulness of the "dance" that she woke up laughing.

If we are in touch with this erotic power, we are capable of empowering others, an important aspect in the analytic process. We can understand Eros as the psychic transformative energy that fuels a deep longing for union with the other.

But like all archetypal forces, Eros is a double-edged sword: there is a positive side and a negative side to it. As much as Eros creates relationships, it also destroys them. Falling in love might feel like going crazy, erotic infatuation is often experienced as a mini psychosis; love is a "divine madness," a state of being outside one's self. Bernini's beautiful sculpture *The Ecstasy of Saint Teresa* reveals the bittersweet pain of erotic passion, of the soul's burning desire for an encounter with God, of ecstatic abandonment of self to the Other. The Christian mystics described Eros as the foundational unifying principle that links God and humanity. In Greek mythology, the story of Psyche and Eros deals with the awakening of spiritual passion. By uniting with Eros, the soul connects with the source of life and love. The wounding of Eros has also been a major theme of the Romantic poets. Last year's Odyssey addressed Novalis's cryptic saying: "To love is always to feel the opening, to always keep the wound open."

Erotic energies can be very unsettling, yet there is a "healing, whole-making dimension of Eros," which moves from fragmentation towards integration and wholeness to generate and nurture new life. Erotic power is nurturing; it heals our alienation and has an empowering, liberating quality that leads us towards life-giving co-creation. Our culture needs Eros to overcome its estrangement from self and the world.

The urge to reach out beyond ourselves and dissolve the boundaries that separate us, to touch and be touched, to recognize each other through our intersubjectivity, these are the promptings of Eros that enable us to reach higher levels of personhood and consciousness. In our relatedness lies the power to heal and to be healed. This is why Eros is vital to the analytical relationship and the individuation process.

## Analysis as an Erotic Encounter

I believe the erotic to be an archetypal energy at the heart of the therapeutic relationship, rooted in the deepest layers of our psyche. I have already alluded to the Book of Genesis and its insight that knowledge and sexual awareness belong together in the process of becoming conscious. The psychoanalyst David Mann has written two illuminating books highlighting how the erotic pervades most analytic encounters and is largely a positive and transformational influence.[18] I want to look at both sides: the transformation through the erotic, and the dark side of the erotic, the betrayal of Eros, his tears and broken wings.

Eros lies at the heart of all our desires and creative activity. Love seems to be the healing agent that overcomes our human separateness. Freud even confessed in a letter to Jung, dated December 6, 1906, "Essentially, one might say, the cure is effected by love,"[19] and he defined the goal of analysis as being to broaden the capacity for work, play, and love. I personally also subscribe to the idea that analysis is an expression of love as compassion, joy, and equanimity.

Individuation and psychic growth emerge when pathways to intimacy are opened. Analysis assists in the unfolding of the self through erotic engagement. The emergence of the *We* takes place in the sacred space of analysis, the *temenos*, a space filled with great emotional energy and power, a vessel full of hope for true intimacy, respect, acceptance, and estimation.

Eros speaks to our primal interrelatedness; it makes us vulnerable through our openness in the presence of others, and at the same time it opens up the possibility of reciprocity, the co-creation of relationship, which is akin to the modern understanding of transference and countertransference as a mutual process of co-creation. Empathy, compassion, and love build structure, and in order to achieve this building, distance is required. In supervision we learn to keep one foot inside and one foot outside the analytic relationship; we are required to maintain a distance in the midst of our union, otherwise we might be swept away by the archetypal erotic forces that influence the erotic field between analyst and analysand and endanger them by dissolving the boundaries needed for both to feel safe in the *temenos*.

Being aware that the person I face is a subject—not an object at my disposal—protects me from committing abuse. If a relationship is to develop, I must open myself to this encounter with my whole being, but I must also allow the other to remain the other. This is an important distinction for us to make, otherwise we might end up in a destructive fusion or perverse regression. Accepting the boundaries between self and other is in fact a precondition for "knowing."

We as analysts in particular need to be aware of these boundaries. I must not engulf my patients in the process of absorbing their otherness. I need to be aware of the danger of exploiting the other for narcissistic ends. My own wounded Eros might make me particularly vulnerable, so that I feel an intense need to use my patients as a mirror for myself, and I will then try to engulf them. If the wings of Eros are broken, I, as the analyst, cannot rein myself in. I will want to feed on the patient, thus breaching boundaries and disempowering him or her, and thereby preventing a self from being born in the fluid mutual interaction, as Kohut would say.

As much as we need to be alert to the many faces of Eros emerging in the analytic encounter, we also need to be on our guard if the erotic seems to be missing. This might be a sign of an impasse, a situation in which no transformation and growth can take place. We have to ask ourselves in these situations why it is that nothing about this patient arouses our love, because the erotic is in fact "the most transformational opportunity in the analytic process," as David Mann, in his reflections on erotic transference and countertransference, has pointed out.[20] In analysis, analyst and analysand are unconsciously related to each other by an erotic bond that structures and gives color to the relationship unfolding between them. It is in some way a love relationship, though we might hesitate to use the term "love" in connection with the analytic encounter. Julia Kristeva in *Tales of Love* calls psychoanalysis "an infinite quest for rebirths through the experience of love."[21] Freud, for his part, asserted that "[o]ne could effect far more with one's patients if one gave them enough of the love which they had longed for as children."[22] Jung declared in his commentary on the *Rosarium* that if no bond of love exists, there is no soul and no relatedness.

In Jungian practice, we consider analysis to be a process of death and rebirth, a work of love in which the archetypal yearning to be known and seen unfolds; it is an individuation quest for knowledge, a wisdom path even. It assists us in seeing through the veils of the conditioned mind and to recognize our ultimate nature. In the analytic encounter, this "Tantra of Dialogue," we plunge into the depths of the heart hoping that our true nature will be revealed and our yearning to be seen and heard will ultimately be gratified.

A Jewish analysand of mine in her late seventies, reflecting on being seen, felt that she was coming from the opposite end of the world, where "being seen" in any manner, shape, or form, was anathema, dangerous, a trespass. Her proudest achievement, even as a small child, was making herself as invisible and inaudible as possible. Only through the long process of her individuation journey was she eventually able to believe and feel that it is all right to "be there," that she was not "in the way," and that her presence was not harmful to other people. She began to feel for the first time that it is acceptable to exist with all her particular attributes, name, age, place of birth, gender, etc. Originally, she felt she had to hide, even "delete" parts of herself in any given situation, so as to present a figure that had a hope or a chance of being tolerated. For her, individuation meant being able to integrate a sense of herself as being truly lovable for what she was and not for what she did; it meant trying out new ways of being in this world, new ways of relating to others. Her transformative journey of individuation has been a quest for new ways of experiencing relationship. It reminded me of a comment Jung made on a successful analysis of his. He said that the patient became himself, he was able to accept who he was and his inner truth came to light again: "My aim is to bring about a psychic state in which my patient begins to experiment with his own nature—a state of fluidity, change, and growth where nothing is eternally fixed and hopelessly petrified."[23]

We need to have Eros to imagine the inner experience of our clients, to decipher what is really going on inside them, and to resonate with what we have intuited and perceived. We need empathy based on the appreciation of differences if we are to enter imaginatively into their unique inner worlds. Putting oneself in the position of another human being requires the suspension of the ego, a letting go of the conviction that we know the ways of the psyche. "Great God, keep me from judging another human being until I have walked a mile in his moccasins," an unknown Apache warrior prayed. We need to experience inwardly what the patient is feeling and needing, looking for where he or she is most whole, most genuine. This is possible only if I have a calm mind and if I let go of all my presuppositions about the other.

Sometimes I think of our analytic work in terms of "listening with the third ear" (Theodor Reik), listening intuitively to the inner voice of our clients as well as to our own inner voices that arise from the encounter. There is a beautiful sculpture by Rodin, *Meditation* (or *The Inner Voice*), which inspired Rilke to describe the artist's way of working as follows: "This work ... had to be carried out so humbly, so obediently, so devotedly, so impartially ... that no specified parts remained and the artist worked at the form without knowing what exactly would result, like a worm working its way from point to point in the dark."[24] In my own experience as an analyst, I often feel this wormlike quality, this letting go of the logical, verbal mode, this diving into dark, unconscious terrain, into the world of feeling and imagination. If Eros gets wounded, we are cut off from our intuition, from the ability to see with the third eye and listen with the third ear. Without this capability we no longer relate to the visionary. We cannot discover the essence of life, because Eros is the eye opener that helps us to see deeply into the ground of being.

In the analytic encounter, Eros connects the inner and the outer, breaks down defenses, and creates an openness of the whole person to the world at large. A different way of seeing emerges—an awakening of the heart and all its senses. Jane Wheelwright, describing analysis as a heart-to-heart encounter in which mirroring takes place, referred to her personal experience face to face with Jung as deeply erotic and numinous. She wrote that in his presence she felt

> ... as though all the surrounding matter had turned into whizzing molecules. Everything there seemed to be moving, melting, changing forms. Everything stirred .... I felt someone, not me, spoke through me and someone, not Jung, was speaking through him .... Whatever it was, it seemed to be creating before my eyes and ears and senses a model of the changed person I was meant finally to become. Trying the new me on me, so to speak .... Two people were caught in a vice that was forcing them to undergo an important rearrangement of themselves that had significance—some meaning far beyond them.[25]

## C. G. Jung and His Wounded Eros

Sometimes, when we ourselves as analysts are not in touch with our own erotic energies or when we have suffered an early wounding of Eros, we feel uneasy about dealing with the erotic. Perhaps if our own wings of Eros are broken, we might not be at home in the language of affection, which provides containment in the analytic encounter; we might defend ourselves against Eros, act out sexually, compulsively seduce the other, or take flight by spiritualizing and desexualizing Eros. When I first published my work on incest and sexual abuse, I dealt with Jung's own damaged wings of Eros.[26] First, there was a lack of sufficient mirroring in his very early years, and second, there was a betrayal of Eros when an older man he had trusted abused him sexually. He had to endure his mother's periodic abandonment throughout his early childhood, as well as her sudden uncanny changes in personality. Jung later commented: "From then on, I always felt mistrustful when the word 'love' was spoken. The feeling I associated with 'woman' was for a long time that of innate unreliability."[27]

I consider this an early wounding of Eros, an absence of mirroring leading to difficulties in relating and a lack of basic trust. In his early years, he experienced himself as unworthy and unlikable and withdrew into his own world. Any failure of original affection and insecure bonding leads to basic mistrust, breaks the wings of Eros, and impacts one's capacity to engage in deep erotic relationships.

This relational problem later shaped Jung's theories and influenced his way of relating to his clients. He did not trust very much in intersubjectivity on account of his subjective experiences in childhood, but focused more on interiority. For him, the "… most decisive experience of all … is to be alone with his own self, or whatever one chooses to call the objectivity of the psyche. The patient must be alone if he is to find out what it is that supports him, when he can no longer support himself."[28] The total inwardness that Jung often sought has its shadow side. A childhood friend of Jung's, Albert Oeri, remembered Jung as "an inhuman monster," capable of shutting others completely out of his world.[29]

As an adult, in a letter to Freud, Jung talked about the other fateful and traumatic experience that deeply affected his relation to Eros. He wrote on October 28, 1907:

> My veneration for you has something of the character of a "religious" crush. Though it does not really bother me, I still feel it is disgusting and ridiculous because of its undeniable erotic undertone. This abominable feeling comes from the fact that as a boy I was the victim of a sexual assault by a man I once worshiped. Even (when my wife and I visited you) in Vienna the remarks of the ladies ("enfin seuls" etc.,) sickened me ….[30]

Jung referred to his childhood abuse again in a later context, explaining why he refused to treat a homosexual man who had dreamt that he was swimming with him in Lake Zürich. Jung adds: "That's also the reason why I was afraid of Freud's approaches."[31]

Broken wings of Eros impacted Jung's analytical stance, colored his theory, and prevented him from developing intimacy with men. We might also look at his seductiveness towards women and the boundary violations he committed as a reenactment of his own experience of childhood abuse and betrayal of trust.

### Broken Wings and Betrayal

Betrayal is about love's opposite: the lust for power. It is about personal advantage over the well-being of the other, about being driven by the ego and not acting in response to the Self. Betrayal happens when the desire for the deepest well-being of another is perverted into gratifying only one's own needs; it occurs when we are not assisting in the process of bringing to birth our spiritual being, when we as analysts fail in our maieutic function, when we do not nurture what is given to us. To betray means to be a traitor to our wholeness, to be unfaithful to ourselves as a living organism of becoming. On the basis of my understanding of humans as bio-psycho-social-spiritual beings, the broken wings of Eros refer to splitting, alienation, and estrangement from self and the world, from thinking, feeling, and bodily and spiritual rootedness.

In analysis we encounter these wounds as a deep split between head and heart, head and body. Clients who suffer from a betrayal of Eros often feel stifled and compressed to the point where they seem not to be alive, devoid of any life energy. A client of mine described this condition as follows:

> I am not aware of having anything more than a head. The rest is so far not part of me. I don't feel or relate to it. It's beyond my influence, as if it were anesthetized, deadened. I feel unable to want and desire. It is like living death, frustration, despair, as if I were cursed.

In therapy, the absence of Eros in the client is often revealed in his or her inability to relate to the therapist. A deeper commitment and union seem to be missing, while a fixation on the false-self mode is predominant. Wounded Eros manifests in disruptions, in our body being out of balance. We lose energy, we become depressed, and we suffer from a sense of meaninglessness. Broken wings of Eros may be experienced as loss of soul, emptiness, a psychic desert, an attitude that leads into objectification and rationalization. When Eros's wings are broken, no coherent sense of self can develop, and no personal meaning-making myth can unfold. Where Eros is betrayed or absent, the dark face of Eros, the lust for power, creeps in and anxiety and fear reign, preventing the love cure from working. With Eros undeveloped, we tend to become sentimental, giving in to undifferentiated feeling.

Wounded Eros can be seen in the supremacy of Logos and the devaluation of the feminine spirit. Abstract reasoning becomes divorced from our feelings and intuitions, and we develop a one-sided preference for Logos over Eros, with the result that our capacity to relate is diminished. These broken wings of Eros create an imbalance, and this personal and collective one-sidedness prevents the individuation of the individual and of society as a whole. We can see this wounding in our culture at large in the general indifference to human and environmental destruction, as well as in the widespread incidence of borderline personality disorder or dissociative identity disorder. Broken wings of Eros are also at the core of addictions, where addiction substitutes for relationship.

The failure of Eros manifests as self-estrangement, an incapacity to relate—individually and collectively. Alienation is the disease of modern human beings; Fromm was of the opinion that all neuroses are caused by a sense of alienation. We experience alienation as estrangement from ourselves, our feelings, our fellow humans, and nature. We become susceptible to despair and self-destruction. We lose creative expression and authenticity because we lack the energy that comes with relatedness, with being in contact with other human beings and the world at large. Estrangement from ourselves robs us of the possibility of realizing our own potential, of expressing our true authentic self, and it leads to the development of a split between a true and a false self, to depression, grandiosity, and extreme vulnerability.

At the same time, estrangement paradoxically holds out the possibility of ultimate at-one-ment. As human beings, we strive to unite with that to which we belong and from which we have been separated. Authentic life strives for what it lacks. Jung strongly believed that since we are separated from the whole we desire union with the whole. "Originally we were all born out of a world of wholeness and in the first years of life are still completely contained in it. There we have all knowledge without knowing it. Later we lose it, and call it progress when we remember it."[32]

When the wings of Eros are broken, our sensitivity to the numinous, the miraculous, is dulled. The hypertrophy of reason blocks the flow of creative Dionysian energy, suppresses desire, and leads to the devaluation of emotions and a crisis of feeling that values narcissistic self-love over altruistic love. This brokenness of Eros's wings at the collective level ends ultimately in some kind of fixation on individualism and in an erosion of ethics in the absence of respect for the other and for the dignity of nature. We become emotionally and spiritually barren, infertile.

Mending the broken wings of Eros can also be spoken of as tending to and restoring the jeweled net (or web) of Indra, a Hindu metaphor for the interconnectedness of all things.

Without Eros, we fall out of the cosmic order; stagnation reigns and Eros is reduced to an instrument of manipulation and seduction. Absence of Eros means lack of fecundity, diminished creativity, and a state of dispiritedness and alienation from the realm of becoming. Sometimes a taste of the wounding aspect of Eros is needed; the soul needs to suffer in order to get in touch with the other pole. A union of divine Eros and chthonic Chaos is a precondition for the healing of the splits. We need to integrate the erotic, the destructive, and the creative aspects of Eros. Only a reconciliation of these opposing forces will make it possible for them to take their playful and creative place in the individuation process. If Eros is repressed, it will become our shadow, a dark inner force that disrupts life and creates a rift between erotic and sexual desire, a split between mind and body.

I have written and often lectured about the shadow side of our profession, when the goldmine of Eros turns into a minefield. Unethical behavior between therapists and clients can be conceptualized as a betrayal of Eros, a breaking of the soul's wings. Sometimes the fear of Eros in therapy becomes apparent when the therapist dissipates the hot, erotic energy through reductive interpretations. We attempt to control the energy field either by not attending to Eros in the analytic encounter or by pathologizing or infantilizing the erotic desires of our clients.

## The Broken Wings of Eros in the Christian Tradition

Much has been written on the denial of desire within Christian ethics. In Christianity, the dual aspect of Eros embracing heaven and hell has been torn apart; sensual and sexual love and desire have been condemned as coming from the devil, and spiritual love as rooted in

God overvalued. St. Augustine regarded sexual passion as a dangerous force that threatens the purity of spiritual life. Friedrich Nietzsche lamented: "Christianity gave Eros, the god of love, poison to drink. He did not die of it, it is true, but he degenerated into vice."[33]

The Christian tradition harbors a deep suspicion of *Eros*. The Church has systematically suppressed *Eros* and denounced the erotic, replacing it with something "higher," something the New Testament calls *agapé*—a purely spiritual, non-physical form of love. Traditional Christian teaching devalues the embodied experience of love and overemphasizes the dangerous, non-spiritual character of sensuality and sexuality. Instead of integrating sexuality into a holistic understanding of life, Christianity has fallen into a profound dichotomy that separates spirit from flesh and raises the spiritual above the physical. Shrouded in suspicion and shame, the erotic has become marginalized. The implications for our culture of this dichotomy of flesh and spirit have been far-reaching: it became the basis not only for the denigration of sexuality but also for the oppression of women and the eroticization of power in a society characterized by structural violence. Feminist theologians today, however, take a positive attitude to erotic power and intimacy that comes from the subjective engagement of the whole self in a relationship. They are critical of our culture of broken-heartedness and the misidentification of Eros with lust or sexuality. Erotic power is seen as the fundamental life-giving power of existence, empowering and liberating, creating and connecting hearts, involving "the whole person in relationships of self-awareness, vulnerability, openness, and caring."[34]

## Wounded Eros in Fairy Tales

We often find the archetypal motif of wounded Eros and the path to integration in fairy tales. "Bluebeard," for example, is about the destructive effects of an unconscious encounter with Eros. "The Nixie in the Pond" (a Grimms' fairy tale) deals with a split-off erotic complex that pushes the man and the woman into an individuation process in which they have to discover and embrace their split-off Eros. Many fairytale princesses, stuck in narcissistic grandiosity and unable to relate and surrender to true feelings, are victims of the breaking of Eros's wings.

*Turandot*, Puccini's last opera, based on a Persian tale from the collection *The Thousand and One Days*, is also a very good example. Princess Turandot is a beautiful but cold young woman, totally cut off from Eros. In revenge for the slaying of her ancestor, Princess Lou-Ling, by a conquering prince, she has sworn an oath that she will not consent to be the bride of any suitor who cannot successfully answer the three riddles that she puts to him. Icy, ruthless, and tyrannical, she refuses to submit to love. All of her several suitors so far have failed the test and have been subjected to the punishment of death by beheading. The last suitor, however, a handsome stranger, is able to answer all three riddles and Turandot is left confounded. Thwarted and humiliated, she begs her father not to give her to the stranger, but the father insists that the oath is sacred and cannot be broken. The princess recoils from the intimacy of the impending conjugal union and the resulting dissolution of her isolated sense of self. Having long since banished Eros, she can now react only with rage and anxiety at the prospect of love and surrender. In her attempt at self-preservation, she seeks to destroy her husband-to-be and everything that might emerge between them—but it is love that wins her over in the end. The stranger offers to forfeit his own life and thereby release her from the obligation of her oath if before dawn she can discover his name; he does not want to take her by force, but desires her love. Despite her tyrannical power and fierce determination, she is unable to find out the stranger's name, but just as dawn is breaking the young man kisses her passionately, breaking down her defenses, and as she weeps, he reveals himself to her as Prince Calaf. He makes himself vulnerable; he gives himself totally into her hands. This loving surrender of the prince breaks the spell, and Turandot becomes human once again. With Eros integrated, her deep-seated longing for redemption through love can finally be fulfilled.

Catastrophe and betrayal seem to be the necessary trigger for the individuation process of the princess, wounded as she is and totally cut off from her feelings, her intuition, and her feminine instincts. She is driven only by a lust for power. She is in a state of possession, governed by Thanatos, devoid of Eros. She is in desperate need of a new attitude, a separation from her identification with the past. The *coniunctio* is possible only if the princess sacrifices her old egocentric attitude and discovers the essential value of relationship by learning to listen to the voices of the self.

Eros calls us to dissolve our narrow ego-boundaries and restricted sense of self. Eros pushes us beyond, to reveal our true selves to one another. The dissolution of our old personality is called for in the process of becoming one with the other—destruction in the service of creation, as Sabina Spielrein put it. Sacrifices must be made on our way to reclaiming our lost unity by surrendering to a larger unknown whole,

I see Eros as the healing energy of existence. When we become reconciled to Eros, we learn to care and bond, we speak of a connected self that represents an ethics of connection and commitment to the well-being of the other. Erotic love is an action, a way of being in this world. It is a vital life energy, an act of deeply respecting all created beings and acting to promote the well-being of those we love. Reconciliation to Eros brings to us an openness to our yearnings and desires, allowing spontaneity and the joy of being alive to enter our heart. Living erotically is like swimming in the river of life, giving in and giving over, being capable of surrendering to the unknown, being true to one another and revealing to one another our original face. If Eros is liberated, transformation can occur through an awareness of our interconnectedness and a balancing of our unregulated energies.

In serving Eros, we might develop our consciousness, entering into the *unus mundus* field, which—to borrow the words of physicist David Bohm—can be felt as "an ocean of energy," where "folding and unfolding moves together," where the "unity of unity and diversity" can be experienced along with the paradox of the "wholeness of the whole and the part."[35]

Speaking of paradox, I recall having learned in my Zen training that a Chinese Zen master from the Tang Dynasty once said:

> When I did not yet practice Zen Buddhism, to me a mountain was a mountain, and water was water; after I got an insight into the truth of Zen, I thought that a mountain was not a mountain and water was not water; but now that I have really attained the abode of final rest, to me a mountain is really a mountain and water is really water.

May venturing into the uncertainties of the heart awaken your yearning to know who you are and may delving into intimacy help you to come closer to the insight that the mountain here in Beatenberg, the Holy Beatus, really is a mountain, and the lake in front of us really is a lake, and your "You" and my "I" truly are a We!

---

## *NOTES*

[1] Domin Hilde, "Es gibt Dich," in Hilde Domin, *Ich will dich. Gedichte* (Frankfurt am Main: Fischer, 1995), p. 75. English translation approved by publisher.

[2] Donald W. Winnicott, *Playing and Reality* (New York: Basic Books, 1971), p. 134.

[3] The Jungian analyst Judith Pickering gave a fascinating paper on Levinas entitled "Here I Am" at the IAAP Congress in Cape Town, 2007.

[4] C. G. Jung, "Problems of Modern Psychotherapy," in *The Practice of Psychotherapy: Essays on the Psychology of the Transference and Other Subjects, The Collected Works of C. G. Jung*, trans. R. F. C. Hull (Princeton, NJ: Princeton University Press, 1916/1958/1969), vol. 16, § 163 (All future references to Jungs's *Collected Works*, abbreviated to *CW*, will be followed by chapter title, volume, paragraph.)

[5] Esther Harding, *The Parental Image* (Toronto: Inner City Books, 2003), p. 136.

[6] C. G. Jung, "The Psychic Nature of the Alchemical Work," *CW* 12, § 381.

[7] Wilfred Bion, "Notes on Memory and Desire," in *Psychoanalytic Forum*, 2 (1967): 271-280.

[8] Trusting our yin qualities in the analytic process is important. See Lorie E. Dechar, *Five Spirits* (New York: Chiron Publications, 2006).

[9] C. G. Jung, "Lecture IV," in *Nietzsche's "Zarathustra": Notes on the Seminar Given in 1934-1939*, ed. James L. Jarrett (Princeton, NJ: Princeton University Press, 1988), vol. I, p. 102.

[10] Mario Jacoby, *Individuation and Narcissism: The Psychology of the Self in Jung and Kohut* (London: Routledge, 1990), p. 205.

[11] C. G. Jung, Letter to M. R. Braband-Isaac, 13 July, 1939, *C. G. Jung Letters, Volume 1: 1906-1950*, ed. Gerhard Adler and Aniela Jaffé, trans. R. F. C. Hull (Princeton, NJ: Princeton University Press, 1973), p. 274.

[12] C. G. Jung, Letter to Upton Sinclair, 7 January 1955, *C. G. Jung Letters, Volume 2: 1951-1961*, ed. by Gerhard Adler, trans. Jeffrey Hulen (Princeton, NJ: Princeton University Press, 1976), p. 207.

[13] See Moojan Momen, "Abdu'l-Baha's Commentary on The Islamic Tradition: 'I was a Hidden Treasure ...,'" in *Baha'i Studies Bulletin* 3, no. 4 (1985): 4-35.

[14] See John R. Haule on the "Self field," in *Pathways into the Jungian World*, ed. Roger Brooke (London: Routledge, 1999), pp. 255-272.

[15] C. G. Jung, *Memories, Dreams, Reflections*, ed. Aniela Jaffé, trans. Richard & Clara Winston (New York, NY: Random House, 1989 [1961]), p. 325.

[16] Jung, "The Eros Theory," *CW* 7, § 32.

[17] Jung, "Woman in Europe," *CW* 10, § 255.

[18] David Mann, *Psychotherapy: An Erotic Relationship* (London: Routledge, 1997); David Mann, *Erotic Transference and Countertransference* (London: Routledge, 1999).

[19] C. G. Jung, *The Freud/Jung Letters: The Correspondence between Sigmund Freud and C. G. Jung*, ed. William J. McGuire, Gerhard Adler and Aniela Jaffé, trans. Ralph Manheim and R. F. C. Hull (Princeton, NJ: Princeton University Press, 1974), p. 12f.

[20] Mann, *Psychotherapy*, p. 12.

[21] Julia Kristeva, *Tales of Love* (New York: Columbia University Press, 1983).

[22] Paul Roazen, *Freud and His Followers* (New York: Knopf, 1976), p. 363.

[23] Jung, "The Aims of Psychotherapy," *CW* 16, § 99.

[24] Rainer Maria Rilke, *Essay on Rodin and Other Prose Pieces*, ed. and trans. William Tucker (London: Quartet Books Limited, 1986), p. 52.

[25] Jane Wheelwright, "Jung," in *C. G. Jung, Emma Jung, and Toni Wolff: A Collection of Remembrances*, ed. Ferne Jensen (San Francisco, CA: The Analytical Psychology Club of San Francisco, 1982), pp. 97-105.

[26] Ursula Wirtz, *Seelenmord: Inzest und Therapie* (Stuttgart: Kreuz Verlag, 1989).

[27] Jung, *Memories*, p. 8.

[28] Jung, "Introduction to the Religious and Psychological Problems of Alchemy," *CW* 12, § 32.

[29] Albert Oeri, *Ein Paar Jugenderinnerungen* (Berlin 1935) quoted by John R. Haule in "Freud and Jung: A Failure of Eros," in *Journal of Analytical Psychology*, 39 (1994): 147-158.

[30] Jung, *Freud/Jung Letters*, p. 95.

[31] Linda Donn, *Freud and Jung: Years of Friendship, Years of Loss* (New York: Charles Scribner's Sons, 1988), p. 151.

[32] Jung, *Freud/Jung Letters*, pp. 274-275.

[33] Friedrich Nietzsche, *Beyond Good and Evil: Prelude to a Philosophy of the Future*, IV, § 168. See also Alfred Ribi, *Eros und Abendland: Geistesgeschichte der Beziehungsfunktion* (Bern: Lang, 2005), p. 380.

[34] Rita Nakashima Brock, *Journeys by Heart: A Christology of Erotic Power* (New York: Crossroad, 1988), p. 26.

[35] See for instance David Bohm, *Wholeness and the Implicate Order* (London & New York: Routledge Classics, 2002).

Mario Jacoby, Dr. phil., maintains a private analytic practice in Zürich. He has given lectures and seminars all over Europe, the U.S.A., South Africa, Latin America, and Israel. He is the author of numerous articles and books on Analytical Psychology, including *The Analytic Encounter* (1984), *Individuation and Narcissism* (1989), *Shame and the Origins of Self-Esteem* (1993), and *Jungian Psychotherapy and Contemporary Infant Research* (1999).

# 7

# Intimacy and the Arrows of Eros

*Mario Jacoby*

## Eros in Ancient Mythology

Eros is a difficult and elusive being—especially when you want to do some writing or talking about him. I, personally, experienced this more-or-less theoretical treatment of Eros as very challenging and difficult, tiring and resistance-provoking. It seems that Eros does not want to be talked about. In the lovely myth of Eros and Psyche, he comes only at night, in the dark, and he sets a stringent condition on the beloved Psyche, namely, that she is strictly forbidden to shine any light on him; love can take place only in absolute darkness. Yet world literature and poetry have been feeding themselves for centuries on the tenderness, but also the cruelty, of Eros and his arrows. But precisely that may be the reason why I experience such difficulty in putting words down on the blank sheet of paper in front of me. From which angle—considering the infinite variety of angles there are to choose from—shall I try to tell you, and basically also myself, something new? Of course, that is impossible. But there must be at least something we could find to speak of that may evoke an "Aha!" reaction—at least for those among us who have felt the exhilarating but often also painful penetration of the arrows shot by Eros.

As you will recall, in the ancient myth of Eros and Psyche, told us by Apuleius of Madaura[1] in *The Golden Ass*, the beautiful Psyche falls in love with Eros and vice versa. But, as mentioned before, there is one condition: he will appear only in the dark and it is strictly forbidden for Psyche to light a lamp, otherwise he has to leave her immediately. But Psyche has envious sisters, and they continue to suggest to her that she has to find a way to see this mysterious lover of the dark. He may be a vile, venomous snake, who in the end will kill her. And so one night poor Psyche, believing her sisters, takes an oil lamp and a razor in order to see and possibly to kill Eros. But what she sees is the kindest and sweetest of all the wild beasts, Eros himself. In her over-happy shock, she pricks herself accidentally on his arrow, which is lying next to him, and begins to bleed. And thus, "unwittingly, yet of her own doing, Psyche fell in love with Love."[2] But the beautiful boy, after he has been seen, immediately flies away without saying a word. He has to get back to his mother Aphrodite. But now Psyche has to become active and fulfill the tasks demanded of her by Eros's jealous mother. It was Erich Neumann[3] and also Marie-Louise von Franz[4] who first interpreted this myth and the meaning of Psyche's tasks in terms of the process of individuation.

But I want to stay with Eros, the hero of the title I have chosen for my talk. There are two major stories in the Greek tradition about the beginning of all things that include the birth of Eros.[5] Both of these mythological accounts show the intimate relation of Eros to the night and the dark.

One of these is the account that was passed down in the secret writings preserved by the disciples and devotees of the singer Orpheus. It starts off: "In the beginning was 'Night', and she was one of the greatest Goddesses. Even the great God Zeus was standing in sacred awe of her."[6] According to this tale, Night appeared in the form of a big bird with black wings. Then appeared the Wind, who apparently was in love with Night, and she conceived through him and laid a silver egg in the gigantic lap of Darkness. From the egg sprang the son of the rushing Wind, a god with golden wings. He is called Eros, the god of love, but this is only one of his many names, the loveliest of all the names he has borne.

Hesiod tells us a slightly different story: First there was Chaos. From Chaos appeared broad-breasted Gaia, the firm and everlasting abode of all divinities. Then Eros emerged in like manner, the loveliest of the immortal gods, who loosens the limbs and rules the spirit of all gods and men.

In psychological terms, Eros is imagined from early on in both traditions as being aroused from a dark, deep place in the unconscious.

Now, a few words have also to be said about the arrows that Eros carries with him and shoots on certain occasions. What do they symbolize? The arrows stand for penetration and opening up. They signify also the power of thought to clarify and of the penis to penetrate. However, as Ovid informs us, Eros uses two types of arrows, which always hit their mark: if they are tipped with gold, they kindle passion; if they are tipped with lead, they extinguish it. Thus, they can either fuel passion or bring sorrow and pain. Sometimes they hit with happy elation, sometimes with intense suffering, and sometimes even with both at the same time.

The French speak of "*coup de foudre*," a bolt of lightning—a sudden emotional pang, "love at first sight." Think of all the great tragic love stories in our literature: Romeo and Juliet, Hero and Leander, Tristan and Isolde, etc. All these lovers are struck by the most passionate love, but they all have to die, because such passion cannot be sustained in the long run in our daily reality. Thus, the arrows of Eros may have the most delightful and passionate effects, but also the most tragic and deadly consequences.

## Intimacy

But now, what do we understand by "intimacy"? John Hill, who is responsible for finding a particularly attractive title to convey the theme of our Odyssey gathering each year, combined the idea of intimacy with the heart. And he is right. We do not *think* intimacy with the mind. Rather, we *feel* a longing or a need for it with the heart. However, feeling is not something that can be sharply or precisely defined. Feelings may contain innumerable nuances, so a definition of something like intimacy is never complete.

Of course, I was curious to find out what our great master Jung had to say on this subject. So I looked in the General Index to his *Collected Works*, and was surprised to discover that the word "intimacy" is not to be found there. From "intestinal canal" the list goes directly to "intolerance." The word "intimacy," apparently, was never used by Jung. Of course, it is well known—and he admits it himself—that feeling was not his strong suit.

Luckily, something Jung said that points in the direction of feeling came to my mind. I suddenly remembered that in "The Psychology of the Transference," in Volume 16 of the *Collected Works*, which he dedicated "To my wife," he writes (in the chapter on "king and queen") the following:

> To the extent that transference is projection and nothing more it divides quite as much as it connects. But experi-

> ence teaches that there is one connection in the transference which does not break off with the severance of the projection. That is because there is an extremely important factor behind it namely the *kinship libido* [italics added]. This has been pushed so far into the background of the unlimited expansion of the exogamous tendency that it can find an outlet, and a modest one at that only within the family circle, and sometimes not even there, because of the quite justifiable resistance to the incest .... Everyone is now a stranger among strangers. Kinship libido—which still could engender a satisfying feeling of belonging together—as for instance in the early Christian communities—has long been deprived of its object. But being an instinct, it is not to be satisfied by any mere substitute such as a creed, party, nation or state. It wants the *human* connection [Jung's italics]. That is the core of the whole transference phenomenon, and it is impossible to argue this away, because relationship to the self is at once relationship to our fellow man, and no one can be related to the latter until he is related to himself.[7]

## Kinship Libido and Attachment

In this passage Jung refers to something that he never mentions anywhere else in his writings, and of course never elaborated further. It seems to me that this "kinship libido" is something extremely important. In using the term "kinship libido," Jung here brings up something that John Bowlby later characterized as the essence of healthy experience and development, namely, what he called "attachment." I do not think that these two terms are completely synonymous, but they are close enough, nonetheless. Kinship libido puts the emphasis on mutuality (kinship has to do with blood-relations, a feeling of belonging together, or also a soul-relatedness). Attachment, on the other hand, is not necessarily mutual, and is often one-sided. Nevertheless, both concepts point to a basic anthropological fact. They confirm Aristotle's claim that humans are social animals. By our very nature, we need to live in a social context, to be part of a society.

John Bowlby,[8] to whom we owe attachment theory as mentioned earlier, started with the observation that the infant has an inborn tendency to seek nearness and security by being with a trustworthy person. The newborn child has a deep-seated need for a so-called "secure base." If an infant feels tired, sick, insecure, hungry, or just lonely, it reacts by crying or giving out other signals in the hope that Mummy will be present to protect, help, and console it. If this "primary trust"[9] is missing in early infancy, the infant is likely to develop an abandonment complex, which later manifests itself in the form of great timidity, and many other symptoms such as anxiety, guilt, shame, unbearable loneliness, etc., which can persist even through adult life. What we have here is Early Damage Syndrome, or, as Erich Neumann called it, "Disturbance of the Primary Relationship."

To recapitulate, Eros is born from *night*, in *darkness*. We may say that it has its origins deep in the unconscious, or at least that it gets awakened from there, and once it is aroused, it can have a profound effect on us—we may be smitten by Eros's arrow.

## An Attempt at Psychological Interpretation

I have, so far, gathered together the *dramatis personae* for the exposition—as one would do in classical dream interpretation. Having done that, can we now somehow connect the dots in the puzzle? We have: (a) Eros born out of Night and her silver egg, carrying his bow and arrows; (b) the Wind, which together with the Goddess Night is responsible for the birth of Eros (wind symbolizes movement from mild to wild; it stands for spirit, since one can have only indirect knowledge of it, yet it can have an enormous impact); and (c) the situation we call intimacy, perhaps also kinship libido or attachment needs. How do they all hang together—if at all?

If we are to interpret a myth psychologically, we have to do it, first of all, on an archetypal level. Eros, Night, Wind, etc. are all collective, archetypal experiences, and as such they may constellate a certain general meaning. Eros, for instance, begins to be felt, its movement triggered within us, when we meet another person who seems particularly attractive to us. We may become highly *motivated* to meet that person and get closer to him or her. This interest is fuelled by what in psychological terms is called motivation. Here we come to a term that has sparked considerable interest among researchers and may also be relevant to our context.

## From the Primacy of Sexual Drive to Innate Sensual-Sexual Motivation

Within the past two decades, the psychoanalyst and specialist in infant research Josef Lichtenberg has worked out a quite convincing scheme of what he calls "Motivational Systems." Through his research, he has identified five basic innate motivational systems working in the human psyche. I will not go into all of them. For our theme of Eros, only one of these innate motivational systems is pertinent and of great interest. Lichtenberg calls it *innate sensual-sexual motivation.*[10]

As is well known, classical psychoanalysis since Freud has attributed fundamental importance to infantile sexuality as a factor in whether an individual is successful or unsuccessful in achieving personal maturation in adult life. By contrast, Jung, (as mentioned earlier) attributes to the infant a polyvalent predisposition.[11] He could not accept sexual drives as the primary motor of our entire psychic life, from early infancy on. The conclusions of Lichtenberg—that there are five distinct innate motivational systems that have a part to play from early on in the development of a sense of self and later on in the development of a sense of personal identity—come somewhat closer to the Jungian position. For Lichtenberg, sexuality, together with sensuality, forms the basis of one of the five innate motivational systems. Now, interestingly enough, he believes that it is important to differentiate *sensual* needs from the more strictly *sexual* needs. According to his observations, the sensual joy or physical pleasure of the newborn is released by an innate program and is normally part of day-to-day occurrences, as reflected in the infant's ongoing dialogue with the mother or other primary caregiver. But sexual excitation, although it follows *the same innate pattern*, begins to operate as part of the regular daily experience of the infant only much later, from the age of about 18 months on.

Infant research confirms what has long been recognized, namely, that there is an innate program of *sensual-affectional* needs, which plays a decisive role in the mother-infant relationship. These needs are much more significant than has generally been assumed, and constitute a vital part of our overall life cycle. In normal development, we are utterly dependent on our parents' devotion to us during infancy and early childhood. This dependency expresses itself quintessentially in our need for sensuality and affection. We now know that the satisfaction of these sensual-affectional needs also advances the consolidation of our sense of self and our sense of security and containment right into adulthood.

Now, in the original drive theory of Freudian psychoanalysis, sensual-affectional needs are seen as coming into play only in the build-up to sexual coitus. According to Freud, the goal of the sexual drive is always the release of sexual energy through orgasm. More recently, infant research has begun to investigate the origins and development of the need for genuine sexual excitation. We have learned from the work of James Kleeman that it is common for male infants to discover their penis for the first time around the age of 10 months.[12] They play with their genitals, stroking them very tenderly in a way quite similar to how they touch their mother's breasts. But such behavior is scarcely differentiated from other games that satisfy the infant's curiosity and need for exploration. Kleeman's conclusion is that in the first year of life these "sexual" games serve the purpose merely of establishing physical contact with the body. Yet, at about the age of 18 months, boys as well as girls start manipulating their genitals deliberately, and the purpose changes from exploration to genuine physical excitation, now of a masturbatory nature. It is at this point that it may properly be said that an awakening of the sense of sexual pleasure occurs.[13]

## The Differentiation between Sexual Drive and Sensual Pleasures

Although sensual pleasures and the drive to achieve orgasm are goals of the same motivational system, their differentiation in adult experience may play an important role in the development of intimacy. I want to offer a few pertinent observations. In intimate relationships, one often hears complaints such as: "My partner is not able to be tender and affectionate. All he wants is sex, all the time, on demand, the whole thing." Usually, such complaints come from women, who feel that they are loved only when their partner shows, in a sensitive manner, both tenderness and passion. Whenever their partner does not succeed in being tender enough by their feminine standards, they feel humiliated and used as mere sexual objects, needed only for the release of their partner's sexual energies. As a consequence, they often have difficulty opening themselves up to their own sexual energies. The complaint may, of course, come from the other side of the gender divide as well, even if not as frequently. Such conflicts can be accounted for by the differences between sensual-affectional needs and orgiastic sexual impulses. They also show that that these two forms of intimate behavior are not always integrated into the sense of self in tandem, as a matter of course.

It is of the utmost importance here that we question the conventional wisdom and the old clichés that attribute tenderness to the female gender and orgiastic driveness to the male. Such collective prejudices can operate in parenting too, and with detrimental effect. For example, many parents impose stereotypical sex-roles on their children from very early on. Thus, for the male child, the so-called feminine need for tenderness and affection is devalued. Likewise, for a girl, sexual abandon and wanton sexuality are frowned upon.

As analysts, we find quite often that such rigid ideas about masculinity and femininity determine a person's basic sexual motivations from early on in infancy, steering them in certain directions and not others, and then exerting perhaps a problematic influence on the later development of sexual identity. One may see this evidenced in the development of frigidity in women or a kind of personally unrelated male chauvinism in men, who become more occupied with their own sexual potency than with authentic intimacy.

As mentioned before, the feeling of intimacy is usually related to what Bowlby called attachment. In many adult love relationships, attachment and tenderness on one side, and sexual passion on the other, all operate together in harmony. But, as is well known, this is not always the case. As analysts, we often see people who suffer from conflicting needs in this area. On the one hand, there are many strong attachments that are not sexualized, but on the other, we find a great deal of personally unrelated or non-intimate sexual behavior. Thus, many people, typically (though not exclusively) men, believe that sexual adventures outside of marriage constitute no breach of the promise to be faithful to their life partner, because in their experience such liaisons have no bearing on, nor call into question, their deep-seated motivation to "belong together." This of course raises the question of whether the expectation of absolute sexual fidelity has any place in a fully integrated sexuality, or whether it may not have more to do with possessiveness or narcissistic vulnerability. Clearly, each case needs to be examined on an individual basis.

It would take us too far astray at this point to delve seriously into the question of why we humans so often have such enormous difficulties in coming to terms with something like sexuality. Already in archaic times, people had to obey certain rules and taboos connected with sex. It is, nonetheless, a fact that all too often sexuality is related—whether consciously or unconsciously—to the central problem for which clients come in for therapy, though not of course to the totalizing extent propounded early on by Freud. No matter how we look at it, today the phenomenon of sexuality cannot be considered in isolation. Indeed, sexuality reaches into many realms of life and may even insinuate itself, albeit unconsciously, into virtually any experience. In this latter case, we speak of sexualization.

## EROS IN ANALYTIC-THERAPEUTIC PRACTICE

I'd like to go back for a moment to the mythical figure of the god Eros we discussed earlier. Sexuality is really just one expression—although, of course, a very central one—of this archetypal force. Yet I find this myth of Eros emerging from an egg laid by the Night and fertilized by the Wind to be very illuminating. I support Jung's idea that Eros is not to be considered as synonymous with sex, but neither should it be divorced from sex. Ideally, Eros "participates" as an aspect of sex, as well as of most other couplings or group activities of a psychic nature, be they social, aesthetic, or spiritual.

I also want to deal briefly with something that many of us have experienced, namely Eros as part of our reality in our work as therapists and analysts. We all know about this strange and complex phenomenon called transference/countertransference. I shall begin with Jung's understanding of the four stages of "erotic phenomenology."[14]

In the first stage, Eros is purely biological. The second stage continues to be dominated by sexual feelings, but Eros has moved on to the aesthetic and romantic level, where the other acquires some value as an individual. In the third stage Eros is raised to the heights of religious devotion and is thus spiritualized. In the fourth and final stage, Eros reaches the level of Sapientia, a form of Wisdom. I think today we have to take these ideas *cum grano salis*—with a grain of salt. But here Jung articulates an insight that was already known in antiquity, namely, that Eros is an emotional entity capable of transforming itself on different levels of experience. Freud, who discovered—to his dismay—that sexualization in the transference can at times reach high levels of intensity, observed, nevertheless, that certain of his patients seemed to have the gift of achieving something he called "sublimation." They were able to raise the biological imperative of the sexual drive to a different, more conscious level and direct it towards more creative ends.

But what about intimacy within the analytic encounter? As most of you probably know, people usually enter into analysis to share intimate details about themselves that cannot be discussed elsewhere. The analyst is at first usually an unknown entity, a stranger. But as the analysis progresses, the analyst continues to be relatively unknown, while the patient reveals more and more of himself or herself, often in intimate detail. After a while, some patients begin to complain about the unfairness of the relationship: they know nothing about the therapist's private life, while they themselves are expected to reveal intimate details about their own personal affairs. Furthermore, they may find it humiliating to discover that the analyst has become such an important part of their life, while they themselves mean very little to the analyst—or so they imagine. They see themselves as just one of a number of clients in the analyst's pool. They begin to doubt the authenticity of whatever attention, praise, encouragement, or empathy they may receive from the analyst, regarding it—rightly or wrongly—as merely part of the analyst's "professional" behavior. This perception may in fact be true in some cases. I always try my very best to stick to my true reactions and observations—but this does not preclude the possibility that certain observations, usually those at the beginning of the analysis, may have to be tactfully overlooked, not mentioned. Jung was of the opinion that analysts should meet their patients as far as possible on their level—"not too high nor too low."[15] He promoted the idea of the therapeutic "partnership." He said that in deeper analyses, "the doctor must emerge from his anonymity and give an account of himself, just as he expects his patient to do."[16] He also insisted that "[b]y no device can the treatment be anything but the product of mutual influence, in which the whole being of the doctor as well as that of his patient plays its part."[17] This sounds good, fair, freeing, and encouraging for therapists. Patients should be "enabled" to "make use" of the therapy and the therapist. They should be as free as possible to communicate their troubles, their conflicts, their needs, and their love for the analyst, as well as their hate, their disappointments, and their criticisms. They may behave as infantile as is necessary within the boundaries of the therapeutic setting.

Psychotherapists, on the other hand, can never permit themselves just to "let go." They must keep a certain control over themselves, never react thoughtlessly, nor requite the patient's love, nor punish or retaliate. Jungian analysts, accepting mutual influence as an important psychotherapeutic fact, and relying to a great extent on "spontaneous reactions," may not have sufficient protection against the danger of getting into quite risky emotional entanglements in the name of spontaneity, mutual openness, or an "honest" dialogue.

I want to share with you a practical example of how difficult this task can be in practice. An analysand of mine, a young doctor, was suffering from periodic bouts of depression—falling at times "into a deep hole," as he described it. Often, it took only the slightest mishap for him to feel "as if the rug had been pulled out from under me," as if he had been tossed into an abyss of absolute worthlessness. Whenever this happened, he would feel so completely unworthy that he would be too ashamed even to show his face at work, where he had major responsibilities. It was clear that his self-degradation had little foundation in reality, but derived from his own unrealistically high demands on himself.

Therapeutically, it was important not to leave him alone and isolated in the middle of such "holes." He needed empathic understanding of his suffering and, in the long run, a working-through of his vulnerability and its roots in an emotionally deprived childhood. One day, when he had fallen into one of his "holes," I followed a spontaneous impulse and told him that I knew very well how he felt, *having experienced something like it myself*. It was only a brief hint, but—this is important—a true one, though perhaps more true of my past than my present. I offered it in a moment when I believed I could comprehend especially well how it must feel to be in this dungeon, rejected by God and the world. It just came on as a spontaneous impulse of identification and a certain sense of intimacy that comes with the feeling that you and the other person are "on the same level."

But in the next session he complained that he had felt badly misunderstood and was offended by my remark, because when I said I was acquainted with such depressed states from personal experience, it only proved to him how incapable I was of imagining the extent of his suffering. It was simply inconceivable to him that I could ever fall into such a hell. Obviously, he still needed to idealize me, and this made it impossible for me to do my part in bringing us "to the same level" in a moment of intimacy. At the same time, I felt pleased and satisfied that he could at least give vent to his emotions by telling me how he felt.

Somehow, he was probably right. It is not the analyst's personal confessions that bring greater mutuality or intimacy in the therapeutic situation. Rather, it seems to me that "the same level" is more a matter of the analyst's attitude to the analytic process. True mutuality comes about when analysts discover what part they themselves play in any difficulty that may arise in the transference situation, instead of attributing the problem to the pathology of the patient.

Undoubtedly, Eros in all its many forms plays a central role in the analytic encounter. That is why, to my mind, the analyst needs to be as aware as possible of the intensity and nuances of his or her own feelings, needs, and shortcomings. This calls for a thorough self-analysis on the part of the analyst. Only such sensitive self-awareness can allow him or her the spontaneity that is needed, because it is, first of all, the analyst's job, whatever happens, not to lose the empathic connection to the patient's inner reality.

Having said this, it is high time to end my talk. But our subject will never let us come to a real end. I am sure you know this as well as I do.

---

## *NOTES*

[1] Apuleius of Madaura, "Amor and Psyche," in *Metamorphosis, or the Golden Ass* (Oxford: Clarendon Press, 1910).

[2] Erich Neumann, *Amor and Psyche: The Psychic Development of the Feminine—A Commentary on the Tale by Apuleius*, trans. Ralph Manheim (Princeton, NJ: Princeton University Press, 1971 [1956]), p. 79.

[3] Neumann, *Amor and Psyche.*

[4] Marie-Louise von Franz, *A Psychological Interpretation of the Golden Ass of Apuleius* (New York: W. W. Norton, 1970).

[5] Karl Kerényi, *The Gods of the Greeks* (London: Thames and Hudson, 1951).

[6] *Ibid.*, p. 16.

[7] C. G. Jung, "The Psychology of Transference," in *The Practice of Psychotherapy, Essays on the Psychology of the Transference and Other Subjects, The Collected Works of C. G. Jung*, trans. R. F. C. Hull (Princeton, NJ: Princeton University Press, 1969 [1916/1958]) vol. 16, § 445. (Future references to Jung's *Collected Works*, abbreviated to *CW*, will appear with chapter title followed by volume and paragraph number.)

[8] John Bowlby, *Attachment and Loss* (New York: Basic Books, 1969).

[9] Erik Erikson, *Childhood and Society* (New York: W.W. Norton, 1950).

[10] Joseph D. Lichtenberg, *Psychoanalysis and Motivation* (Hillsdale, NY: The Analytic Press, 1989), pp. 222ff.

[11] Jung, "Foreword to 2nd Edition of Psychic Conflict in a Child," *CW* 17, p. 5.

[12] James A. Kleeman, "A Boy Discovers His Penis," *The Psychoanalytic Study of the Child*, 20 (1965): 239-265.

[13] *Ibid.*

[14] Jung, "Psychology of the Transference," *CW* 16, § 361.

[15] Jung, "Tavistock Lectures," *CW* 18, § 337.

[16] Jung, "Principles of Practical Psychotherapy," *CW* 16, § 23.

[17] Jung, "Problems of Modern Psychotherapy," *CW* 16, § 163.

Allan Guggenbühl, Prof. Dr. phil., received his degrees from the University of Zürich in education and psychology, and afterwards his diploma from the C. G. Jung-Institut Zürich in 1994. He was editor of the Jungian journal *Gorgo*. Currently, he is director of the Institute for Conflict Management in Zürich and is well known for his methods of Mythodrama and crisis intervention at the institutional and individual level. He has many publications, including his celebrated *Men, Power, and Myths: The Quest for Male Identity*.

# 8

# Love: Our Most Cherished Anarchist—or Path to Failure?

*Allan Guggenbühl*

"The more you talk about love, the less there is of it!" goes the famous proverb. This might also apply to writing about love. Is it possible to write something essential about love without losing the essence of our personal experience of love? There are obstacles to overcome. In contrast to transference, defense mechanisms, how to fix fuses or cook lasagne, love is an *immensely personal topic*. We have all experienced romance, falling in love, and being in a love relationship. We dream of eternal love and are devastated when our expectations are not fulfilled. When we are disappointed in love, we often feel like a wreck and life loses its meaning. When we fall out of love, we experience sleepless nights, desperation, anger, and even feelings of revenge. We lose our composure, become silly, and might even behave irrationally. Most people would not admit publicly to doing the things that love drove them to do. For example, a well-known medical professor sends thousands of text messages to her lover pleading for forgiveness; a leading public figure posts sex ads in the name of his former girlfriend in revenge for her dumping him.

Given such experiences, we would have to say that love is a *complex*. Love is a topic that arouses emotions, personal convictions, and blissful or painful memories. It is difficult to discuss love in a rational, sane way. Statements or generalizations are quickly denounced. What we think makes sense, someone else may consider gibberish. Theories about love cannot compete with the personal conclusions we draw. *What we experience, we consider to be true*. In order to digest our love experiences, whether exhilarating or traumatic, we construct *personal theories*. We create a story or develop an idea about the dynamics, the secrets, the psychology of love. We wish to comprehend the overflow of emotions, the irrational behavior, or loss of control. Generally, we consider our explanations as our very personal theory. This is why we often hesitate to analyze our love stories. What we have experienced is unique and ultimately true! To scrutinize our experiences would be to betray them. "I know why my relationship with my former boyfriend failed! He did not appreciate me enough!" Or: "Don't try to connect my feelings for this man to my father! There is certainly no connection at all!" Ongoing love affairs or loving relationships are often hidden from the undiscerning eye of the analyst or psychologist.

Love is experienced in different ways. Falling in love is usually an intoxicating adventure. Our emotions overflow, we feel light-hearted, optimistic, humorous, and energized. We laugh at every silly joke and feel transformed. Subjectively, we experience love as a force that strikes us out of the blue. Often, the power of love seemingly alters our attitudes towards life or makes us change our decisions. Ambivalences evaporate. We stop loathing dancing, start loving flowers, or even develop an interest in angels or *feng shui*. Charged with the energy of love, we feel full of zest and vigor. We sacrifice time and money just to be with our beloved for a few minutes, and we feel that our existence finally has purpose. When we are in love, we consider it eternal bliss to be close to the cherished person, even if all we do is just stare at each other. We drive for hours by car overnight, wait interminably at airports or on park benches. Being in love makes us forget our egotistical ways.

Love connects us with our body. We are alert to bodily sensations. Our heart beats faster; we sweat and feel warmth in our chest. We may even start to tremble and our voice cracks when we address the loved one. When we are in love, we feel sexually aroused. Eros appears and transforms a hand movement into a magic gesture, a casual pat into a gentle caress, and an impromptu touch into a subtle sign. Sexual imagery floods our mind and the fluids in our body begin to flow. We want to connect physically and feel sexy and horny. We turn into sexual beings.

Love releases hitherto unknown energies. Suddenly, we become adventurous and are willing to take unprecedented risks. A married woman in Thun had a fling with an Italian musician. After a telephone call from her adored one, she jumped into her car and drove more than 300 kilometers to Turin in order to meet her lover and spend one delightful, sensuous, forbidden night with him. The next day she was back in Thun, of course, and he returned dutifully to his wife.

Love invites craziness. We sing in the rain, dance in the street, or start telling inappropriate jokes. We might make harsh decisions, cut off ties with our own family and forget our friends, because we think love demands it. Love can blind us and even lead us to commit crimes. A thirty-year-old woman stole half a million francs from her employer. Her lover needed the money and promised to pay her back immediately. Unfortunately, he disappeared after she gave him the money.

When love strikes, our perceptions change. Trivial events become highly significant—a look, a sigh, an impromptu touch all become invested with meaning. We become extremely sensitive to any movement, word, or action from the beloved one. We begin to *interpret* events around us. "Why did he wear a yellow shirt?" "Why did the background music change, the minute I sat beside her?" When we are in love, we light-headedly relinquish rational thinking. The world is filled with magical signs and hidden messages. "Unknowingly, he chose my favorite colors!" We search for links: "It must have a meaning that his mother's birthday is the same as mine!" "It is certainly no coincidence that I met him the moment my grandmother died!" Lovers discover synchronicity! When a song is played during a romantic moment, then this is of course considered as an endorsement of the relationship! The gods are with us! The things that happen in the outside world seem to be connected with the inside world. "This bird came deliberately to greet us!" whispers a love-struck man to his girlfriend. The moment he kissed her, a bird flew by. Another couple declares a highly frequented café to be their own private spot. Love brings out the mystical, supernatural in us. We refer to thinking categories that under normal circumstances we would abhor. We talk of signs and enchantments, and become mesmerized by scenes that develop around us. In other words, love turns us into perfect fools.

### A Cynical Outsider's View of Love

The outsider's view differs from the lover's perspective. For people who are not in love, lovers can be a nuisance. Passing time with people who have just fallen in love can be an unbearable experience. As the two lovers indulge themselves and have eyes only for each other, they live in their own private bubble. It is usually impossible for an outsider to enter their private world. They seem to retreat into their own realm and are oblivious to anything that happens around them. Their language degenerates rapidly. "You!" says a man in love. "Yes! What were you saying?" she replies. "Oh!" he answers, "I only wanted to say, 'You!'" Lovers often develop a depreciative view of the outside world and grandiose fantasies about themselves. Of course, no one understands them. They consider their experience as a couple unique. "I never met a woman who understands me better!" marvels a young Swiss about his new girlfriend from Thailand, disregarding the fact that they do not even share a common language! They communicate in substandard pidgin English. If an outsider politely points out that a mutual language is a prerequisite for understanding between two people, this comment will most certainly be unwelcome. People in love irritate outsiders because they are obsessed with themselves. Other human beings barely stimulate any interest. Lovers are prone to a *folie à deux*.

But that is not enough. Lovers are not only self-centered, they behave irresponsibly. Often their decisions are not based on sound judgment, but are hurried and flippant. A family man living in Zürich went on a business trip to Tokyo. At the airport, his wife and children bade him farewell. On the plane, a flight attendant served him. Her eyes intrigued him. They began to flirt. Over India, their feelings got deeper. Over the China Sea, they discovered they were in love, so upon reaching Narita airport in Tokyo they decided they spend some time together. Two days later he called his wife and informed her that he wanted to change his personal situation, needed a time-out from family life. The new relationship flourished, despite the fact that the businessman and the flight attendant had different backgrounds, interests, and personalities. After two years, the passion was gone. Actually, it was obvious from the beginning that they were not suitable for each other. Irrational decisions are often made when love strikes.

## Tragic Love

Of course, love is not just blissful and joyful, but includes the tragic. The absence of the loved one feels like torture. Disappointed lovers are confronted with the abysmal and dark sides of life. Often, tragedy follows the blissful moments. Love stories nearly always have a tragic ending, except in fairy tales. Romeo and Juliet perish after a fatal misunderstanding. In Whitehorse, Yukon there is a house that is officially haunted by a ghost. During the Klondike Gold Rush, hundreds of young prospectors flooded the town. A young woman fell in love with a handsome prospector. They had a tumultuous love affair. When he left, he promised to return. He never came back. She waited until her dying day, and apparently still keeps waiting. The tragedy of love manifests itself in the wake of the frequent absence of the loved one. The most tragic example is that of the famous historian Jane Morris. She fell desperately in love with an English admiral. The problem: they did not share the same century. He lived more than a hundred years before her. While doing research for a book on the Royal Navy, she read his letters and accounts of his exploits. The more she got to know about him, the stronger her love for him grew.

## Love beyond Passion

Of course, the feelings in the examples given above could be labeled *infatuation*. Love is not just passion, but something deeper: commitment, mutual understanding, and attraction to another person. We select someone to be the most important person in our life. Love can mean that we care deeply about a person, accept his or her faults, and put him or her at the center of our life. Love implies a deep feeling of understanding and helping another person. The person becomes a part of us.

An elderly woman was suffering from Alzheimer's disease. She lived in a nursing home. Her husband visited her daily, drove her around, tried to converse with her, and fed her. Sadly, she did not recognize him or appreciate his help, but was nasty and unkind to him. Despite this treatment, he continued to look after her lovingly. Finally, his daughter asked him how he could cope with this situation and if he ever felt frustrated. He answered calmly: "To me she is still my little girl!" He was able to endure this situation because he had kept this image of her in his heart.

This idea of eternal love is expressed in the Greek myth of Philemon and Baucis. The couple lived happily together, having truly found themselves, and after their death they continued to live close to each other as two trees.

## A Clinical View of Love

Perhaps the secrets and craziness of love can be unraveled with the help of psychiatry! A clinical approach might lead to new insights. Could it be that the drama, the tragedy, the emotional turmoil, and the bizarre behavior of lovers are symptoms of a psychological disease or a mental derangement? Naturally, to think in these terms is slightly absurd. Falling in love is an existential event, one of the most cherished experiences we encounter. Thus, to make love into a psychiatric issue might seem bit inappropriate. Taking this viewpoint, however, may help us to uncover the specific dynamics that manifest themselves in people who are in love.

Perhaps love is a sign of a *dual narcissistic syndrome*. A cynic could argue that lovers are primarily focused on themselves. They talk about each other, dream about each other, and direct their interests almost exclusively to one person only. If we regard lovers as a single entity and analyze their behavior accordingly, love can be seen as a sign of *mutual overindulgence*. Constantly, they give each other positive feedback, flatter each other, and praise themselves; this must lead inevitably to *mutual inflation*. As the couple's main interest is the significant other, they fence themselves off from harsher realities. The relationship becomes *self-delusional*. They live in a *folie à deux*. Being selected exclusively by another individual and declared to be the greatest person on earth enhances one's personal self-esteem. One can devour feelings of grandeur and uniqueness. Since lovers are allowed to be absorbed with themselves and oblivious of other people, their antisocial behavior is accepted. Lovers are permitted to shun social events, which would require them to be more accommodating of others. Coupling is considered superior to socializing. The dual narcissistic syndrome leads to *dependency*. Lovers lose their autonomy. The relationship has to be confirmed by constant phone calls, dozens or more text messages, and a heap of presents. The attention of the significant other becomes vital. When he or she withdraws his or her attention, the world falls apart. Feelings of sorrow, anger, and grief follow. The narcissist cannot live without being mirrored by the other. He or she remains stable only when someone woos and admires him or her emotionally.

The *romantic love syndrome* is a term that applies to a specific form of love.[1] The term is used to express an extreme form of one-sided and unrealistic love. A person *imagines* he or she is having an intense love affair with another person. Typically, the object of passionate adoration is someone in the vicinity, or a public figure.[2] When the romantic love syndrome strikes, the person is convinced he or she is engaged in an intense love affair with a celebrity, a colleague at work, or an acquaintance. Even if he or she has *never* met the other person, the one who is in love is certain that the intimate relationship exists. The movements, words, clothing, and actions of the adored are constantly scrutinized for proofs of the relationship. Everything the chosen one does is interpreted accordingly. One woman, a patient, was certain that the rock star Meat Loaf was her lover. She was absolutely convinced that the songs he wrote were addressed exclusively to her. The words of his songs were the proof that he was her lover. However, she did have her limits. When Meat Loaf gave a concert in her hometown, she locked herself up in her room and shoved a cupboard in front of the door, so no one could force their way in. After an imagined argument with him, she was mad and not willing to receive him into her apartment!

Can love be viewed as an *hysterical syndrome*?[3] From the perspective of a cynic, the overreaction, the sensitivity, the drama, and the demand for personal attention are all possible symptoms of a hysterical personality or reaction.[4] Perhaps one is just overly emotionalized when one falls in love. The longing to be the center of someone's attention, the yearning for a reaction, and the craving for personal intimacy might just be signs that sane judgment and the ability to control oneself have vanished.

## The Point of View of Evolutionary Psychology

From the point of view of evolutionary psychology, passionate love has yet a different meaning. *Survival of the fittest* is the key phrase of evolutionary psychology.[5] Men seek women who are healthy and fertile and can pass on their genes. Men want their women to be younger than they are and, of course, sexy. In contrast to men, women seek partners who are good providers and promise security and stability. According to Darwinian theory, men do not need to be good-looking in order to attract women—what is more important is the status in society that they have achieved. There is a small difficulty though: men and women are psychologically different! They think, act, perceive differently and do not communicate in the same way. The gender gap developed because of the way families were structured in prehistoric times: the men went out hunting and the women stayed at home and cared for the children. The diverging activities and interests of this division of labor made it more difficult for males and females to approach each other for the purposes of procreation. The danger was that they would remain locked in their separate worlds. In order to overcome the breach between males and females, biology evolved a ruse. It set women and men emotionally on fire, so that their perceptions would become blurred and their judgments weak. In the heat of overflowing passion, it is suggested, men and women forget their basic differences. The overdose of feelings enables them to get close to each other. They get confused and overlook the fact that they do not really understand each other. Passionate love turns humans into irrational beings so that they can, despite their differences, come together to propagate the species.

## The Autonomy of the Soul—Erotic Love as Soul's Message

Jungian psychology offers another perspective. Crucial in Jung's thought is respect for the *autonomy of the soul.* Jungian psychology emphasizes that psyche is a force *sui generis.* In order to understand our behavior, emotions, and problems, we have to presuppose that the psyche has its own agenda. Our actions and emotions are not determined entirely by society, genes, personality, or biology, but arise from *unconscious motives.* We are influenced, and sometimes even steered, by patterns that are embedded in our psyche. Our actions are not the result of rational decisions either, but are influenced by our personal psychodynamics, which *transcend* our consciousness and are therefore difficult to pin down. Our feelings, perceptions, and actions attune automatically to deeper, unconscious forces. What we feel and think are often an enactment of a deeper script, which is hidden in our inner self. The scope of consciousness is limited. Our unconscious operates on its own rules. We can never fully understand its dynamics. When we limit ourselves to "hard facts," we become alienated from the true nature of the psyche and become narrow-minded. We become victims of the illusion of control. We try to objectify processes that are by nature *luminous* and *ambiguous.* They continue to be beyond our perception. This is the reason Jungian psychology employs terms that are multifaceted and open to the mystery of the psyche. For psychology, the language of rational, scientific discourse is inadequate. Clear definitions are not required, but rather, terms that can act as mental movers, terms that enable us to decipher unconscious motives, to *read* instead of understand our self. Vague terms such as "image," "symbol," and "myth" help us to interpret soul without being seduced by clear-cut answers.

The notion of *teleos* is of prime importance. Our inner psychodynamics are goal-oriented. Our dreams, fantasies, and ideas are not just results of causes, but possibly the first steps towards a specific outcome. They might indicate the direction in which a process is heading. Our psyche selects topics and themes with a specific intention. Thus, everything we experience has the potential for meaning. Our lives are often an enactment of an archetypical script.

In this script, consciousness has a specific role to play. It is not independent and unbiased, but has to respect certain boundaries set by the unconscious. We cannot think up *whatever* we want; the range of our conscious thoughts is limited. Whatever violates our personal belief system or the core myths of our peer group or society, whatever contradicts personal or cultural bonding, is automatically ruled out. Our unconscious complexes act as a censor, protecting us from inner conflict. Ideas and notions that contravene our unconscious profile will *not* enter our consciousness. Anything that might disturb us or contradict our values is fenced off. Irritating thoughts must be expelled, because they might cause distress or malfunction. Our stability is in danger. We can think only what our personal psychology allows us to. Consciousness is not an entity unto itself. Insights that are against the interests of our ego are banned from entering it. Ideas that might discourage us are not wanted. The duty of consciousness is to provide us with a cogent theory that enables us to prosper and face the challenges of life. Critical thoughts and strong doubts have to be excluded. Our consciousness developed along rational lines precisely in order to exclude shadow issues, which are typically relegated to the unconscious. However, our ego-consciousness is not superior to but intertwined with our unconscious dynamics.

Analytical psychology wants to understand the intricate relation between hidden motives and our behaviors and thoughts. It is *not* satisfied with the objective and the concrete in the external world, but delves into underlying and unseen forces that reside in our inner world. One of its basic assumptions is that our conscious thoughts and insights are often skewed, influenced by unconscious desires and motives. When we start developing sound, logical psychological theories, it is time to be skeptical. Depth psychology is termed as such because it wants to see *beyond* the obvious or objective. *Seeing-through* is a key term for analytical psychology. We have to try to identify *hidden* motives, to search for the myths that pattern our lives. Jungian psychology wants to discern the connection between *outer facts* and the *inner realities of the soul*. According to analytical psychology, we should always doubt the objective "truth," because it is often merely a pale reflection of what is really going on inside. Our thoughts, our beliefs, and our perceptions may be the enactment of unconscious patterns.

## Reducing the Complexities of Life in Order to Live

The problem is that the Jungian approach does not help us to cope with the challenges and issues that confront us in our everyday lives. The conclusions of analytical psychology are of little value when we have to make ends met, pursue a career, or run a business. The vast majority of the issues we have to tackle in our private or professional lives *don't* require in-depth psychological thinking. On the contrary, if we wish to meet the expectations that come with our roles in society, we would do well to avoid in-depth reflection.[6] Heavy thinking hinders us because it leads us to de-objectify our realities. Nobody expects a banker to philosophize on the mercurial quality of money or a police officer to contemplate the importance of not breaking rules. We function better when we *avoid* speculation about our inner and the outer realities. It is prudent to stick to facts. Societies function because they define distinct roles and duties for their members. Philosophy is a nuisance. Societies are successful when they manage to *simplify* the matters they deal with. Elaborate thinking is *not* required. Most of the scientific psychological research done in academia adheres to the same principle. By concentrating on "hard facts" and accepting only "scientifically sustained" results, scientific psychology narrows the complexity of human nature down to simple and comprehensible truisms. It complies with the laws that govern our societies. If we start to mull over the dynamics of our psyche, we might not be able to go on functioning normally. We lose our effectiveness when we de-objectify our surroundings, search for hidden motives or purposes. Using categories such as "projection," "inner and outer realities," and "seeing-through" leads to confusion and irritation. Societies can function smoothly precisely because they have a narrow view of human psychology.

The vast majority of us accept this principle. We assimilate the basic social codes of the group we belong to. We learn in school, during professional training, and often even at universities to trust society's explanations. The values and attitudes of our society define our personal profile. We tune in to the expectations of our peers. Our self-image is usually a product of our upbringing and our adaptation to the expectations of our peer group.[7] We are therefore biased when we attribute qualities and talents to ourselves. They do not reflect our actual complexes, but rather, the way we have to see ourselves in order to survive. As mothers, we of course love our children, and when we work as teachers, we believe that grading children helps them in their lives. Our self-image must conform to the tacit and unwritten assumptions of our peers and society, otherwise we would be ostracized. We cannot allow ourselves a wacky, abnormal self-image, because that would perturb us. We would lose our stamina. When we are sane and healthy, we *blot out* memories and insights that remind of us our shadow. Anything that could harm or destabilize us has to be suppressed. Our self-image has to be delusional, since immoral or deviant qualities are not considered desirable. Provided that we are not clinically depressed or suicidal, we *purify* our image of ourselves. Our self-image cannot really mirror our true personality, because we all need a self-image that will empower us and help us to reduce the complexities of life. Complicated thinking and self-doubt hinder us.

But what does all this have to do with love? When we fall in love, this perfect arrangement is disturbed. Love ignores the rules and regulations that are set by our peers, our upbringing, and society. When we fall in love, our attitude towards life changes. We might even violate social norms and boundaries. Love leads us along dangerous paths. It induces us to act irrationally. We break out of the confinement of our ego-boundaries. We disregard sound advice and shun logical thinking. As described above, even the most diehard rationalist begins to believe in magic and dreams and to ignore reality when he or she falls in love. Lovers adore images and create stories for themselves. "You remember when we met?" "You recall our time on the Isle of Arran?" Our world becomes *animated* when we are in love. The distance between outer reality and our inner world collapses. We connect to our surroundings. We "personify" soul.[8] Trivial details and trifles become significant. The entrance ticket to a show attended together is kept as a precious memento on a shelf, and it arouses warm feelings every time we pass it. We are not just functioning, but the world *resonates* in us. Words and places carry meanings, and we relinquish control. Soul takes over, while social codes and objective reality lose power. We live in a world of symbols.

Love reconnects us with soul. We are confronted with psyche. We break out of the ego-confinement that our society, upbringing, and peers force us to respect. Love connects us with realms that are *not* usually represented in our society. The magic, the irrational thinking, and the sensations are an expression of the power of the psyche. The love experience cannot be comprehended adequately in relational terms and it does not originate in causes. Lovers realize that *something more, something inexplicable* is happening to them. Soul has chosen the encounter between two people to express its power and energy. The love experience connects us with our archetypical core. We get involved in the dynamics, the mystery, and the fascination of our psyche. Psychic energy emerges, an energy that is always in us but must otherwise be hidden away as a sacrifice to social roles and duties.

This may explain why even great loves often fail or end in tragedy: Romeo and Juliet, Frank Sinatra and Ava Gardner, John Lennon and Yoko Ono, or Julius Caesar and Cleopatra. Even these relationships are apparently not strong enough for the energy, fascination, and passion that emerge. As weak, mortal human beings, even the greatest among us are just not prepared to integrate these forces. How much less can the average relationship contain these energies! Rather helplessly, we start thinking in terms such as "relationship," "communication," "understanding," or "partnership." In vain, we try to emulate the great lovers of literature and history and love as passionately as they did. Perhaps their love was doomed because they tried to soar too close to the sun, to experience love beyond the limits of what is humanly possible, to love as the gods love. As humans, we all have to adhere to codes, social norms, expectations, and the games people play. We are not equipped to participate in the games of the gods. When transcendental qualities emerge, as in love, we are out of our depth. The gods allow us to peek at other realities every now and then, but they do not want us to get too accustomed to them.

---

## *NOTES*

[1] *Mental Health Digest* (Washington, D.C.: U.S. Dept. of Health, 1991), p. 7.

[2] William Jankowiak, *Romantic Passion* (New York: Columbia University Press, 1997).

[3] Edward Shorter, *From Paralysis to Fatigue* (New York: Free Press, 1992).

[4] Elaine Showalter, *Hystories: Hysterical Epidemics and Modern Media* (New York: Columbia, 1997).

[5] Robert Wright, *The Moral Animal: Why We Are the Way We Are* (New York: Vintage Books, 1994).

[6] George Ritzer, *Enchanting a Disenchanting World* (London: Pine Forge Press, 1999).

[7] David Livingstone Smith, *Why We Lie: The Evolutionary Roots of Deception and the Unconscious Mind* (New York: St. Martin Press, 2004).

[8] James Hillman, *Re-Visioning Psychology* (New York: Harper and Row, 1975), p. 32.

Urs H. Mehlin, Dr. phil., received his doctorate in Psychology and German and French literature from the University of Basel. He became General Stage Manager and Assistant Director at the Grand Theatre of Geneva in 1967. In 1969 he began working as a teacher at the Institute of Applied Psychology in Zürich. From 1972 to 2002 he taught psychology and was an instructor in Musical Theater at the Teachers' Training College of Zürich. He received his diploma at the C. G. Jung-Institut Zürich and subsequently became a training analyst there. He has given lectures and seminars on diverse topics. He is now a member of ISAPZURICH and serves there as a training analyst. Among his publications are *Psychology, Psychoanalysis and Theater* and *Analytical Aspects of Artistic Creativity*.

9

# Love and Hate, Intimacy and Estrangement: Patterns and Pathologies in Human Relations

*Urs H. Mehlin*

Some time ago I read about a study done in the United States which found that conversations between spouses lasted approximately 2½ minutes per day on average! I must say I have difficulty believing this statistic, but I do believe that the polarity between intimacy and estrangement and the frightful proximity between love and hate are basic topics not only for every man and woman, for every community and society, but also for every culture—past, present, and future.

In her novel *Clélie*, written in France in the 17th century (an epoch very much interested in studying human manners and relationships), Madeleine de Scudéry (1607-1701) drew and commented on a map showing the different ways and places in which loving relationships can grow. She identifies three rivers, along whose banks are situated *"Tendre-sur-Inclination," "Tendre-sur-Estime,"* and *"Tendre-sur-Reconnaissance"*: tenderness based on inclination, tenderness based on esteem, and tenderness based on recognition.

So, following broadly this "precious" ("précieuse" in the 17th-century literary sense) example, we will explore some paths through the landscape of human passion, climb the heights of peak-experiences and dive into the abyss of hatred, follow the twists and turns leading to the salvation or destruction of relationships, and, last but not least, go some way back into the depths of the roots (both biologically and archetypally conditioned) of conflicts that may seem to be limited to the present or to be only personally constellated.

## Longing for Home: The Ruling of the Great Mother

How many sighs have been uttered, how many bitter tears shed, how many letters sent, bearing high hopes and most intense wishes, how many poems and immortal works of art created out of the feeling of longing—an archetype that seems to me to be composed of the poles of hope and despair, and which, in consequence of its inherent tension, manifests itself in so many and varied archetypal images. The poem, *The Pilgrim*, by Joseph von Eichendorff, ends with the following four lines:

| | |
|---|---|
| *Und ein geheimes Grausen* | And a secret horror |
| *Beschleichet unsern Sinn:* | Creeps onto our mind. |
| *Wir sehnen uns nach Hause* | We long for home |
| *Und wissen nicht, wohin?* | And we don't know where. |
| | (My translation) |

I am convinced that this form of expression gives voice to that basic longing more eloquently than psychological amplifications can, since it preserves in a wonderful way the openness of a real symbol. But since we are here to do justice to our science, psychology, which might well be considered a servant of art and poetry, we cannot help but see behind the longing for the loved one the longing for the (great) mother.

Basically, a loving relationship consists in the polarity of caring and passion, of longing and desire. Exposing oneself to the dynamics of love entails holding the tension that results from these polarities. The pole of longing, if it becomes predominant, leads to nostalgia and regression, and this eventually ends in depression or self-destruction, as death and self-dissolution seem to hold out the promise of release and redemption. This romantic approach to love is found for instance in Goethe's *Werther*, which fails to acknowledge the seductive power of the devouring, destructive aspect of the Great Mother. One-sidedly identifying with passion and desire allows for progressive dynamics and thus, seemingly, for development; however, it also involves the risk of falling into a repetitive pattern, and this ends up inflicting depression and destruction. Taken one-sidedly instead of as mutually dependent, both poles lead to an absence of lively, real, mutual participation and tend to generate an empty routine—some sort of more-or-less ill-fitting arrangement, in which depression, torment, and agony substitute for the happiness and suffering of a committed relationship.

Now if we concretize these reflections, we might very well assume that both men and women look for a mother as well as for a lover in a relationship. One of Freud's more interesting findings was that in marriage men inherit the feelings the wife had towards her mother to a greater extent than the feelings she had towards her father. For the sake of simplicity, I will, for the moment, develop this theme and the paradox it entails from the male perspective. The power of the so-called positive mother-complex consists in its being detached from the real mother as a person and being transferred in its essence to a possible partner. As an old psychoanalyst put it, in a formula that impressed me in my youth, "A wife can be like mother, but she cannot be Mother." Nevertheless, even if this condition is fulfilled, the shadow aspects of the basically "positive" complex should not be overlooked. The unconditional acceptance, caring, and nurturing—all these functions denoting the very essence of mothering—inevitably create dependency. And this dependency prevents progress and diminishes autonomy. Moreover, the incest taboo is inevitably connected with the transference of mother-related feelings. And thus the boy of course has to, and even desires to, grow up eventually. The structurally felt feelings of impotence and castration tend to be compensated for with the only-too-well-known extramarital affair or with quarrels and discussions about trivialities, which become more persistent and damaging to the extent that their function has not been understood. The "attraction" of an "erotic" extra-conjugal relation for a married man is, paradoxically, its always imminent termination and, even more so, the illusion that the boy finally has become an "independent" and fully-grown adult. But beware! Even a common cold can make him return home and regress to the joys of a warm bed, sweet tea, and a hopefully ever-present, understanding, forgiving, nursing mother-figure.

The real danger of long-lasting extramarital affairs lies in their subjective simulation of autonomy, and in the objective damage done by this simulated autonomy to both relationships, for both partners are reduced to a very limited role and ultimately to an illusion of hope. A particularly common—and particularly devastating—pattern is the male attitude of neither making a commitment nor letting go and thus constantly sending out mixed messages and thus preventing clarity of feeling and attitude in the partner.

To switch now to the female perspective, it is precisely the corresponding lack of autonomy of the women involved that allows the perverse game to go on, in a mostly unconscious collusion—if not forever, then at least for longer than it should. Puer and puella usually do not unite in a happy and stable relationship.

If a positive tie to the mother does not guarantee a good marriage, we cannot draw the opposite conclusion for detachment from the mother and an identification with autonomy. The latter option very often also lacks a solid base on which growth, whether individually or in a relationship, is possible.

## Forcing Relations: The Power of the Great Father

According to La Rochefoucauld (1613-1680),

> *La plupart des femmes se rendent plutôt par faiblesse que par passion. De là vient que, pour l'ordinaire, les hommes entreprenants réussissent mieux que les autres, quoiqu'ils ne soient pas plus aimables.* (From *Maxime supprimées.*)
>
> (Most women yield because of weakness rather than passion. It follows that sexually aggressive men are more successful than others, even if they are not more likable.)

This dictum from 17th-century France spells out clearly the male role in sexual activity, namely, aggression—a notion that has its cognate in the term "conquest," used in most European languages to describe the success of a "sexual entrepreneur." There is a tiny element of ambivalently experienced "force"—and often a considerable element of power—present in most intense relationships. To put a taboo on it, and along with that, to banish fundamental archaic "male" drives and impulses, as is clearly the trend today, does not necessarily eliminate all the inherent problems and risks. We are faced here with a delicate and difficult dilemma: how to distinguish clearly between an element that seems always to have been part of the "game" on the one hand, and instances of its getting out of control and thus becoming devastating on the other. Could we, in Jungian terms, speak of an "integrated father-power" in one case and an "acted-out father-pretension" in the other?

Psychologically speaking, excessive male aggression shows not only a pathological lack of impulse control, but also a deep fissure and disturbance within the relationship. Legal measures certainly (and fortunately also successfully) fight the symptom, but often without inquiring into its root causes. For violence, wrath, and rape signal the breaking through of not only personal repressed anger and uncontrolled impulses, but the archetypal shadow of the great father. It is man in his weakness who is exposed to this eminently threatening danger; and it is generally unacknowledged fear that forces men into this weakness. In modern psychopathological terminology, we would of course speak of narcissistic wounding and narcissistic rage: it is Othello becoming the prey of his complex who stands as an archetypal image behind the analysand who loses himself in the fantasy of suffocating his unfaithful wife with a pillow. According to an old psychological maxim, if a woman's most fundamental fear is the fear of abandonment, that of a man is the fear of becoming impotent. In cases such as Othello's we discover not merely an addition, but a multiplication of both fears. That the phenomenon is not limited to men is well illustrated in the experience of Medea and other fearful and terrible wives and mothers who have been left deprived of everything. The difficulty in dealing with the impulse to power and violence (a difficulty that is at the same time the antidote to this impulse) is developing the ability and willingness to accept a "no," recognizing that precisely in that same "no" lies also an element of power!

"Sound and fury," however, do not necessarily signify the end of a relationship; they can also lead to a more authentic and lively exchange than the constant repression of anger in the interests of maintaining a superficial, often false, harmony. Indeed, fighting that is engaged in mutually as a form of intense relating can in some cases function as an erotic stimulus, and can, occasionally, even set in motion the transformation that is needed. This is the real meaning of the word "entertainment." Fighting in this sense has to be clearly distinguished from painful, chronic quarreling and muttering over nothing and everything, which are entirely devoid of the transforming possibilities just mentioned, but follow the same repetitive pattern, after which each partner retires disappointed to his "I am right and I am not understood" position. Observed from the outside, it may seem rather strange that a situation in which both partners are obviously discontented is nevertheless neither resolved nor abandoned. However, the relationship often proves to be astonishingly stable right through into old age. A "senex" couple who have lost their connection to joy and caring might be seen as the passing shadow of the happily transformed and thus everlasting Philemon and Baucis.

Another form of power operating within the dynamics of couples—seemingly more subtle, but nevertheless equally ambiguous—is money, which, according to Bert Brecht, makes people sensual. The common use of the possessive adjective "my" with husband/wife/boyfriend/girlfriend implies not only attribution, but also ownership. Seen from this perspective, all reactions of jealousy can be understood more easily. But the attempt to "buy" love and acceptance by offering expensive gifts can also be in the interests of gaining power. The institution of "Morgengabe" (the gift given to a bride by her husband after the wedding night) and, on a different level, the institution of prostitution show that connection quite clearly. With reference to the "Carte de Tendre," another 17th-century author wrote a poem in which he made the point that "Tendre sur Bijou" (jewelry) is the safest way to access the loved one. Thus we occasionally find desperate attempts to "save" a relationship by offering expensive gifts or adopting an extremely luxurious lifestyle. Both reveal themselves in the long run to be substitutes for the energy that should be flowing directly into the relationship rather than into the acquisition of material goods. It is as if a commonly fed vampire would drain the "blood," the life-force, out of the couple. Of course, there is nothing to be said against mutual spoiling, and according to a German proverb, little gifts maintain friendship. Perhaps, the shadow of giving is the hope of getting in return. However, the main impetus for giving gifts should, clearly, be the desire to bring happiness rather than the hope of a reward.

## Idealization and Beauty: Seduction, Deception, and Disappointment

Historically, probably the most convincing example of idealization can be found in the medieval tradition of the Troubadours in France and the Minnesänger in Germany. Typical of this tradition is the differentiation between "high" and "low" love, "*Hoher und Niederer Minne*." In high love, the beauty, the cultivation, the outstanding moral virtues, and generally the unparalleled qualities of the admired woman are praised. This idealization, of course, can be maintained only so long as the actual woman behind the idealized image never becomes "real," never materializes. In our terms, we would speak of the purest possible projection of the anima on a seemingly near, but in reality unobtainable, woman. The result of this awkward situation is beautiful poetry on the one hand, and a rather "ordinary" and common love and everyday life with other women on the other. Paradoxically, much larger problems arise when modern men try to overcome this split as they experience the painful incongruity between image/anima and real object. It seems to me that generally speaking women have less difficulty accepting a partner who falls short of their "animus." It is sometimes a ridiculously tiny detail that deters men from idealizing their female partner. "Beauty," on the other hand, while undoubtedly an important feature of attraction, not only implies inconstancy (a quality attributed to both Venus and Helen of Troy), but is also subject to change and decline. As such, beauty, so long as it is not experienced and developed along the lines of the Greek duality of *"kalos k'agathos"* (beautiful and morally good), becomes a pure aspect of the persona. This identification with the persona, collectively cherished today in the form of cosmetics, fashion models, and plastic surgery, fosters precisely this kind of estrangement from the self and from partnership, a state of affairs that is the polar opposite of intimacy.

Women, however, are generally prone to a different kind of idealization: against all evidence, they cling desperately to the hope that their partner will eventually give up his undesirable attitudes, his unrelatedness, his lack of understanding, his unfaithfulness, or his drinking. Thus, they allow themselves to become the unintended victims of their own idealization. By being faithful to their animus, they risk the failure of a real partnership, being either unwilling or unable to acknowledge the ever-present and ever-growing estrangement, until it finally can no longer be denied.

It is an important task for both men and women not only to try to accept those respects in which their partner falls short of their idealized image, but also to maintain the idealization. This not only can, but must, be done by building up a shared lifestyle that is not reduced to routine and trivialities. Sharing and working towards common interests and ideals helps keep a relationship alive as much as jointly solving common problems and fulfilling common tasks. This kind of idealization is far removed from poetry, which, in its freedom, lacks realism. It is also far removed from the attitude of relaxing into passive pleasures and blaming the partner for not measuring up to whatever one expects of him or her. It means work, patience, commitment, and, not least, a healthy dose of tolerance for frustration.

## Nasty-Little-Boy Eros: The Big Demon

> In the cosmogony of Hesiod, Eros was born out of Chaos and was the most beautiful of all the immortals, the deity who inspired his own sweet passion in all human beings. Physical desire, as personified in the figure of Eros, was thus seen as a primordial element present before the world itself came into being—indeed, as an element which was partly responsible for the world, since its power of attrac-

> tion gave life to living creatures. There were many other traditions which describe Eros as the son of Uranus and Ghia, or of Chronos and Rhea, and even of Iris and Zephyrus. However, the most popular version of all is that in which Eros was the son of Aphrodite, the goddess most closely associated with love, and fierce Ares, god of war.[1]

"Some Cupid kills with arrows, some with traps," wrote Shakespeare in *Much Ado about Nothing*. His use of the verb "kill" in this seemingly light-hearted context shows the truly demonic effect of the childish delight that the little son of Venus derives from his weapon. I don't remember who it was that once said that whoever believes in free will has never suffered from toothache or been in love. This demonic aspect is also an essential part of the beauty mentioned above, as expressed by Rilke: "Das Schöne ist nur des Schecklichen Anfang. … Ein jeder Engel ist schrecklich." (The Beautiful is only the beginning of the Terrible. … Each Angel is terrible. [My translation.])

The "demonic" effect of being struck by Amor's arrow is in practice first felt as a loss of independence and is experienced negatively as a possible one-sided dependence. Mutuality in a relationship can never be forced, but can only be given and received as a gift—moreover, as a gift that is by no means harmless. "Both Love and Art are, according to their essence, criminal, or they are not," says Paul Valéry. The Swiss author Meienberg, in a similar vein, maintained that "each and every love is a scandal"—a scandal in the sense, I think, that it throws or pulls us out of the generally accepted boundaries of what we and those who surround us are accustomed to. Goethe, at over 80 years of age, fell passionately in love with the teenager Ulrike von Lewetzow. He became depressed when he was refused permission to marry her. This is a clear example of the "scandalous" nature of love, but the episode resulted in one of the deepest and most beautiful poem sequences ever written, the so-called "Marienbader Elegie." The fear of stepping outside generally accepted boundaries, the fear of becoming ridiculous—or, expressed positively, the inclination to follow collective rules and maintain one's public persona—protects one to a certain extent from Amor's intrusions. And society tends to get back eventually to "business as usual" whenever the nasty boy finds an occasion to shoot one of his arrows. Therefore, as a result of this collective influence, but also because passion is so time- and energy-consuming, we feel the urge to dominate the wildness and turmoil by channeling them into institutionalized and therefore seemingly safe vessels, where insurance and assurance, heritage included, are guaranteed by state and law. I wonder if the attempt to institutionalize homosexual relationships, thereby making the scandal acceptable but also limiting freedom, reflects basically the same tendency: the tendency to escape from the fatal reach of mighty Aphrodite and her unruly son to the safety, continuity, and household routine guaranteed by Hera. Jung wrote:

> In certain differentiated persons a purely biological interpretation and evaluation of sexuality can also have this effect [of devaluation]. Any such conception overlooks the spiritual and "mystical" implications of the sexual instinct. These have existed from time immemorial as psychic facts, but are devalued and repressed on rationalistic and philosophical grounds.[2]

Setting limits to the depth of the wounds created by passion—the hell of despair as well as the heaven of ecstasy, bliss, and paradise—is achieved not only by regression into institutionalism, but also by turning back to routine. This routine can be achieved by consistently focusing one's attention on side activities such as work, career, money-making, sports, children, relatives, or, seen from the outside, very peculiar but complex-loaded trivialities. As necessary as all these activities may be or indeed are, they should also be seen as an unconscious attempt to escape the urgency of the demand to keep the couple alive. Another (typically male) way of evading that demanding task is to adopt an attitude of detachment. Thus, after making love, many men experience not just the usual "sadness" ("*omne animal post coitum triste*"), but real boredom instead of the hoped-for peak experience. Devaluation serves the purpose of avoiding commitment, and of avoiding suffering as well. But suffering (in both senses of the term) the tension that passion puts us in is the one condition for achieving and maintaining intimacy. Watzlawick's dictum that people who are not able to live without each other also cannot live with each other can easily be misunderstood in the sense that indifference might be seen as a condition for coupling. Now, indifference is a means of living *beside*, not *with*, each other, whereas suffering, even when the two are together, must be accepted as a condition for achieving intimacy. And here the autonomy, the masculine as well as the feminine autonomy lost in the first moment of being wounded by the arrow, has to be re-established, precisely in the service of the common healing of that same wound.

## Treason and Trickery: The Attractive Denying of Faithfulness

We would probably all agree that fidelity is an important condition for building and maintaining trust and intimacy in a relationship. And yet when one of Jung's new patients, apparently wanting to impress him, quoted *Faust*: "Two souls live in my breast," Jung replied: "That's the least one might say of oneself"! So, things would be comparatively simple and controllable if we followed only one goal, if we were completely consistent and reliable—in short, if we could and would disregard the complexities of life and soul. However, disregarding these complexities might not only endanger us on the difficult path towards individuation, but also make us victims of precisely that shadow that we desperately wanted to avoid in the first place. And that shadow has manifested itself through time and in all cultures in a number of archetypal images, of which we will briefly examine Carmen and Don Juan as the female and male representatives respectively.

Ladies first: Carmen, like her famous screen sister Lola as the Blue Angel, warns men to beware of her for she represents the young witch's fatal activity of enslaving and finally emasculating her partners, reserving for herself the right to stay free, independent, and completely unpredictable.

And Don Juan, in his macho way, without any warning, ruthlessly does the same. Let me first present him along with his "shadow" in terms of their respective characteristics:

| DON JUAN | MONK |
|---|---|
| Extraverted | Introverted |
| Libertarian/greedy | Restrictive/abstemious |
| Individual | Collective |
| Agnostic | Religious |
| Restless | Calm |
| Selfish | Altruistic |
| Denying existential conditions | Escaping from life |
| Insatiable | Sacrificing |
| Dynamic of Addiction | Dynamic of Regret |

Interestingly enough, both representatives of what we can consider an archetypal image are unable to enter into a real human relationship in its fullness and with all its complexities. When we step away from this abstract and idealistic perspective and try to come closer to more down-to-earth reality as it can be observed in everyday life, we can establish the following "typology":

| **SEDUCER** | **CONQUEROR** | **HENPECKED HUSBAND** |
|---|---|---|
| Active-passive balance | Overactive | Passive |
| Mother-bound | Father complex | Stagnating |
| "Narcissistic" | "Macho-type" | Stuck/Blocked |
| Seeks play & pleasure | Seeks success | Seeks happiness |
| M.: "Casanova" | M.: "Don Juan" | M.: "Pasha" |
| F.: "Hetaira"/"Helena" | F.: "Vamp"/"Carmen" | F.: "Little Mother"/"Hestia" |
| Attitude: Amoral | Anti-moral | Moralistic/Conventional |

Each of these "types" can enter into at least temporary relationships, but a fulfilling and lasting relationship requires a combination of characteristics of the three types, a combination in which every element finds its place and has its function. And here, fortunately, a literally unlimited number of combinations and individual variations are conceivable. The most important consideration is that both partners should suit each other on both the conscious and, probably even more so, unconscious levels. There are, in my experience, quite a few real (as well as theoretically conceivable) relationships that are long-lasting, stable, and even intense, based on what would commonly be called "symbiosis," "collusion," or even "co-dependence." Thus, not only the Seducer, but also the Seduced, not only the Conqueror, but also his or her victim, and not only Pasha and Little Mother, but also their mostly discontented partners would be worthy of closer examination. We must not, however, fall into the trap of imposing psychological censorship on everything that does not fit our own image of the ideal couple and forcing this image on our analysands, but rather, we must undertake the difficult task of finding out what makes a good couple.

## What Makes a Good Couple, or How to Live Happily Ever After

In order to make complex matters a bit simpler, let me suggest an A-B-C of intimacy in relationships, where:

A stands for Amor's Arrow,
B for Blush, Bliss, and Bitterness, and
C for Contract and Commitment.

One of my analysands, a young woman of 30, described the following experience she had as a young girl: from the time she was in Grade 1 to the time she was in Grade 4 she felt an intense and ever-present unrest and animation in the presence of her classmate Max, and even when she was away from him. In adulthood, she is still seeking that same feeling, and she keeps asking herself whether a relationship that does not provide such a feeling is the right one for her, even when so many other elements seem to fit. *"Il y a des jours, où Cupidon s'en fout,"* sings Georges Brassens—and nobody and nothing can force Cupid/Amor/Eros to take aim if he isn't so inclined. Perhaps we should not long for the wound caused by Cupid's arrow, with all the fire of suffering but also of passion that it brings, but if the arrow strikes, it should be welcomed and certainly not be covered up with the dullness of daily routine. Married couples run the risk of becoming saturated, of ignoring or shunning that disturbing little boy—and then wondering where the once-fiery passion has gone to.

But it is precisely that childhood feeling described by my analysand—containing exactly that treasure of bliss that brings on an inner or outer blush at not feeling or behaving like a real adult, always mixed with an element of bittersweet longing—that keeps us and our relationships alive. It is not limited to our dyadic relationships, but enriches our whole life. My professor of French literature taught us a phrase I will never forget: "Whatever you do in life, whether it be love or literature, do it with passion!" Happiness certainly is a wonderful effect of being "in love"; however, happiness cannot be sought as a constant state. At best, it is a series of ever-returning moments encountered between the "dangerous sea of passion" and the "lake of indifference."

Becoming dependent is the reward as well as the prerequisite for entering into a relationship. This entails, on both sides, the bitterness of sacrifice. Wanting to have freedom, to get everything, always, and at once, is not childlike, but infantile. Staying faithful in times of crisis and sickness is a condition for a passionate "being together," even, or especially, if suffering is involved. On the other hand, trying against all the evidence to maintain a relationship that one party has quit does not promise healing and wholeness, but torment and delusion.

The value of a relationship is, in my opinion, determined to a large extent by what it brings out, by what it constellates in us and our partner—in Jungian terms, by the extent to which it fosters individuation. Could we go so far as to posit behind the individual "Self" a "Relational Self," prefigured in the very first and most intense life-permitting mother-child relationship? And later, the cultivation of this "Relational Self" requires constant work to stay faithful to the situation we have chosen, because destiny has chosen it for us. This means above all a commitment to counterbalancing the change and turmoil of passion with a mutually accepted contract. When interviewed on French Radio, an older woman looking back on her successful marriage said: *"Il faut être poli l'un avec l'autre et il faut avoir du respect l'un pour l'autre."* ("It takes mutual courtesy and mutual respect.") The shadow of each loving attitude is precisely that lack of courtesy and respect for the other.

In my own formula, falling in love is primarily wanting to have, being in love is wanting to give in order to get—and loving is wanting to share. Schematically, love and relatedness along with their respective shadow can be represented as follows:

| **LOVE / RELATEDNESS** | **(SHADOW)** |
|---|---|
| Renouncing | Dominating |
| Forgiving | Bearing grudges |
| Wanting to give | Wanting to have |
| Fascination | Despair |
| Relatedness | Egotism |
| Saving/Helping | Destroying |
| Patience | Greed |
| "Young Girl" | "Young Witch" |
| "Hero" | "Don Juan" |
| "Positive" Animus/a | "Negative" Animus/a |

Well, as in everything, knowing is much easier than doing. Intimacy in relationships is not a permanent gluing together of the two partners, but rather a constant circling and revolving around each other, around the secret that I have tried to name the "Relational Self," maintaining the presence, even in temporary distance, and staying faithful, even or especially in a crisis. There are, certainly, painful periods of estrangement in every relationship—and there are also, hopefully, in all relationships intense and fulfilling moments of shared intimacy.

## *NOTES*

[1] Maria Mavromataki, *Greek Mythology and Religion* (Athens: Editions Haitalis, 1997), p. 123.

[2] C. G. Jung, "The Structure and Dynamics of the Self," in *Aion: Researches into the Phenomenology of the Self, The Collected Works of C. G. Jung*, trans. R. F. C. Hull, vol. 9ii, (Princeton, NJ: Princeton University Press, 1978 [1959/1969]), § 357.

Deborah Egger-Biniores, MSW, is a training analyst at ISAPZURICH. She maintains a private practice in Stäfa. She is president of the Association of Graduate Analytical Psychologists (AGAP), and was a member of the Executive Committee of the International Association of Analytical Psychology (IAAP). Her professional areas of interest include adult development, transferential fields, spiritual growth; she is currently writing on the role of the couple in adult development.

# 10

# What's Wrong with Anima and Animus? Exploring the Uncertainties of Inner and Outer Relationships

*Deborah Egger-Biniores*

When I first saw the title of this year's Odyssey, "Intimacy: Venturing the Uncertainties of the Heart," I immediately thought of a favorite greeting card of mine which reads: *"Der Verstand kann uns sagen, was wir unterlassen sollen. Aber das Herz kann uns sagen, was wir tun müssen"* (Joseph Joubert). Translated: "The intellect/mind can tell us what we should refrain from doing. But the heart can tell us what we must do."

This sounds lovely, until we realize what it means. These two ways of knowing come from the same psyche but from different spaces and sometimes from different intentions, and they often have to be honored in tandem. The statement always gives me a sense of what it is like to live with one foot in the inner world and the other in the outer world.

For some ten years I have been aware of an active inner dynamic movement within me that has resulted in a conscious decision along the way to open myself, as totally as I am able, to following and questioning the intentions of my soul. This undeniable process, set off by my inner response to the death of my mother and an initiation dream that followed her death, has been extremely challenging. This has led me, among other things, to a renewed confrontation with, and interest in, the manifestations of anima and animus. My struggle with "anima" and "animus" comes from having had a life of constant growth and change, but not necessarily a happy one, although it is not without glimpses of joy and contentment. This kind of inner journey, of course, has a profound bearing on my outer world, and this in its turn is reflected again in my inner world. It is this back and forth, this sometimes exhilarating, sometimes devastating dance of life and all its inherent chaos and confusion that I want to talk about today.

"Suffering is the fastest horse that can carry us to perfection"—so said Meister Eckhart. To accept and at the same time question our suffering—and the life of soul and anima/animus bring a lot of it—is to experience the birth pangs of a new inner being. This is tantamount to understanding that life and growth are *emergent* and not merely programmed into our genes. It is also tantamount to walking the postmodern fine line between meaning and meaninglessness.

Today I am going to muse around the suffering and joy that I have experienced in my own life, and also that I have witnessed in my practice, as the human soul struggles to establish a relationship to what we so often refer to so carelessly and glibly as "anima" and "animus." While we share the experience and feeling level of our topic, we must also consider, on the theoretical and intellectual level, what is wrong with anima and animus, in our effort to examine these concepts for their relevance to the present.

The longer I work in the field of analytical psychology, the more problematic I find the language we employ in our attempt to speak about the basically ineffable. Matters of soul and psyche are ineffable not because they are taboo. Rather, it is because speaking of processes and dynamics that occur primarily in the unconscious and are by nature subjective seems to require a use of language that is vague and prone to projection and therefore subject to misunderstanding. On the other hand, the ego also has a tendency to want to be definite and decisive in language, and this is exactly what can kill any nuanced relationship with the inner world and its manifold manifestations.

Speaking of the anima, Jung said: "The concept of the anima [and, it goes without saying, the animus] is a purely empirical concept, whose sole purpose is to give a name to a group of related or analogous psychic phenomena."[1] If Jung had been living in this century rather than in the last, he would almost certainly have worded that statement differently. He would probably not have used the phrase "purely empirical concept" to characterize the anima/animus, given that "empirical" means "based on observation and experiment rather than speculation." Empirical evidence gathered over the past two decades has shown that

Jung's "concept of anima" is somewhat flawed and needs to be revisited in the light of contemporary experience. Today we see more clearly the challenge and the importance of listening to our own experience and not being in a hurry to codify experience. As I hope to demonstrate today, our tendency to systematize experience and observation, thus encasing and reducing their power and potential, is a luxury we can no longer afford in a postmodern world.

Jung's way of observing and defining anima and animus has, in my opinion, become outdated over the past fifty years, not because it was incorrect back then, but because then is not now, and we are not Jung, and the collective we live in today is not the collective Jung lived in back then. I'd like to see if we can move beyond Jung's binary understanding of anima and animus to a more fluid understanding of the *life of soul embodied*. The ways in which Jung defines and speaks about anima and animus are varied, contradictory, and confusing. They also display strong personal, cultural, and *zeitgeist* biases, especially in attributing inherent psychological characteristics to biological gender. This is a point at which we encounter major difficulties and uncertainties.

Boston analyst Susan McKenzie puts the problem this way:

> Jung's anima/animus (A/A) thinking leads us into the trap of linear orderliness, fixed identities, androgynous symmetries, and archetypes that are differentially inherited, based on sexual anatomy.[2]
>
> In the last few decades there has been a rapid growth in the scientific understanding of conscious and unconscious processes inspiring a new Jungian exploration of archetype and complex.[3]

We will look a little more closely at this in a few minutes. Several other theorists, including James Hillman and Verena Kast, have also developed this more open version of Jung's original idea. McKenzie herself notes that Jung's "gender theory does … allow for both genders to reside in an individual but posits a slow and sex-appropriate emergence of the contra-sexual from the unconscious."[4] However, many authors, both male and female, have taken issue with the concept of the contrasexual in relation to anima and animus, and although it may feel like blasphemy to some of you, we must delve into this difficult issue here.

We live in an era in which reality is seen as emergent, not fixed, and Jung's anima/animus scheme is, as McKenzie says, a "terrible fit" for our times. It does not embrace wholeheartedly the experience of homosexuals, bisexuals, and the transgendered, who occupy both the fringe and forefront of our society's emerging acknowledgement of sexual ambiguity in men and women. This state of affairs throws Jung's animus/anima dichotomy into disarray.

It has been suggested by McKenzie (and some other postmodern Jungian thinkers) that we focus on the Jung that is symbolic and mythical and transcendent, so we can begin to envision a theory that describes "identity *under construction* and the individual in the act of *perpetual becoming*"[5] (italics added). A revised Jungian gender theory would transcend some of the limitations of Jung's anima/animus gender thinking, allowing us to contribute to contemporary gender theory in the spirit of the Jung of the symbolic and the subtle body. *This is the Jung who invites us to the medial place of the soul, bridging the realm of the physical body and the realm of the spirit.* This is what anima and animus do for us, but we have to move beyond the binary opposition of male/masculinity and female/femininity when we explore the world of gender and sexuality openly.

Let's look at the difference between sex and gender to begin with. Sex is the difference of embodiment—the structural and functional properties of the human body. "Gender is the identity club," as Polly Young-Eisendrath termed it—"the social category … we are assigned at birth … based on the sex of the body." She continues: "Whereas sex is inflexible, gender identities vary from culture to culture"[6]— and even over the course of a lifetime, an individual's understanding of what his or her gender requires of him or her may change in subtle ways. So gender is flexible in today's world, certainly more flexible than it was a hundred years ago, and, moreover, we (both as individuals and as a collective) are more *conscious* of this flexibility:

> The idea that the cultural gender artefact co-evolves with the gender experiences of individuals in the culture is readily illustrated by the same-sex marriage debate in America. As homosexuality and transgender become more visible in that culture—in TV shows, movies, music, and political debate—it seems that the prevailing gender belief that only one man and one woman can define a marriage is changing.[7]

The rapidity with which this kind of co-evolution is taking place (and before our very eyes!) confronts us as depth psychologists with the imperative to interface with other disciplines like never before. I want to touch briefly upon two of these disciplines (neuroscience's emergence paradigm and philosophy's postmodern thought), in order to prepare for a more in-depth exploration of our personal and individual connection to anima and animus later in this lecture and this afternoon in the seminar.

## Emergence Paradigm: Neuroscience and Analytical Psychology Interface

Daniel Siegel, Allan Schore, and a host of other researchers at the Lifespan Learning Institute in California, are bringing together the latest developments in neuroscience, attachment theory, and psychoanalysis to explore the emergence paradigm in human relationship. Consider this from Daniel Siegel's book, *The Developing Mind*:

> There is an entity called the "mind" that is as real as the heart or the lungs or the brain, though it cannot be seen with or without a microscope. The foundation of the mind parallels a dictionary [*Webster's*] definition of the psyche: "1. the human soul; 2. the intellect; 3. psychiatry—the mind considered as a subjectively perceived, functional entity, based ultimately upon physical processes but with *complex processes of its own*: it governs the total organism and its interaction with the environment. (Italics added.)
>
> The mind emerges from the activity of the brain, whose structure and function are directly shaped by interpersonal experiences .... In other words, human connections shape the neural connections from which the mind emerges.[8]

And this happens all throughout life. This understanding of emergence within the human psyche not only substantiates our work in the consulting room via the transference but also challenges us to re-think our theories of archetypes and complexes. It should therefore come as little surprise that many Jungians and researchers from other areas are working to reformulate and gain a better understanding of the current theories of gender, archetype, and emergent mind processes. (See for instance Hogenson, Hauke, McKenzie, Samuels, Wilkinson, Schore, etc.) I, too, believe anima/animus must be reconsidered in the light of this notion of emergent process if we wish to continue the work of depth psychology via personal individuation within the collective.

The idea of the archetypes as "emergent properties of the dynamic developmental system of brain, environment, and narrative" has been put forth by George Hogenson, for example.[9] His dynamic systems model includes "the physiological characteristics of the infant, the intentional attributes of the caregiver and the cultural or symbolic resources that constitute the environment."[10]

Hogenson understands myths and symbols to be cultural artifacts and "part of the system that bootstraps the infant, and subsequently the developing individual, into the world of intentional objects, meaningful action, and relationships."[11] Or as McKenzie has put it, "Artefacts are the creative products of a culture, created by collective minds and handed to each new generation through cultural memory. Artefacts are an *external* inheritance, our cultural inheritance"[12] (italics added). These in-the-moment, here-and-now descriptions and understanding of the elements of archetypal manifestation, enliven our psychology and help make it relevant for the world in which we live. They also challenge us immensely.

Susan McKenzie mentions several writers who have, as she puts it, "explored the idea that same-sex love might be a viable path to individuation, posing a challenge to Jung's heterosexist anima/animus theory."[13] (See her references to Hopke, Carrington, and Wirth,[14] and Kulkarni.[15]) But with the advent of the concept of mind as an emergent process and the new understanding of early, preverbal attachment, McKenzie and others are postulating a new theoretical understanding of gender, which would open up and de-literalize Jung's original anima/animus theory, making it applicable to and relevant for today's postmodern culture.

McKenzie employs a gender theory that "deconstructs the assumed natural link between core gender identity (biological sex) and subsequent gendered feelings."[16] She also sees gendered identity positions "... as somewhat temporary ego platforms from which to explore and expand one's gender capacity."[17] She states:

> My post-Jungian theorizing leads to a final phase of rediscovery and conscious integration of the innate potential for masculinity and femininity within every individual, regardless of biological sexual beginnings or initial gendered positions. ... I also draw on the sciences that have a lot to say about gender determinants that are outside of the psychosocial/sexual realms: in particular brain development and prenatal hormonal influences that may turn out to be the most powerful determinants of gendered feeling.[18]

How can her attempts to develop and articulate a postmodern Jungian gender theory based on her experience with transgendered, homosexual, and bisexual individuals bring value to our reflections on anima and animus today?

The first thing McKenzie's work does is bring real life, real flesh and blood, to our thinking. Consider this example from her article:

> Many of my lesbian analysands preferred boy play, dress, and physicality in childhood. This preference did not disappear after the tomboy years. It frequently went underground in early adolescence as a forbidden gender desire and was often followed by same-sex sexual attraction. In my analytic work with these women, on occasion I stumbled in my gender assumptions. Beth, a midlife lesbian whose gender presentation was conventionally female, was recounting her early gender experiences to me. As she was describing her lusty tomboy experiences of being the best athlete among her many male cousins and the heroic defender of her little brother on the school playground, I referred to the little girl of her interior world. Beth stopped me and said, "Oh no, it's a little boy and his name is Jim." Jim turned out to be an important character in her current struggle to defend herself against the homophobic bullies she perceived in her adult world.[19]

Secondly, it seems to me that the decoupling of gendered feelings from biological sex opens up new life for all of us, regardless of our sexual orientation. Instead of defining and integrating "my animus" or "my anima," I can look for, actually *live for*, the syzygy, the "coupled" energy flow between consciousness and unconscious, between being and becoming, between multiplicity and unity, between chance and necessity, between individual and collective, between chaos and stability, between I and not-I, that comes my way, that crashes in upon me, as I live my individual life in the collective around me.

I choose the term *syzygy*, as I learned it in my student days from Verena Kast, because it requires the energy to flow both ways in the coupling for there to be animation. Animation is a main attribute in dealing with anima and animus, and I suspect that in both men and women animation is the product of anima and animus operating in tandem. This understanding puts us on common ground with a number of other disciplines, which employ the term *syzygy* in similar ways:

> In astronomy, a syzygy is the alignment of three or more celestial bodies in the same gravitational system along a straight line. ... In Gnosticism, a syzygy is a divine active-

> passive, male-female pair of aeons, complementary to one another rather than oppositional; in their totality they ... characterize aspects of the unknowable Gnostic God. ... In mathematics, a syzygy is a relation between the generators of a module .... In medicine, the term is used to signify the fusion of some or all of the organs.[20]

And, of course, in psychology, Jung used the term *syzygy* "to denote an archetypal pairing of contrasexual opposites ...: the conjunction of two organisms without the loss of identity."[21] Verena Kast has explored the idea of the syzygy, the anima and animus as a couple. She has also pointed out that Jung never maintained that archetypes are gender-specific.[22] It follows that anima/animus must exist in individuals of both sexes. Kast amplifies this idea, alluding to the neurobiological discoveries of such renowned neuroscientists as Antonio Damasio:

> But we are nonetheless aware that both sexes need the talent both for relationship and for discrimination. In other words, it makes no sense to assume that autonomy comes naturally to one sex any more than it does to assume that relationship comes more naturally to the other. In addition, we must surely ask whether it makes any sense to speak of consciousness as being 'male' or 'female'. I doubt this, and support the above argument—which, interestingly, is corroborated by the findings of modern neurobiology ....[23]

While McKenzie is working with a specific population and her ideas, for some, come from an extreme position, her efforts to present "... a more suitable Jungian gender theory, one that will fit all genders and sexualities"[24] push us into creative and meaningful reflections.

## Postmodern Thought

Jung realized that modern cultural conditions "... had set a limit upon the permitted scope of the human psyche."[25] In his phenomenological approach to the unconscious, not only did he re-awaken attention to the irrational and instinctual (as opposed to the rational) in humanity, he also heralded the importance of "subjective experience as a legitimate approach to concerns of the wider, collective culture and to 'scientific' investigation in general."[26]

For postmodern thinkers, according to Christopher Hauke, Jung used his psychology, "the method of the individual ... to critique not only the modern psyche but its cultural setting as well.[27]

> In doing so, Jung's psychology challenges the splitting tendency of modernity: the splitting of the "rational" and "irrational", the splitting of the social, collective norm and individual, subjective experience, the splitting of the Human and the Natural, of mind and matter, and perhaps above all, the splitting of the conscious and unconscious psyche itself.[28]

This is a paradox that I had not grasped completely until quite recently. The very thing that Jung was trying to accomplish—the challenging of the split in humanity—his psychology has not yet succeeded in achieving, even among those of us who have studied it. We pay lip service to it, we teach it, we theorize about it, but to live it is another matter altogether. We cannot challenge the dissociation in the collective if we hang on to the assumed reality of polar opposites.

It is quite unnecessary to genderize aspects of psyche and then assume sexist hierarchies between them. Postmodern thought values pluralism, that is, the acknowledgement of differences without hierarchy, and this leads us to question the notion of the unitary self based on a fixed gender identity. Jung's views on gender tend towards essentialism and are therefore outdated.[29]

> The shift detectable in postmodern feminism and postmodern Jungian psychology is one away from biology, away from opposites and also away from simplistic metaphorical assumptions that ... keep not only men and women in their opposed places, but also keep *one style of rationality* empowered over any other versions of the "truth".[30] (Italics in original.)

So if we are not referring to gender opposites when we use "anima" and "animus," have these terms lost their meaning? This is surely not the case, for anima and animus carry specific functions in psychic life and growth. These functions include, but are not limited to, development of identity, experiences of soulful living, connectedness between conscious and unconscious life, opportunities for new creativity, and the process of individuation. Psychologically and emotionally, they represent our direct dealings with the "other" in both the inner and outer worlds.

Andrew Samuels, in *The Plural Psyche*, describes it like this:

> ... [A]nimus and anima images are not of men and women because animus and anima qualities are "masculine"

> and "feminine". No—here, for the individual woman or man, anatomy is a metaphor for the richness and potential of the "other". A man will imagine what is "other" to him in the symbolic form of a woman—a being with another anatomy. A woman will symbolize what is foreign to her in terms of the kind of body she does not herself have. The so-called contrasexuality is more something "contrapsychological"; anatomy is a metaphor for that.[31]

But body as metaphor doesn't quite do it for me—I think it needs to be taken a step further.

Polly Young-Eisendrath, in *Hags and Heroes,* while still framing anima and animus as contrasexual, does take it a bit further. "These contrasexual complexes are organized around the identity archetype of Not-I: the animus or anima is a complex of habitual actions, symbol, image and emotion organized around the core of Other or Not-I in regard to excluded aspects of gender identity."[32]

However, to my way of thinking, even Not-I is too static. I prefer to consider contrasexuality in terms of the Dominant Psychic Principle (DPP) operating in the individual at any given time. One's relationship to one's sexuality is fluid rather than fixed. Furthermore, this fluidity encompasses constantly varying shades of self-identity and the self's shifting relation to "other than I." The DPP is being continually "updated" by the passage of data flowing over the threshold between consciousness and unconsciousness, and therefore relegating anima and animus to fixed unconscious complexes does an injustice to men and women alike. While it is valid to link the anima to female psychology in terms of how the projection of a male-conceived anima onto women contours women's self-image, to do so without a recognition of the bias imposed by patriarchal culture results in an essentialist view just at the point where Jung could in fact be revaluing the "feminine."[33]

Under patriarchy, the female ego clearly does not have the same status as the male ego. When the dominant consciousness is "male" the female ego is compromised. Thus, in the analytic process, the rebirth of the personality contingent upon the "death" of the ego needs to proceed differently for men and for women. For example, men may need to undergo the death of an ego that is experienced as separate and distinct from others and be reborn into "relationality." On the other hand, what women need is not so much the death of the ego, but a death to the false self-system that patriarchy has imposed upon them, in whatever form.[34]

Employed throughout human history as a paradigm, the symbolic opposition of male and female has perpetuated oppositional thinking itself. It has also kept chaos and uncertainty at bay. I believe we are moving to a place individually and collectively where psychic chaos and uncertainty can be embraced for their creative potential rather than feared for their potential destructiveness.

James Hillman and Nathan Schwarz-Salant both make a postmodern case for the necessary weakening of the ego, of consciousness, when relating to anima and animus. Hillman, in *The Myth of Analysis*:

> In Jung's language, psychotherapy achieves its ultimate goal in the wholeness of the conjunction, in the bisexuality of consciousness, which means, as well, conscious bisexuality, that incarnation of durable weakness and unheroic strength that we find in the image of Dionysus. Bisexual consciousness here means also the experience of psyche in all matter ...; it means a world undivided into spirit and matter, imaginal and real, body and consciousness, mad and sane .... The therapeutic goal of the *coniunctio* would now be experienced as a weakening of consciousness, in the former sense of that notion, rather than an increase of consciousness through "integrating" the anima. The *coniunctio* now would be weird and frightening, a horror and a death, inclusive of psychopathology.[35]

And Schwartz-Salant, writing about both therapeutic and personal (intimate) relationships, states:

> If the process of discovery contains the rhythm of both the "scientific" and the "imaginal," and if the fleeting nature of imaginal perceptions is trusted without being reified, then two people experience their relationship as a vessel containing both of them. Both people attempting to glimpse the mystery of their relationship are, alternatively, scientists and alchemists, perceiving on the one hand with objectivity and on the other hand with the vision of the imagination. When two people acknowledge that each is both rational and mad, they are prepared to enter the "third area" that has its own mystery and that is far larger than both of them together.
>
> A person dealing with "third areas" has to learn to "see" differently, to see through the eyes of the unconscious, and especially through the vision of the self.[36]

I want us to come back, in the seminar this afternoon, to the realm of destruction, a destroying down to one's essence, as I experience it, for it is also one of the aspects of anima and animus that can feel "wrong," but is nevertheless essential to a full life.

## Personal Lives—Mythic Lives

I would now like to attempt a postmodern interpretation of Dionysus and Ariadne, the half-divine couple. The story of Theseus conquering the Minotaur in the labyrinth in Crete is usually told and understood as a hero myth, with Ariadne playing a supporting role that is often glossed over. Ariadne loves Theseus, who, as a representation of the hero, takes up burdens and defeats monsters. But, as Deleuze said, "[A]s long as woman loves man [which indeed Ariadne does], as long as she is mother, sister, wife of man … she is only the feminine image of man: the feminine power remains fettered in man."[37] However, when Ariadne is abandoned by Theseus, she is free to have her encounter with Dionysus, and her transmutation is thus accomplished: the feminine power is emancipated in each of us, in all of us. As Hauke so aptly points out:

> The myth, arising it seems from a period when patriarchy was well established, suggests a complicated dynamic that involves the effort of the woman to free herself from the oppressive Father, not directly under her own steam, but through empowering another male—the hero Theseus—who is there to "correct" the father's errors. In this we should remember how it is through the hubris of King Minos that he keeps the bull lent him by Neptune, and it is through the copulation of Minos's wife, Ariadne's mother, and the bull that the Minotaur is born [as a punishment]. Like the father in *Beauty and the Beast* or "The Handless Maiden", Minos features as the foolish father who makes mistakes that usher in the events that lead to his daughter's path of individuation and fate. Beauty and Ariadne, while pursuing their individuation [by the happenstance of love at first sight], do so in reference to, and within the context of, the Father whose order remains. These stories confirm a state where woman, despite her own efforts in empowering the man, is trapped within the Law of the Father.[38]

Men are trapped within this law as well, of course. Hauke continues:

> Although Ariadne's ... individuation, such as it is, is accomplished within conditions that are dominated pervasively by the masculine, initially, there is a spark of hope in the *activity* displayed by the feminine in Ariadne's empowerment of Theseus. That this leads once more to Ariadne's abandonment, and not marriage to Theseus, may be viewed ambiguously as, on the one hand, a loss, or, on the other, a blessing achieved through the "divine" marriage with Dionysus.[39]

Ariadne's relation to Dionysus, a god, as opposed to the mortal male, Theseus, is quite another story. As long as we are stuck in the part of the story where Ariadne is tethered to Theseus, a large portion of our psychic and emotional energies remains trapped in a meaningless labyrinth, and our creativity, smartness, sensuality, altruism, and resourcefulness are consequently diminished. By abandoning the "Ariadne-in-us" at this point in the story, we place ourselves beyond the possibility of achieving the divine marriage. As Stacy Wirth observes, "Ariadne's 'achievement by loss' and the resulting 'ambiguity' ought not to worry us, but give us pause to consider their necessity in a larger and more meaningful dynamic."[40] Indeed, in loss and uncertainty, the numious Dionysian way already makes itself felt. It is only in *bearing with* these unsettling emotions that Ariadne is wed to Dionysus, the Lord of Souls,[41] and becomes one with that divine being in which "male and female are *primordially united*"[42] (italics added). Thus, in the figure of Ariadne we glimpse the chance to recover an undivided consciousness that is specifically "... not an attainment but a given. It is not a goal to be sought but an a priori possibility, always there for anyone."[43] Decidedly not the active hero's path to marriage (or psychic wholeness), Ariadne's way can be well imagined as one that subverts the "Law of the Father."

Ariadne's myth, as Hauke notes, "is rich in a greater imagery that is relevant for the affirmation of life, the development of consciousness, and co-terminously, the integration of the feminine or anima."[44] He goes on to say:

> While still linked to her lover Theseus, Ariadne, "is only the feminine image of man: the feminine power remains fettered in man" [quoting Deleuze] ... But when the god Dionysus finds Ariadne abandoned on Naxos and places a non-earthly crown of nine bright stars on her head, the feminine power is emancipated in the form of the beneficent and affirmative Anima.[45]

But what does this "beneficent and affirmative Anima" look like in real life, in concrete terms? I believe she might very possibly look like the new emerging female hero of the latter part of the 20th century. I see her prefigured in the character Dorothy, in Victor Fleming's 1939 film, *The Wizard of Oz,* based on the children's novel by L. Frank Baum, published in 1900. Not only does this female hero return home to the farm one step closer to wholeness herself, but she also redeems the lives of four males within the sphere of her influence: the three inept farmhands and the charlatan magician from Kansas, otherwise known as Scarecrow (no brains), Tin Man (no heart), Cowardly Lion (no courage), and the Wizard (no integrity).

In my practice I see this "beneficent and affirmative Anima" at work in men of all ages, struggling with the ambivalence of external success and the internal dehydration that all too often accompanies it. These men are looking courageously for ways to resolve the conflict, where the capacity to earn a living in the patriarchal workplace comes at the price of being forced to abandon their own emotions, partners, and families—and indeed the planet as well.

We are all trapped in the Law of the Father, men and women alike, regardless of our gender or sexual orientation, or the level of integration of the masculine and feminine aspects of ourselves. This is a universal psychic reality of our times. To help move our world towards a new reality, to escape from this trap of the patriarchy, we must untether "woman from man"—each in our own way, and all of us together. We must respect her sovereign agency in this process of untethering (in *each* of us) as well as in her subsequent suffering of abandonment—and honor her opening to something completely other, namely, to that Dionysian way of being that seeks an undivided life, a life in which "I" and "the other" are, paradoxically, not so separate after all, and in which soul and psyche are present and acknowledged in all human endeavor.

---

## *NOTES*

[1] C. G. Jung, "Concerning the Archetypes and the Anima Concept," in *The Archetypes and the Collective Unconscious, The Collected Works of C. G. Jung*, trans. R. F. C. Hull (Princeton, NJ: Princeton University Press, 1959), vol. 9i, § 114.

[2] Susan McKenzie, "Queering Gender: Anima/Animus and the Paradigm of Emergence," in *Journal of Analytical Psychology* 51, no. 3 (2006): 407.

[3] *Ibid.*, p. 412.

[4] *Ibid.*, p. 407.

[5] *Ibid.*, p. 403.

[6] Polly Young-Eisendrath, "Gender and Contrasexuality: Jung's Contribution and Beyond," in *The Cambridge Companion to Jung*, ed. Polly Young-Eisendrath and Terence Dawson (Cambridge, UK: Cambridge University Press, 1997), p. 225.

[7] McKenzie, p. 405.

[8] Daniel Siegel, *The Developing Mind: Toward a Neurobiology of Interpersonal Experience* (New York: The Guilford Press, 1999), pp. 1-2.

[9] George B. Hogenson, "The Baldwin Effect: A Neglected Influence on C. G. Jung's Evolutionary Thinking," in *Journal of Analytical Psychology* 46, no. 4 (2001): 591–611.

[10] George B. Hogenson, "What Are Symbols Symbols of? Situated Action, Mythological Bootstrapping and the Emergence of the Self," in *Journal of Analytical Psychology* 49, no. 1 (2004): 67.

[11] *Ibid.*, p. 75.

[12] McKenzie, p. 405.

[13] *Ibid.*, p. 409.

[14] Robert H. Hopcke, Karen Lofthus Carrington, & Scott Wirth, eds., *Same-Sex Love and the Path to Wholeness* (Boston, MA: Shambhala, 1993).

[15] Claudette Kulkarni, *Lesbians and Lesbianism: A Post-Jungian Perspective* (London: Routledge, 1997).

[16] McKenzie, p. 410.

[17] *Ibid.*, p. 411.

[18] *Ibid.*

[19] *Ibid.*, p. 416.

[20] "Syzygy," in *Wipikedia*, http://en.wikipedia.org/wiki/Syzygy (accessed 6 January 2009).

[21] *Ibid.*

[22] Verena Kast, *The Nature of Loving: Patterns of Human Relationship*, trans. Boris Matthews (Wilmette, IL: Chiron Publications, 1986), p. 94.

[23] Verena Kast, "Anima/Animus," in *The Handbook of Jungian Psychology: Theory, Practice and Applications*, ed. Renos K. Papadopoulos (Hove, UK: Routledge, 2006), p. 126.

[24] McKenzie, p. 412.

[25] Christopher Hauke, *Jung and the Postmodern: The Interpretation of Realities* (London: Routledge, 2000), p. 1.

[26] *Ibid.*

[27] *Ibid.*, p. 2.

[28] *Ibid.*

[29] *Ibid.*, pp. 114–121.

[30] *Ibid.*, pp. 139–140

[31] Andrew Samuels, *The Plural Psyche: Personality, Morality, and the Father* (London: Routledge, 1989), pp. 103-104.

[32] Polly Young-Eisendrath, *Hags and Heroes: A Feminist Approach to Jungian Psychotherapy with Couples* (Toronto: Inner City Books, 1984), p. 124.

[33] *Ibid.*

[34] *Ibid.*, p. 125.

[35] James Hillman, *The Myth of Analysis: Three Essays in Archetypal Psychology* (London: Routledge, 1999 [1960]), pp. 293–295.

[36] Nathan Schwartz-Salant, *The Mystery of Human Relationship: Alchemy and the Transformation of Self* (London: Routledge, 1998), p. 223.

[37] Quoted in Christopher Hauke, *Jung and the Post Modern: The Interpretation of Realities* (London: Routledge, 2000), p. 81.

[38] Hauke, pp. 143–144.

[39] *Ibid.*, p. 144.

[40] Personal communication.

[41] In *The Myth of* Analysis, Hillman uses the epithet "Lord of Souls" to stress Dionysus' essential link to the Underworld and the life of soul itself. See for instance pp. 277, 294.

[42] *Ibid.*, p. 259.

[43] *Ibid.*

[44] Hauke, p. 144.

[45] *Ibid.*

# Part IV

# Uncertain Heart—Unbounded Heart

Murray Stein, Ph.D., is President of ISAPZURICH, where he is also a training analyst. He is a founding member of the Inter-Regional Society for Jungian Analysts (USA) and the Chicago Society of Jungian Analysts, and was president of the International Association for Analytical Psychology (IAAP) from 2001 to 2004. He has written several books, including *Jung's Treatment of Christianity; In Midlife: A Jungian Perspective; Transformation: Emergence of the Self*; and *Jung's Map of the Soul: An Introduction*. He is the editor of *Jungian Analysis* (Open Court) and of the Chiron Clinical Series, which he has published through Chiron Publications.

11

# When you Venture There, Uncertainties and Mysteries Abound

*Murray Stein*

My first and nearly immediate reaction to the title of this open and public gathering, "Intimacy: Venturing the Uncertainties of the Heart," was to imagine the sign one puts on the door of hotel rooms for privacy: *Please do not disturb!* It seemed to me almost wicked to propose a conference on a topic that belongs so deeply to the private sphere of life. Are we not breaching the walls of a sacred *temenos* when we talk with strangers in public about intimacy?

Harold Bloom makes the keen observation that Shakespeare in his late masterpiece, *Antony and Cleopatra*, never shows the two intimates alone together. That is left off stage, veiled, sealed by silence. Bloom surmises that, this being of course deliberate on Shakespeare's part, the poet wanted the audience to imagine for themselves what these two vivid personalities did in the hours and days spent hidden away in their private places. I imagine them as engaged in "liminality dialogues"—naked exchanges between lovers in a space out of sight and hearing of the public world. Here they step out of their public identities as General and Queen; here their hearts and souls meet nakedly and forge their deepest bond. Should one speak of such things in public? Perhaps an affirmative answer can be justified if we can learn something from such discourse, if talking about such matters can stir into consciousness something that is important for our own lives.

In Shakespeare's tragedy, Antony is torn apart by the brutal opposition between his Roman identity as a man of war with a strong sense of duty and his unconventional and indeed adulterous love of Egypt (as Cleopatra is metonymically referred to in the play), where his longing for intimacy takes him. Shakespeare proposes no resolution for this pair of warring opposites in Antony's psyche; no healing symbol emerges. For Antony, it is a choice, stark and absolute: either public life and action in the Roman style, or intimacy in a liminal world with the Egyptian Queen. Caesar *or* Cleopatra, Rome *or* Egypt. Lost in confusion and caught fast in emotional bondage to Cleopatra ("My heart was to thy rudder tied by th' strings, / And thou shouldst tow me after" [3.11.57-58], he cries out bitterly and in desperation at a crucial moment in the play), Antony is then abandoned by his supreme inner guide, his daemon ("Peace, I say! / What should this mean? … 'Tis the god Hercules, whom Antony lov'd, / Now leaves him" [4.3.20-22]). Lacking the firmness of an identity based on archetypal sources and in utter despair, supposing that Cleopatra has betrayed him and is herself now dead, he collapses emotionally and takes his own life. Cleopatra follows him into death shortly in her inimitable fashion: "Give me my robe, put on my crown; I have/ Immortal longings in me" (5.2.279-80), she demands royally, and then, whispering to her servant Charmian as she clasps the asp to her breast in a moment of supreme theatrical intimacy, she speaks these breathtaking lines—"Peace, peace! / Dost thou not see my baby at my breast / That sucks the nurse asleep? … As sweet as balm, as soft as air, as gentle— / O Antony! Nay, I will take thee too" (as she applies the second asp to her arm). "What should I stay—" (5.2.309-312)—and dies. In the silence of death they achieve a final intimacy.

In another initial reflection on the topic of intimacy and the need for silence and liminal space to make it work, I recalled my great surprise when early in my first Jungian analysis I learned that what transpired there was not to be discussed anywhere else. Analysis is a *vas bene clausum*, a well-sealed vessel. Not only is it legally protected from intrusions, it must also be privately and personally held inviolate. About analysis, one was instructed, one remains silent, whether one takes part there as analyst or as analysand. I did not understand the importance of this at the time, but over the years I have decided that this is a good policy. The reason is that silence *without* increases intimacy *within*, and with intimacy there comes into being a process that we as Jungians believe offers the deepest healing and greatest satisfaction for the soul, the process of individuation. Individuation depends critically on finding sheltered spaces in life where one is free to be all that one can be, to discover what lies in the shadows, and to reveal what is found in the most hidden and private recesses of the psyche, in dreams, in fantasy, in feeling, and in thought. Individuation cannot achieve its full potential without an opening of the secret places of mind and heart to self, and, where intimacy with another is concerned, to a trusted other. It is what Antony, the aging warrior, now well advanced into the second half of life, sought with Cleopatra and what he most needed for his further individuation. For some, analysis is a kind of Egypt in the modern world, and therefore it is also a threat to the Roman in us.

In what follows, I will offer some thoughts on the magic that dwells in a few of the many kinds of intimacy that can be identified. Let me begin by observing that something strange and uncanny happens when one becomes deeply absorbed in a relationship, intimately so, whether with another person, with one's own unconscious, with texts, with received religious symbols, or with other specific objects in the cultural or natural world. And this can be frightening and disturbing, as well as deeply moving and transforming. It is something people often will not talk about openly because it sounds so strange, especially to the modern ear. There might even be a sense of guilt for betraying an esoteric mystery by divulging such things publicly. One can understand this reticence and why people often shy away from such terribly self-disclosing revelations about the secrets of the soul.

## Two Tales

Karl Barth (1886-1968), the great Swiss Protestant theologian of the 20th century, whom Pope Pius XII called the greatest Christian theologian since Thomas Aquinas, was an immensely imposing and important public figure in the academic and theological circles of his day. He also lived a quite complicated private life with wife, five children, and mistress (a true *soror mystica*) under one roof. Throughout his adulthood he suffered off and on from quite serious bouts of depression. One dimension of his private life that he never referred to or disclosed in his professional writings was his own personal dreams, which he recorded and occasionally discussed with his intimates, especially with a pastor friend whom he looked to as his *Seelsorger* (pastoral counselor), Eduard Thurneysen. His interest in dreams and their relation to his conscious life may well have stemmed from his early years. As a teenager growing up in Basel, he was exposed to the advice and informal analysis of a psychiatrist and psychoanalyst named Dr. Ewald Jung, a nephew of C. G. Jung's, whom his mother had taken into their home as a boarder when the young Karl was 12 years old, shortly after his father had passed away. Dr. Jung lived with the family for six years and so came to play the role of a father figure of sorts for the young adolescent. Through him, Barth was introduced to the world of the unconscious complexes, dreams, and much that depth psychology at the time was interested in exploring.[1] Later, he attended some lectures by C. G. Jung's Zürich colleague, Dr. Alfonse Maeder, and so became further acquainted with depth psychology. Although officially and in public highly critical of what psychology and psychoanalysis had to offer modern man, and disdainful of dreams and the unconscious as sources of assistance and wisdom, Barth found that in the intimacy of his friendship with Thurneysen he could allow himself "to approach the uncanny-attractive world of dreams."[2] As it turns out, he took his dreams surprisingly seriously, though he did not pretend to understand them very deeply.

In a letter to Thurneysen, Barth wrote that while he was most intensely engaged in his study of the doctrine of God as Trinity[3] and struggling mightily to place this most difficult Christian symbol (considered to be a "revelation") at the very center of his multivolume *Church Dogmatics*, he had a dream that brought with it a most unsettling experience. "All this past week," he related,

> I have repeatedly been pulling my hair out wondering how this would all be possible [he was struggling with creating a whole new theological statement, an immense undertaking]: recently I woke up suddenly in the middle of the night because I dreamed so very vividly about the scandalous subjectivity of this revelation [i.e., God as the object of His own self-knowledge], which somehow was literally (and unfortunately also objectively!!) coming towards me, when suddenly the wind ripped open the door of the room and slammed shut the window (in reality), so that the racket and the dogmatic vision miraculously came together.[4]

As Wolfgang Schildmann, a Jungian psychoanalyst and close student of the relation between Barth's dreams and his theological works, comments,

> His [Barth's] "melancholy" brooding over the ancient runes of dogma, his numinous dream experience with synchronistic accompaniment, and his feeling that he must follow his inner necessity confirms Jung's opinion that the Trini-

> tarian developmental process has to do with "fateful transformations" that "as a rule have a numinous character."[5]

In his studies, Barth had inadvertently tapped into an archetypal level of the psyche, and his intense broodings over an ancient definition of the Godhead constellated numinous and synchronistic effects in his bedroom. To use religious language, the Transcendent became immanent and incarnated. The Transcendent entered and disrupted the ordinary flow of life. Barth never published this account; he shared it only with his close longtime friend in private correspondence. He thus observed the rule of silence.

In the face of such ruptures in the fabric of everyday reality associated with intimate engagement with a religious symbol that has entered the world of time and space with awe-inspiring reverberations, silence generally prevails. It is said the Saint Thomas Aquinas himself, the great Doctor of the Church, stopped writing and studying after he had a numinous vision while saying Mass. This occurred towards the end of his life, after he had spent many years working intensively on the mysteries of Christian theology. He explained his puzzling silence to a confidant: "I have seen things which make all my writings like straw."[6] More than that he never disclosed. To this day, no one knows what he saw in his vision, but his death followed shortly thereafter.

Carl Jung (1875-1961), an almost exact contemporary of Karl Barth's and a fellow Baseler as well, reports in his writings several experiences that are quite similar to Barth's. In breaking the rule of silence, Jung risked a great deal, mainly his scientific reputation, since these self-disclosures would only serve to confirm the accusations of his harshest critics that he was a "mystic." He chose to use himself and his experiences to teach others about what can happen when one enters into this domain of intimate relations with symbols.

In all of these incidents, we find three vertices overlapping to create a quite unforgettable event: (1) a conscious preoccupation with a traditional symbol (the conscious vertex); (2) a dream (or dreams) or a vision (the unconscious vertex); and (3) a corresponding external phenomenon (the synchronistic vertex). This complex event begins when the subject enters into an intimate relationship with an object—in these cases the object is a received symbol of a religious tradition—and broods long and hard upon it. The unconscious responds with a dream or spontaneous image (a "vision"), and synchronistic events then cluster around.

In one highly significant instance for Jung, this convergence occurred in relation to his brooding preoccupation with the Christ symbol, which he began considering intensively in the late 1930s and continued, though at a lesser intensity of laser-like focus, off and on to the end of his life. "In 1939 I gave a seminar on the *Spiritual Exercises* of Ignatius Loyola," he writes in *Memories, Dreams, Reflections*. He continues:

> One night I awoke and saw, bathed in bright light at the foot of my bed, the figure of Christ on the Cross. It was not quite life-size, but extremely distinct; and I saw that his body was made of greenish gold. The vision was marvelously beautiful, and yet I was profoundly shaken by it.[7]

As in Karl Barth's experience, a powerful and compelling image presented itself to Jung in his bedroom on the heels of intensive study of a specific religious symbol.

Jung continues this passage in his autobiography by reporting a number of further dreams and images related to his steady preoccupation with Christian imagery. In 1949, ten years after the vision of Christ at the foot of his bed and while again deeply immersed in the study of the Christ symbol and its relation to the astrological Age of Pisces—thus, while in a state of brooding over the meaning of the Christ-as-fish symbol—he made the following observation in his diary:

> I noted the following on April 1, 1949. Today is Friday. We have fish for lunch. Somebody happens to mention the custom of making an "April fish" of someone. That same morning I made a note of an inscription which read: "Est homo totus medius *piscis* ab imo." In the afternoon a former patient of mine, whom I had not seen for months, showed me some extremely impressive pictures of fish which she had painted in the meantime. In the evening I was shown a piece of embroidery with fish-like sea-monsters in it. On the morning of April 2 another patient, whom I had not seen for many years, told me a dream in which she stood on the shore of a lake and saw a large fish that swam straight towards her and landed at her feet. I was at this time engaged on a study of the fish symbol in history.[8]

This is the synchronistic element, the third vertex.

It is around this "third thing" that I have tried to cast a net of reflections about what happens in intimate relations with ideas, people, and things. It has the qualities that Jung finds in the alchemical Mercurius: "Like the Trinity, the alchemical 'triunity' is a quaternity in disguise owing to the duplicity of the central figure: Mercurius ...."[9] Its duplicity, or dual nature, consists in its having an intimate relationship with the subjective and psychic realm on the one side (it is closely bound up with the image being contemplated in consciousness and appearing in a dream or vision), but simultaneously it is radically and completely independent of the psychic matrix on the other. The "third thing" is a symbol that is more than a metaphor or any other kind of trope. It breaches the boundary between inner and outer, psyche and world.

## The Third Thing and Transcendence in Personal Relationships

In contemporary Jungian psychoanalytic thinking, the reflection on the transcendent function has been extended to include the interpersonal dimension that gets constellated within the analytic vessel, a *vas bene clausum*. Here, too, Mercurius is present and active. The "third thing" that is spoken of here is the "space between," which assumes an identity, life, and character of its own and influences both partners in the analytic enterprise. The relationship itself, as the third thing, takes on form and quality and assumes a measure of autonomy that to an extent influences and even sometimes controls the thoughts and feelings of both partners in the field. What about the duality of this "third"? Does this also show evidence of *true transcendence*?

In some recent Jungian reflections, synchronicity has been introduced into this discussion notably by Joseph Cambray,[10] and following him, by George Hogenson.[11] The point is that the analytic relationship may constellate uncanny coincidences that have the quality of synchronicity in that they can be meaningful for both partners or at least for the one who is in a position to observe the synchronistic event. Jung's well known example of this is, of course, the appearance of the scarab beetle at his study window as he was discussing precisely this dream image with a young female patient. Many other similar examples have been collected in the Jungian literature since Jung's observations.[12]

Let me add strongly that the intersubjective field is not limited to analytic relationships, and neither is the possibility of what we can think of as a transcendent function building up between two intimates, whatever their professional or non-professional relationship may be. As a possible example of this, I offer the following personal experience.

Several years ago, a quite dear friend of mine died at an advanced age. I will call her Magda to preserve her anonymity. I had known her for over ten years, first as an analysand and later as interlocutor and friend. In the course of these years, we had had many deep exchanges about her life, her feelings, her dreams, and so forth. She was in the process of summing up as she came to the end of a long and productive life. She was a Catholic nun, and believed without reservation in the reality of God and the afterlife.

In her later years, Magda became crippled from having spent too much time on her knees as a younger woman—not only in prayer, but also scrubbing the floors of the convent when she was young—and so she was now confined to a wheelchair. She grieved deeply the loss of her physical mobility and independence, and having to depend on her fellow sisters in the home where she was being cared for made her angry and miserable at times. She had to endure the frustration of being immobile. So she enjoyed telling me with a twinkle in her eye that when she died and went to heaven, the first thing she would do there was dance. She loved to imagine her body whole again and capable of unrestrained movement. This is what she looked forward to most of all, even more than meeting loved ones and famous religious figures.

Shortly before her death, I read in a newspaper that Pope John Paul II had confirmed the sainthood of the Carmelite nun, Edith Stein, and would canonize her in Rome at St. Peter's. Magda had connections in Rome, so I asked her if she thought it would be possible for me to obtain tickets to the canonization ceremony. She made a phone call and assured me that when the time came for Edith Stein's canonization, I would have seats. I thanked her profusely.

Magda died shortly after receiving a diagnosis of terminal pancreatic cancer, having chosen to instruct her doctors to withhold unrealistic treatments. She was prepared to leave her body behind and to go on in the spirit to meet her Maker and loved ones who had gone before, especially a sister who had died at an early age so many years ago. My wife and I did have the privilege of being with her for an hour on the day before she passed away. She was in and out of consciousness and barely showed any awareness of our presence, but I was quite sure she was observing us from another place in her psyche, from up there in the corner. We kissed her farewell, wishing her a good journey through the valley of the shadow of death. I knew she was as well prepared for this final experience of life as anyone can be.

On the day of her funeral, we were surprised to discover that the venue of the funeral service had been changed from the nursing home where she had spent her last months, and which contained a nice little chapel, to a larger church; we had gone to the wrong place and at the wrong time. The service was to be held several hours later in another part of the city. Our car had been parked in a lovely garden behind the nursing home. It was an extremely hot day in Chicago, and we had kept the windows and doors of the car shut tight, since we had the car's air-conditioning turned on. To save the cool air inside the car, we got in and out quickly, but as we drove away I asked my wife to check the back seat. Something, which must unaccountably have gotten into the car, was flapping around in the rear window.

She turned to look and exclaimed in surprise: "It's a butterfly!"

"Impossible," I said. "How could a butterfly have gotten into a car all locked up?"

But, sure enough, it was a large brown butterfly with bits of blue on its wings. I rolled down all the windows, offering it a chance to escape and hoping it would fly away, but it refused to leave. It was determined to stay in the rear window of our car for the whole trip and would not take the opportunity to fly away. When we reached the actual venue of the funeral service, we parked the car and opened the back doors. Still the butterfly would not budge. Even after the funeral service, the butterfly continued to accompany us as we drove homeward. Now we began to speak of it jokingly as Magda.

"Well, OK, Magda has decided to come home with us!"

When we got home it was dark outside. My wife reached her hand into the back of the car hoping that the butterfly would now accept the invitation to make an exit. Previously this had not worked, but this time the butterfly hopped onto her hand and sat tight. We called to our friend Joyce, who was staying with our daughter and dog, and who was inside the house, to come on out and see the butterfly. She also had known Magda quite well.

As we stood together outside under a street light, Magda-the-butterfly flew to the ground and began doing an amazing dance at our feet. Round and round she went in a frenzy of motion. Suddenly I remembered Magda's ardent hope to dance again in eternity, and I burst out, "Well, Magda I see you've made it! You're dancing!"

At this moment the boundaries between this world and the next were breached. I could only feel that in this sacred moment we were living both in time and eternity. Surely this was Magda dancing in the form of a butterfly. The butterfly then flew away, and we knew we had witnessed something extraordinary. The next morning our friend Joyce telephoned. She said, "Guess what happened to the butterfly we saw last night!"

"What?"

"It came home with me in my car! When I got home, there it was in the back window. I let it out of the car and it flew off in the direction of Dorothy's garden." Dorothy lived a few blocks away and had been one of Magda's best friends for half a century.

About a year passed when, thanks to Magda's earlier request to Rome, I was able to get tickets for Edith Stein's canonization at the Vatican. The canonization ceremony took place in St. Peter's Square on October 11, 1998.

I had been interested in the life of Edith Stein for some years. She was a Jewish convert to Roman Catholicism, who became a Carmelite nun in the 1930s and died with her people in Auschwitz in 1942 after having been rounded up along with other known Jews in the Netherlands. She was also a distinguished philosopher and had been a favorite pupil of Edmund Husserl's. I was interested in her life for many reasons and had read some of her works and several biographies. To add to this, I had never attended a canonization ceremony before. So I was in a state of heightened anticipation as my wife and a couple of Roman friends and I made our way to the choice seats reserved for us, thanks to Magda and her connections in Rome.

The ceremony itself was deeply moving, as expected. This aged pope, by then so ravaged by time and physical decline, could barely move forward under his own power out through the doors of St. Peter's to his chair on the platform, but there he presided, nevertheless, for three hours over a ceremony that must have been very special for him as well. Both he and Edith Stein were born and grew up in Poland, and he had been intensively involved in trying to heal the long and bitter rift between Christians and Jews. The ritual, the music, the crowd of 70,000 people from all parts of the world, the colorful cardinals and high-level politicians on the platform with the Pope—all of this contributed to the impressiveness of the event. In that atmosphere of grand ritual, music, and prayer, the sense of an invisible world surrounding us became quite palpable, understandably so. But nothing could have prepared me for what happened as the service drew to a close.

We were all standing upright in the warm sun for the benediction; the Pope was intoning his blessing in Latin. The text of this prayer was printed in four languages in the booklet prepared for the occasion, and I was following the Pope's slurred diction as best I could with the help of the text in my booklet. When he arrived at the line, "Ex hoc nunc et usque in saeculum" ("Von nun an bis in Ewigkeit")— "Ora e sempre" ("Now and forever")—an utterly astonishing thing happened.

A brown butterfly with blue bits of color on its wings appeared out of nowhere from that crowd of thousands and alighted on the open page. It landed on the words "Ora e sempre" and rested quietly there.

At first I could not take in what had happened. It came as a total surprise and left me utterly shocked. I had seen no butterflies in that sea of human faces before this. There were none there. It was impossible. I was stunned. Where had this butterfly come from? We were in the middle of a vast sea of humanity in the midst of a giant city, not a garden.

My wife gasped, too. "It's the same butterfly!" she whispered.

Sure enough, the colors were the same as those of the one in Chicago. Our Roman friends who were with us were not aware of the earlier incident involving Magda and the butterfly and so they did not register the same level of astonishment, but they were, nevertheless, also amazed to see a butterfly in this unlikely place and sitting on my prayer booklet.

"Can this be Magda?" I wondered to myself in amazement.

The butterfly took to the air as the Pope said "Amen" and disappeared in the direction of the altar some 50 meters in front of us. My fantasy was that it joined the other spirits and angels so palpably present in Piazza San Pietro that bright day in October.

Now if we think for a moment about what kind of object this butterfly is, its duality becomes evident: it was a literal, physically real, live insect, and at the same time for me and my wife it was a symbol of Magda's spirit because of what we knew about her and felt subjectively about her as a person. This butterfly was a "third thing."

"Transcendence is a delirious rupture in immanence," writes theologian Regina Schwartz, putting precise words to this experience, "an erotic claim made by it, a gap in the Real, a question put to subjectivity, a realm of the impossible that breaks into possibility."[13] I am left with the unshakeable conviction that transcendence *in the strong sense of the word* broke through the fabric of ordinary conscious life in that delicate, hovering, possibly erotic, and certainly delightful dance of the Magda butterfly. And this leads me to the firm conviction as well that specific intimate relationships are grounded in and touch upon the transcendent in a most unique and particular way. In this resides their strongest claim to permanence and their largest meaning. Montaigne, in his essay, "On Affectionate Relationships," writes:

> If you press me to say why I loved him, I feel that it cannot be expressed except by replying: "Because it was him:

> because it was me." Mediating this union there was, beyond all my reasoning, beyond all that I can say specifically about it, some … [divine] force of destiny.[14]

The finger of God is moving when two souls truly meet and join in the bond of intimacy.

---

## *NOTES*

[1] Wolfgang Schildmann, *Karl Barths Träume: Zur verborgenen Psychodynamik seines Werkes* (Zürich: Theologisher Verlag Zürich, 1991/2006), p. 9.

[2] *Ibid.*, p. 23.

[3] God as Trinity—"His argument follows from the idea that God is the object of God's own self-knowledge, and revelation in the Bible means the self-unveiling to humanity of the God who cannot be discovered by humanity simply through its own efforts." http://en.wikipedia.org/wiki/Karl_Barth.

[4] Schildmann, p. 171, my translation.

[5] *Ibid.,* p. 181, my translation.

[6] G. K. Chesterton, *Saint Thomas Aquinas: "The Dumb Ox"* (New York: Image Books 1933/1956), p. 143.

[7] C. G. Jung, *Memories, Dreams, Reflections*, ed. Aniela Jaffé, trans. Richard & Clara Winston (New York, NY: Random House, 1961/1989), p. 210.

[8] C. G. Jung, "Synchronicity: An Acausal Connecting Principle," in the *Collected Works*, trans. R. F. C. Hull (Princeton, NJ: Princeton University Press, 1916/1958/1969) vol. 8, § 826. (All future references to Jung's *Collected Works*, abbreviated to *CW*, will be by chapter title, followed by volume and paragraph number).

[9] Jung, "The Personification of Opposites," *CW* 14, § 235.

[10] Joseph Cambray, "Synchronicity and Emergence," *American Imago* 59, no. 4 (2002): 409-434.

[11] George Hogenson, "From Moments of Meeting to Archetypal Consciousness: Emergence and the Fractal Structure of Analytic Practice," in *Who Owns Jung*?, ed. Ann Casement (London: Karnac, 2007), pp. 293-314.

[12] Roderick Main, "Synchronicity and Analysis: Jung and After," *European Journal of Psychotherapy and Counselling* 9, no. 4 (2007): 359-371.

[13] Regina Schwarz, "Introduction," in *Transcendence: Philosophy, Literature, and Theology Approach the Beyond*, ed. Regina Schwartz (New York and London: Routledge, 2004), p. xi.

[14] Michel de Montaigne, *The Complete Essays*, ed. and trans., M. A. Screech (London: Penguin Books, 2003), p. 212.

Thomas J. Kapacinskas, JD, NCPsyA, is a 1972 graduate of the C. G. Jung-Institut Zürich. He was a professor of Jungian Psychology in relation to religion in the Department of Theology, University of Notre Dame. He is a founding member and senior analyst in the Chicago Society of Jungian Analysts and the C. G. Jung Institute of Chicago, and the Inter-Regional Society of Jungian Analysts and its training program. His principal area of interest is the psychology of religion and the spirituality of psychotherapy, and as a highly sought-after speaker, he has made many presentations on these themes over the years in the U.S.A. and abroad.

12

# Initiatory Knowing: Reflections on the Lives of Simone Weil and C. G. Jung

*Thomas J. Kapacinskas*

## I

> … [N]ow every man has to carry God. The descent of spirit into matter is complete.[1]

> … [O]ur true dignity … consists in this, that in the state of perfection, which is the vocation of each one of us, we no longer live in ourselves, but Christ lives in us; so that through our perfection Christ in his integrity and in his indivisible unity, becomes in a sense each one of us.[2]

In formulating his psychological theories, C. G. Jung adopted a Kantian empirical stance as a psychologist of religion who contemplates the received God-image as an anthropomorphic metaphor for an ultimately unknowable, transcendent reality, whose operations are inscrutable to the human mind. Jung remains "in character" throughout his writings, and in particular in "Answer to Job," where he speaks of God's operations in the mythopoeic Biblical language in which they were originally couched while at the same time endeavoring to remain faithful to the proposition that whatever else such scriptures might be (for example, "divinely inspired" in their ability to lead the soul to contemplate the divine), they reveal the structure of the psyche's experience in seeking the divine. His project is not an attempt to "reduce" theology or religion to psychology. On the contrary, it is an attempt to understand how the *logos* of the *psyche,* the account the soul gives of itself, is enmeshed in religious language and theological discourse about an ultimately transcendent reality.

In a similar vein, Simone Weil, the French Jewish free-thinking philosopher and unchurched Christian mystic, writes of God's transcendent distance from creation, made necessary by the need for it to exist freely. She writes of God's "desire" that we relinquish the gift of life so as to return the gift and ourselves to him. She says:

> Creation is an act of love and it is perpetual. At each moment our existence is God's love for us. But God can only love himself. His love for us is love for himself through us. Thus, he who gives us our being loves in us the acceptance of *not* being.
>
> Our existence is made up only of his waiting for our acceptance *not* to exist. He is perpetually begging from us that existence which he gives. He gives it to us in order to beg it from us.[3] (Italics added.)

For Weil, God's involvement with us on the earthly plane is "confined" to and mediated through the supernatural gift of grace.

She draws upon the image of the Golden Scales of Zeus, as found in Homer's *Iliad,* where they represent the impartiality of the divine in the destinies of men, and she uses this image to talk about the role of necessity in the individuation of our lives. In her *Notebooks,* she writes: "Golden balance of Zeus, symbol serving two ends. Symbol of blind Necessity, symbol of the decision of the just man. Union of these two symbols [how they come together]—remains a mystery."[4] I propose that the work of analysis may be, in part, an exploration of the "mystery" of how these two things come together. Analysis probes the gravity of what weighs down the scales according to the laws of necessity. Why is necessity necessary? Says Weil: "Necessity is God's veil,"[5] "an image by which the mind can conceive of the indifference, the impartiality of God."[6]

> . . . [I]f we were exposed to the direct radiance of his love, without the protection of space, of time and of matter, we should be evaporated like water in the sun; there would not be enough "I" in us to make it possible to surrender the "I" for love's sake. Necessity is the screen set between God and us so that we can be.[7]

So, as our lives move to their fated outcomes, what individuation requires of us has its necessary "gravitational pull," which, while it "screens" us, adds a weight to one "pan" of the scales. This emergent gravity of our "incomparable uniqueness" determines our life-fate. Aniela Jaffé, echoing Jung, provides this gloss:

> ... [M]an is the only creature given the possibility of a conscious individuation ... the possibility of recognizing at least in part those forces which underlie his own being, thinking, behavior and development, as well as the apparently random whims of fate. Such recognition adds an inner dimension to life. Outer and inner realities inseparably comprise a whole. Both are aspects of the Self that unfold just as much in outer events and physical existence, in destiny and in character, as in the inner psychic world, in dreams, fantasies, visions and moods. These structures of the unconscious provide the meaning-giving complement to the processes of outer life, and through them individuation unfolds ....[8]

Similarly, Simone Weil says: "It is possible for us to be mediators between God and the part of creation which is confided to us. Our consent is necessary in order that he may perceive his own creation through us. With our consent he performs this marvel."[9] The Roman emperor and Stoic philosopher, Marcus Aurelius, put it in terms of "harmony":

> All that is harmony for you, my Universe, is in harmony with me as well. Nothing that comes at the right time for you is too early or too late for me. Everything is fruit to me that your seasons bring, Nature. All things come of you, have their being in you, and return to you.[10]

The "love of fate," or *amor fati*, is then the opportunity that we have of loving and accepting our fate and its inherent decreation[11] through a death that is unique to the life we have lived. Weil writes: "In a sense, God renounces being everything [*so that we might exist*]. We should renounce being something. That is our only good."[12] For Weil, we cannot be "good" because human experience is always a mixture of good *and* evil. Only God can be "good" and we can only aspire to goodness.

## II

In order to follow Weil and Jung better, let us remind ourselves that a mystic is "a person who seeks by contemplation (or other means) to achieve unity with the Deity, or who believes in the spiritual apprehension of truths that are beyond the understanding," the word *mys-*

*tic* being derived from the Greek *mustes,* which refers to "one who has been initiated."[13] Since initiation is intrinsic to the mystic's way of seeing, let us inquire into the initiations of Weil and Jung and survey their qualifications to speak as they do.

Weil's initiation came through her experience of detachment and "affliction." She describes affliction as an inconsolable suffering of the void, which can be redeemed only by the experience of grace. She says: "Thus effort truly stretched towards goodness cannot reach its goal; it is after long, fruitless effort which ends in despair, when we no longer expect anything, that, from outside ourselves, the gift comes as a marvellous surprise."[14] Elsewhere she says: "Affliction in itself is not enough for the attainment of total detachment. Unconsoled affliction is necessary. There must be no consolation—no apparent consolation. Ineffable consolation then comes down."[15]

In grasping the psychological underpinnings of the path to mystical knowing, it is helpful, even if somewhat speculative, to consider Simone Weil from the perspective of Jung's psychological typology. In Jung's typology hypothesis, at one pole of consciousness is sensation, which is the ability to monitor the sensorium and orient oneself consciously by skillful use of this data; it is considered to be at the opposite pole from the intuition function, which is a mode of unconscious perception. Crossing the axis of these two polar opposites is a pair of additional opposites: at one pole of this second opposition is thinking, which is the ability to proceed consciously by means of logical inference; at the other pole is feeling, the function which communicates by means of emotions and feeling states where our values lie.

With regard to Simone Weil, we can conjecture, based on the scant information available about her, that she was very likely an introvert with intuition as her most consciously developed (or "main") function. This enabled her, in her philosophizing, to glimpse the deep *gestalt* of *things-in-themselves,* as in her study of Pythagoreanism, Plato, and the *Bhagavad Gita.* It is likely that thinking was her first auxiliary function, given the logical mode in which she conducts her argumentation. Since she is also "steeped" in values, feeling cannot be far behind as her second auxiliary function. In all likelihood, then, sensation was her most unconscious and most "undeveloped" function, especially the sensorium of the body. We arrive at this assessment by surveying the available information and making inferences, with no disrespect intended. Others viewing the same data may draw different typological conclusions. With this caveat in mind, let us proceed.

Her reckless disregard for her body and its sensorium stands out in even a cursory look at her life. Ironically, but true to Jung's typology, it is for Weil the body and its affliction that induce in her a knowledge of the void and initiates her subsequent experience of the *transcendent function* psychologically, and her religious experience spiritually. In psychological parlance, she experienced the "wholeness-generating" *tertium quid non datur* of the transcendent function as a compensation of the *Self* (Jung's term for the deepest center of the person). Empirically, this would be the evolutionary legacy of what Jung called the "Two-Million-Year-Old" human.[16] For Weil, proper to her psychology and her spiritual predisposition, it took the form of "Christ taking possession" of her as a psychological reality and a spiritual presence.

What was it that tipped the "golden scales of Zeus" for Simone Weil? What was it that was "necessary" to bring about the void that preceded her mystical "knowing"? Consider the complex of affliction in physical, sensorium-related modes that characterized her life.

The first, most salient fact is her apparently untreatable headaches, perhaps migraines, now conjectured to have been part of a chronic sinus inflammation syndrome. She says: "At a certain moment, the pain is lessened by projecting it into the universe, but the universe is impaired; the pain is more intense when it comes home again, but something in me does not suffer and remains in contact with a universe which is not impaired."[17] The headaches evidently drove her to internal psychological splitting as a defense.

In her remarks on headaches in *Heal Your Body*, Louise Hay, an astute observer of the inseparable connection between body and mind, says that headaches have to do with "invalidating the self," "self-criticism," and "fear,"[18] and that migraine headaches have to do with: "Dislike of being driven [as, e.g., by sexuality]. Resisting the flow of life. Sexual fears."[19] It is known that Simone Weil felt "invalid" *vis-à-vis* her brother, Andre, a mathematician of genius, and that her mother did not seem to value her femininity, calling her the family's "second son." Little is known about Simone Weil's sexuality. In her writings she is preoccupied with rising above desire. She says:

> We have to go down to the root of our desires in order to tear the energy from its object. That is where the desires are true in so far as they are energy. It is the object which is unreal. But there is an unspeakable wrench in the soul at the separation of a desire from its object.[20]

We might speculate that Weil's headaches were the physical manifestation of this soul "wrenching."

In *The Healing Power of Illness*, Dethlefsen and Dahlke write:

> Whereas sufferers from tension-headaches are trying to separate their heads from their bodies, migraine-patients are transferring one particular bodily theme into their heads and trying to live it out at this level instead. That theme is sexuality. Migraine is always a displacement of sexuality into the head. The head is reassigned what is really the body's job. In fact this particular displacement is not as irrelevant as all that, for the genital area and head stand in an analogical relationship to each other. They are, after all, the two parts of the body that contain all the body orifices.[21]

If we continue to look compassionately at Simone Weil's life we find other examples of her ignoring the sensorium and the body. There is her absurd, if heroic, attempt as a somewhat frail philosophy teacher to identify with the working classes by forgoing the classroom in favor of working in a factory. This drudgery in an abusive environment was an insult to her constitution, an experience from which, perhaps, she never fully recovered. There is her equally absurd, if no less heroic, participation in the Spanish Civil War, during which she accidentally scalded her feet behind the lines, perhaps inadvertently saving herself from a terrible war-related death.

Later, during World War II, under the German occupation of France and the Nazi restrictions upon Jews, she made a gallant attempt to work on a farm without having the physique for such work. She spoke of harvesting grapes as a kind of "hell." There was also her idealistic and perhaps "disembodied" plan to place female nurses at the battlefront, an idea that de Gaulle dismissed as "madness." Today, with our Aquarian sensibilities, we might consider her plan to be a prophet-like advocacy of gender equality in facing the horrors of war, and regard de Gaulle's assessment as male chauvinism.

Consider next her heroic decision not to stay with her family in the USA after their flight from occupied France. She chose to return instead to the privations of wartime London. This last move, alas, cost her her life, since as a consequence of it she became gravely ill with tuberculosis. Despite her weakened condition, she refused to eat any more than the rations allowed the French in occupied France. She perished in 1943, aged 34, at least in part from malnutrition.

According to the dynamic model of Jung's typology, for a person whose sensation function is so unconscious, the most powerful, wholeness-engendering, compensatory experience would come *through* the body and the sensorium. I would suggest that the cascade of physical catastrophes that dogged Weil's life and culminated in her death created an apparently uncompensated void, a state in which, as she says, "Christ Himself took possession of me." This spiritual reality was based in the psyche's experience. It was a palpable experience of wholeness, spoken of in spiritual terms as "possession" by Christ, an experience generated from the ineffable—the "un-conscious" (the psychological term we use to describe the unknown "other" dimension of human experience). What happened to Simone Weil fits perfectly with what Jung's typology would have predicted for her personality type.

## III

Let us now speak about Jung's affliction and the initiation it precipitated. Jung had a completely different psychological temperament from Weil's and did not seek perfection in the way that she did. He was an "apostle" of wholeness, who considered "perfection" psychologically dangerous, particularly for women. To be frank, it is likely that he would have considered Simone Weil's psychology as an instance of hysterical hankering for perfection. Jung says:

> *Perfection* is a masculine desideratum, while woman inclines by nature to *completeness*. And it is a fact that, even today, a man can stand a relative state of perfection much better and for a longer period than a woman, while as a rule it does not agree with women and may even be dangerous for them. If a woman strives for perfection she forgets the complementary role of completeness, which, though imperfect by itself, forms the necessary counterpart to perfection. For, just as completeness is always imperfect, so perfection is always incomplete, and therefore represents a final state which is hopelessly sterile. *"Ex perfecto nihil fit,"* say the old masters, whereas the *imperfectum* carries within it the seeds of its own improvement. Perfectionism always ends in a blind alley, while completeness by itself lacks selective values.[22]

As Jung sought his own wholeness, his affliction came through the psychic and spiritual suffering identified by Henri Ellenberger as Jung's "creative illness."[23] Shamdasani provides this summary of Ellenberger's view:

> He provided the following general schema of the "creative illness": the illness commences after a period of intense intellectual effort, during the illness, the subject is obsessed with an intellectual, spiritual, or aesthetic problem. The termination of illness is experienced as not only the liberation from a period of psychological suffering, but also as an illumination. Finally, this is followed by a transformation of the personality, and often with gaining followers. He cited examples among the shamans and religious mystics, and also notably, Freud and Jung. The latter, he maintained, had "suffered from a kind of protracted neurotic disorder", after his break with Freud. Ellenberger maintained that "the essential features of Jung's teaching, therefore, are the result of his creative neurosis."[24]

In typological terms, Jung's affliction and consequent *mystical experience* came through the unconsciousness of his emotion-laden feeling function. He says:

> An incessant stream of fantasies had been released, and I did my best not to lose my head but to find some way to understand these strange things. I stood helpless before an alien world; everything in it seemed difficult and incomprehensible. I was living in a constant state of tension; often I felt as if gigantic blocks of stone were tumbling down upon me. One thunderstorm followed another. My enduring these storms was a question of brute strength. Others have been shattered by them—Nietzsche, and Hölderlin, and many others. But there was a demonic strength in me, and from the beginning there was no doubt in my mind that I must find the meaning of what I was experiencing[.] … I had an unswerving conviction that I was obeying a higher will, and that feeling continued to uphold me ….[25]

Jung is reported to have considered himself an introverted thinking type.[26] Shamdasani quotes the following from a 1925 seminar of Jung's:

> … [A] man … likes to give you the finished product of his directed thinking and have you understand that so it was born in his mind, free of weakness. A thinking man's attitude towards his intellectual life is quite comparable to that of woman toward her erotic life. … [A] man centers his power in his thinking and proposes to hold it against other men. He thinks if he tells the truth in this field it is equivalent to turning over the keys of his citadel to the enemy.[27]

Jung's self-described method in his "confrontation with the unconscious" was to free the images in the emotions. "Unpopular, ambiguous, and dangerous, it is a voyage of discovery to the other pole of the world,"[28] he writes. Further, he says:

> I was frequently so wrought up that I had to do certain yoga exercises in order to hold my emotions in check. But since it was my purpose to know what was going on within myself, I would do these exercises only until I had calmed myself ... To the extent that I managed to translate the emotions into images ... to find the images which were concealed in the emotions—I was inwardly calmed and reassured. Had I left those images hidden in the emotions, I might have been torn to pieces by them.[29]

The "creative illness" that Jung lived through was apparently precipitated by the crisis of his break with Freud in 1913. He says: "After the parting of the ways with Freud, a period of inner uncertainty began for me. It would be no exaggeration to call it a state of disorientation."[30] Much of the "illness" may have had to do with Jung's grieving his losses—with the overwhelming loss of Freud screening a cascade of other losses. For example, a few years earlier, Jung had gone through an intense emotional involvement with Sabina Spielrein and the loss of the "Siegfried" fantasy engendered by their relationship. Siegfried was the name that they gave to the child—real or imaginal—who was to be the fruit of their relationship in whatever form it was that they came together.[31] A mediating figure of Jung's "Jewish anima," Spielrein had left Zürich and joined Freud's circle in Vienna. Given her complicated and demanding psychology (Jung may have been referring to her when he spoke of a "talented psychopath"[32]), Spielrein's departure may actually have been a relief for Jung. But whether he grieved the loss of her as woman or the loss of his own innocence in what he had gone through (in what we would later understand as a counter-transference), there was a loss for him to *feel* that was associated with her.

As a first-generation psychoanalyst attempting to understand the intricacies of transference and counter-transference, Jung may have been relieved or haunted by Spielrein's departure. As a human being, however, he would almost certainly have been affected by the experience of having a relationship with her and feeling the loss of his own authority brought about by the necessity of Freud's having to intervene to help resolve the crisis.

In this connection, there are unresolvable questions regarding Jung's 1913 "Siegfried dream," recounted by Jung in *Memories, Dreams, Reflections*,[33] and retold by Shamdasani, who gives Edward A. Bennet's account of the dream.[34] In considering the emotional feeling-losses that Jung suffered, there is the question of the guilt for the "murder" that Jung, the ego-figure in the dream, helps perpetrate. Jung interprets this dream as having to do with honoring the shadow, the primitive part of the Self. But there are many other resonances. For example, it may have to do with the "killing" of Freud in Jung's life: consider the play on words (something the unconscious often indulges in) by which Siegfried would "stand for" Sigmund. Or it may have to do with "killing" the fantasy of the child Siegfried that he shared with Spielrein and the demise of his relationship with her. We will never know the full extent of Jung's polysemous feeling-losses.

We may speculate about the feeling-function loss/gain differential in Jung's marital relationship—precipitated by the intense analytic and personal involvements with Spielrein and Toni Wolff, who followed a few years later. Whatever else they may have been, these relationships were understood by Jung as his attempts to manage his "polygamous" anima tendencies by making them conscious in these and other relationships.[35]

There was also a loss/gain differential to be felt by Jung from another perspective: at the time of the rupture with Freud, Jung was, astrologically, a third of the way through his second "Saturn-return." This means that Jung had met Freud and begun to have contact with him near the end of his first Saturn Cycle of (approximately) the first 28 years of his life. For psychological astrologers, such as Jungian analyst Liz Greene,[36] the transits of the planet Saturn, which take about 28 years in the horoscope, correlate with the presence of the archetypal father energy in one's life. Thus, Saturn (and the associated "father" energy thus signified) returns to its initial placement in the horoscope once every 28 years. Strikingly, this was occurring for Jung at about the time that he and Freud began their relationship.

Jung enjoyed a brief spell as the gentile "crown prince" under the Jewish "father" of psychoanalysis, Freud. As heir-apparent of the so-called "Jewish science," Jung was the envy of many Jews within Freud's circle until his break with Freud brought his "adopted son" status to an end.[37]

By any estimation, *through* the loss of Freud, Jung felt the "death" of a father for the second time since the loss, years before, of his personal father, Paul Jung, which occurred, ironically, over a different crisis of faith—one associated with the tenets of the denominational Christianity in which the elder Jung served as a pastor. In reading what Jung says about his father's demise in *Memories, Dreams, Reflections*, dictated to Aniela Jaffé when Jung was in his 80s, one can see how, even at that late age, Jung remained powerfully affected by his father's loss of faith and subsequent death. Some of his criticisms there of the Swiss Reformed Church and its theology[38] parallel Simone Weil's criticisms of the Catholic Church.

Jung's situation in the "creative illness" period of 1913-17 was immensely complicated, both personally and professionally, and it remains a hotbed of biographical speculation in the absence of hard evidence. According to Shamdasani, the most authoritative and careful writer about Jung's life, the "situation is compounded by the dearth of reliable historical and biographical information about ... [Jung] and the insufficiently realized fact that many manuscripts, seminars, and thousands of letters still remain unpublished."[39] Shamdasani quotes an October 9, 1916 letter of Jung's to Alphonse Maeder, which gives some sense of the climate of stress that afflicted Jung in those days:

> As to what the rumors about my person concern, I can inform you that I have been married to a female Russian student for six years (Ref. Dr. Ulrich), dressed as Dr. Frank, I have recommended immediate divorce to a woman (Ref. Frau E-Hing), two years ago I broke up the Rüff-Franck marriage, recently I made Mrs. McCormick pregnant, got rid of the child and received 1 million for this (Ref. Dr. F. & Dr. M. in Z), in the Club house I intern pretty young girls for homosexual use for Mrs. McCormick, I send their young men for mounting in the hotel, therefore great rewards, I am a baldheaded Jew (Ref. Dr. Stier in Rapperswyl), I am having an affair with Mrs. Oczaret, I have become crazy (Ref. Dr. M. in Z.), I am a con-man (Ref. Dr. St. in Z.), and last not least—Dr. Picht is my assistant. What is one to do? How should I behave to make such rumors impossible? I am thankful for your good advice. The auspices for analysis are bad, as you see! One must simply not do such an unattractive enterprise on one's own, if one is not to be damaged.[40]

The tenor of this letter suggests that what Jung faced in his experience of affliction, which he imaged elsewhere as "gigantic blocks of stone ... tumbling down upon me," was the challenge to be his "own man," to somehow experience the "father" in a way that "restored" the father energy lost to him. Such imagery may appear in dreams in association with the breakdown of Saturnine structures. Enduring this destruction was the "tearing out" spoken of by Simone Weil, the loss of *actual* father-figures as a means of opening the void. As with Simone Weil's affliction through the body, it would appear that the symmetry of necessity "required" Jung's felt-loss of Freud as "father" as a follow-on to the loss of his actual father. With only a few colleagues like Maeder still left in the "Zürich School" of psychoanalysis, without Freud, without Bleuler and the Burgholzli, and with his hopes of a university professorship lost, Jung was more or less professionally alone. As a wounded man knows that he is bleeding, so Jung, as developer of the word association experiment, would have known that on the level of the feeling function he was emotionally draining from the cascade of losses he had sustained. There are, therefore, possibly some personal overtones in his 1913 vision (which he in retrospect chose to take transpersonally as referring to the impending World War I).

> I squeezed past him [a dwarf with a leathery skin] through icy water to the other end of the cave where, on a projecting rock, I saw a glowing red crystal. I grasped the stone, lifted it, and discovered a hollow underneath. At first I could make out nothing, but then I saw that there was running water. In it a corpse floated by, a youth with blond hair and a wound in the head. He was followed by a gigantic black scarab and then by a red, newborn sun, rising up out of depths of the water. Dazzled by the light, I wanted to replace the stone upon the opening, but then a fluid welled out. It was blood. A thick jet of it leaped up, and I felt nauseated. It seemed to me that the blood continued to spurt for an unendurably long time.[41]

*Memories, Dreams, Reflections* is strangely inadequate (apparently by design) in its treatment of Jung's personal relationships. In discussing what sustained him during the "creative illness" years, he says things like: "I needed a point of support in 'this world,' and I may say that my family and my professional work were that to me."[42] It is almost certain that in his affliction, Jung, who was not inclined to celibacy, would have been vulnerable to the anima mediation afforded by the feeling relationship with Toni Wolff. Perhaps, her importance is implied in his reference to his "professional work," since she was his anima/collaborator. Like the relationship with Spielrein (which preceded it), Jung's intimacy with "the Fragrance," as he called Toni Wolff grew out of beginnings in treatment, flowered into professional affinity, and ran parallel to his marriage. Sabina Spielrein wrote of Jung's "preaching polygamy,"[43] and he seems to have practiced what he preached as part of his attempt at wholeness—although it cost him dearly in emotional complications accompanying the feeling function.

But Jung's counter-transference and personal experience of the anima access that women such as Spielrein and Wolff had to his soul were not lost on him. In 1945, in an essay on the transference that drew parallels between transference/counter-transference and alchemy, he expounded his *insider's* understanding of the relationship complications that may arise in the alchemical *coniunctio*. While the partnerings with Spielrein and Wolff, each a *soror mystica*, added emotional gravitas to Jung's search for wholeness, they also brought pain. Thus, speaking of individuation, he says: "The urge to become what one *is* is invincibly strong and you can always count on it, but that does not mean that things will necessarily turn out positively."[44]

Jung, his wife Emma, and Toni Wolff suffered both the "invincible urge to become what one is" and the consequent pitfalls inherent in their triangular relationship. The 1985 documentary film *Matter of Heart: The Extraordinary Journey of C. G. Jung* provides unusual insight into the psychic stress that each of these individuals felt, seen through the eyes of those who witnessed that time in their lives and speak candidly about it.

Despite their respective individuation sufferings, Jung was not psychoanalytically defensive with Wolff, as he had perhaps been in consulting Freud on the uncertainties surrounding his relationship with Spielrein. "Fathering himself," we might say, into awareness of the psyche's prospective quality, Jung trusted the psyche's leading in the case of Toni Wolff. Psychologically, this trust in itself marks a development in Jung's feeling function, because it entailed the painful valuing of Emma Jung and his marriage *vis-à-vis* Toni Wolff as professional collaborator and personal companion. This *increase in valuation* could be achieved only with sacrifice and suffering on the part of all three, and it helped lay the groundwork in trust necessary for Jung to hold together in the midst of his afflictions and, psychologically, enter the void.

Jung's relationship with Wolff had begun with her as a patient trusting him when she had lost her own father (another illustration of the symmetry of necessity, "like curing like"). She was arguably strong enough, virginal enough (in the sense of being her own woman, "belonging to no man"), to trust her own soul and sustain a full relationship with him. In his own highly-stressed condition, this must have been a godsend to Jung. Jung's tribute to Wolff after her death read, in Chinese glyphs: "Toni Wolff, Lotus, Nun, Mysterious ...."

Emma Jung trusted, though not always implicitly it would seem,[45] in the necessity of the shared soul-journey, and this is what made it possible for her late in life to thank Toni Wolff for doing for her husband what she herself could not do—a gesture that is a testament to her generosity of spirit.

We have already seen from Jung's letter to Maeder (quoted above) the kind of turmoil that Jung was going through. As the gravity of the triangular involvement bore down upon all three, Jung did not assess his soul-experience in psychoanalytic "acting-in" or "acting-out" terms, nor did he condemn it in conventional Christian moral terms. We may agree with Ellenberger that Jung's "breakdown" was a "creative illness," but Jung himself, committed as he was to an authentic science of the psyche,[46] chose to honor the prospective quality of the soul as a value engaging him in the love of these women. In itself, this is an achievement of feeling not to be underestimated. Where others may reductively see only the acted-out counter-transference of split-off family-of-origin projections, remarkably supported by the energy of both Emma Jung and Toni Wolff, Jung himself accepted the void of "unknowing." He reports saying to himself in those days: "Since I know nothing at all, I shall simply do whatever occurs to me. Thus I consciously submitted myself to the impulses of the unconscious."[47] We hear echoes of this in Simone Weil:

> To accept a void in ourselves is supernatural. Where is the energy to be found for an act which has nothing to counterbalance it? The energy has to come from elsewhere. Yet first there must be a tearing out, something desperate has to take place, the void must be created. Void: the dark night. Admiration, pity (most of all a mixture of the two) brings real energy. But this we must do without. A time has to be gone through without any reward, natural or supernatural.[48]

Jung felt the "tearing out" that Weil describes in the cascade of feeling-losses and uncertainties, and in the emotional suffering that came in their wake. Of necessity, as it were, his integrity was at stake. He had to face the pressure of uncertainty (imaged as tumbling blocks of stone) regarding whether or not he could *"believe"* in himself *vis-à-vis* his father complex once the cocoon spun by Freudian "ordination" had been sloughed off.

As if all of this were not enough, Jung had to contend with the problem of envy within the triangle itself (which we cannot develop here), as well as the envy generated in the Zürich of those days, evident in the letter to Maeder quoted above. Jung was an internationally known, married professional, coupled in the "anima" companionship of Toni Wolff with his wife's apparent acquiescence. The tabloids of that era would certainly *not* have run the headline: "Jung Engaged in Soul Research"!

As we try to understand how it is that affliction through feeling, Jung's undeveloped value function, brought about an initiatory, wholeness-generating experience for Jung, consider the projective identifications "put into" Jung by the two women involved, afflicting him with their sufferings in addition to his own. Inevitably, each woman would have brought her own family-of-origin expectations and moral conditioning to the triangle. In addition, Jung was dependent on Emma in terms of the financial resources she brought to their marriage. No one who wrote as much as he did could possibly have earned enough from a therapy practice to sustain the kind of life he led—McCormicks and Mellons notwithstanding. Emma Jung was also a "mother" on whom he could rely to look after his children and perhaps even himself. Jung confesses that in his childhood he had anxiety dreams about his mother.[49] In Emma Rauschenbach Jung found a woman who was a "rock" upon whom he and his family could depend. The gravity of her sufferings and the possibility of losing her through divorce or ill-health must have weighed heavily upon him, perhaps crushing him. One is likely to underestimate her importance in the triangle as the fulcrum upon which everything pivoted if one allows oneself to be taken in by the romance of Jung's anima involvements. Emma Jung's individuation sufferings appear to have come through the mother archetype, which she strongly mediated. In the traditional patriarchal culture in which she lived, she herself was reciprocally dependent upon her husband as a woman with young children needing a father.

Entering the void of his creative illness, Jung bound himself to the marital mast as an "Odysseus" who chose to answer the Siren's call (that is, the "confrontation with the unconscious" as he later labeled it) with Toni Wolff as anima companion and Emma Jung as the Penelope who waited at home. For her part, Toni Wolff trusted the individuation path that accompanied Jung's. Whatever sufferings may have afflicted her (a chain-smoking addiction to the nicotine among them), she wrote a monograph, *The Structural Forms of the Feminine*

*Psyche,*[50] to explore the roles that she and Emma Jung found themselves playing in the triangle.

In *Memories, Dreams, Reflections,* Jung chose to describe this time of affliction and initiation in somewhat impersonal terms, presumably so that he could preserve his image as a Kantian-style empirical scientist for whom the descent into the void was merely research into the psychology of religion. But *inter linea* there was much more to it than that.

Blessedly for him, and, by extension, all of us who have tried to learn from him, Jung experienced initiation into "grace" (to use Simone Weil's terminology) through the compensatory "wholeness response" of the unconscious. Jung demonstrated that the experience of the void is a psychological as well as a spiritual reality. As he puts it, "the unconscious is something that reacts."[51] "In a cul-de-sac [here one might substitute Simone Weil's word "void"], then only do you hear his voice,"[52] that is, the voice of what he came to call the "Two-Million-Year-Old Man," who first came to him as Elijah, then as Philemon, and finally as Ka.

One "official" description of what was transpiring in those days is to be found in Aniela Jaffé's essay "Was C. G. Jung a Mystic?" She writes:

> A deeply religious phase began after the separation from Freud, when Jung, then 37, turned his full attention and interest to the images emerging from the unconscious. A series of numinous dreams drove him to this introspection because Freudian psychoanalysis proved insufficient to interpret them. It was a dangerous venture to descend into the realm of the unconscious having no idea where the descent would lead. Jung was in fact spared neither suffering nor terror. This phase lasted more than four years, and he found himself again and again in danger of being overwhelmed by the unconscious and its numinous contents. The unconscious encountered Jung as a *tremendum,* and in retrospect in later writings he quoted the words of Paul several times: "It is terrible to fall into the hands of the living God." ... [L]ooking back, Jung regarded this ... mystical initiation as critical and life-changing. "The years when I was pursuing my inner images were the most important in my life—in them everything essential was decided. It all began then; the later details are only supplements and clarifications of the material that burst forth from the unconscious, and at first swamped me. It was the *prima materia* for a lifetime's work." (C. G. Jung, *Memories, Dreams, Reflections*, p. 191)[53]

It is, perhaps, understandable that Jaffé would want to protect Jung and "tidy up" the messiness of those days and the relationship issues that were part of them. But this fosters the illusion that only the "light" side of the god-image (if we use Jung's mythopoeic terminology) becomes incarnated in the lives of "great" individuals. Expurgation isn't of much value in grasping what really happened to Jung. Thus, Jaffé's speaking of Jung in this critical period as if he were involved merely in a program of stages that he simply had to get through is not very helpful. She writes:

> Integration of the maternal also altered his "soul-image," the anima. A younger anima figure emerged in place of a mother-anima. At that time he met Toni Wolff, who became his helper in the intellectual penetration of the world of psychic images and remained his helper until her death in 1953. Alchemically, she was his "soror mystica."[54]

Neat, clean—but not very helpful.

By Jung's own testimony, it is only through the *affliction* of shadow issues in our lives and the choices that we then make that we come to confront the "dark" side of the god-image in ourselves. How else could it "incarnate" and be wrestled with by consciousness in the struggle for integration and wholeness? Says Jung: "We must live out our own vision of life. And there will be error. If you avoid error you do not live; in a sense even it may be said that every life is a mistake, for *no one* has found the truth."[55]

By studying how exemplars like Jung and Weil negotiated the untidiness in their lives, we can learn how not to be shamed by the darkness that we face in our own. Says Weil:

> Our life is impossibility, absurdity. Everything we want contradicts the conditions or the consequences attached to it, every affirmation we put forward involves a contradictory affirmation, all our feelings are mixed up with their opposites. It is because we are a contradiction—being creatures—being God and infinitely other than God.
>
> Contradiction alone is the proof that we are not everything. Contradiction is our wretchedness, and the sense of our wretchedness is the sense of reality. For we do not invent our wretchedness. It is true. That is why we have to value it. ...
>
> Impossibility is the door of the supernatural. We can but knock at it. It is someone else who opens.[56]

Speaking of the ordeal of "wretched impossibility," where one encounters the Great Man (or Two-Million-Year-Old Man), Jung declares:

> You learn about yourself against the Great Man .... This is the way through things, things that look desperate and unanswerable. ... There one is alone, as one should be, with the highest ethical distinctions. Ethics is not convention; ethics is between myself and the Great Man [the Two-Million-Year-Old Man]. During this process, you learn about ethics versus morality. The unconscious gives you that peculiar *twist* that makes the way possible.
>
> The way is ineffable. One cannot, one *must* not, betray it. It is like the way of Zen—like a sharp knife, and also twisting like a serpent. One needs faith, courage, and no end of honesty and patience.[57]

## IV

Simone Weil's initiation invites us to "retrench," using the traditional language of an "intelligence enlightened by love" (her definition of *faith*). She asks us to understand the limits of intelligence itself and, in faith, "wait" for God to enter spiritually from the terrible psychological experience of affliction (*mysterium tremendum*) and the void thus created. The void *is* a void because it is both a psychological "abyss" and a spiritual dryness that flattens the soul. But it is also the precinct of the divine because God is a *no-thing-ness*, God is found in the void, in "nothing-ness."

Likewise, Jung's initiation is an invitation to have "faith" in the deep unconscious *Self* as something that will inevitably "react" to produce a "wholeness response" through the voice of the Two-Million-Year-Old Man—the "voice" of our evolutionary legacy resonating in its own time with both psychological depth and spiritual "lift."[58]

Both initiations point to a similar phenomenology: the necessity of the void and of affliction in bringing about compensatory wholeness-generating mystical experience. However, their "outcomes" are different. One is reminded of Aquinas's saying that God "governs free beings freely," by which he may have meant that for human beings governance occurs in the terms on which it is sought. This may also account for the premonitory "Christian" governance that Simone Weil finds in Plato's truly "just" man of *The Republic*.

Weil's initiation is in terms of her individuation through her uncompromising (hysterical [?]) perfectionism. Her objective is to get out of this world as quickly as possible since "our existence is made up only of ... [God's] waiting for our acceptance *not* to exist."[59] She would not have us be deluded by imagination "filling up" the gaps with "illusions," such as the "unreal" objects of desire. One can readily see that her individuation, principled and uncompromising, like that of Jesus himself, placed her—like him—on a collision course with the compromises that "average" life in collective settings demands.

Jung, on the other hand, is more tolerant as far as our "wretchedness" is concerned. He maintained that analytic attention in the therapeutic dyad to our illusory imaginings and "errors" heartens us to tease out what the "underlying trend" in our lives *truly* is. It helps us to grasp that our "wholeness" is beyond intellectual understanding, and is in fact an encounter with the "Two-Million-Year-Old Man." Psychologically, this "compensation" is generated from the unknown depths of the *Self.* We remind ourselves that we are naming the unknown by the more unknown. The compensation comes *in the terms on which one enters the void.* Jung had his "confrontation with the unconscious" to find out whether the compensation would come while his ego-structure was gripped by the *mysterium tremendum,* with no guarantees, of course. Thus, he is a testament to allowing initiatory wholeness to orchestrate itself through the afflictions that accompany individuation, since, like Simone Weil, that is precisely what he did.

Archimandrite Sophrony, speaking of St. Silouan, the Athonite, puts it this way:

> The battle-ground of the spiritual struggle is, first and foremost, man's own heart; and he who would explore his own heart will appreciate the prophet David's reflection that "the heart is deep." The real life ... is lived in this deep heart, hidden not only from alien eyes but also in its fullness, from the owner of the heart himself. He who enters these secret recesses finds himself face to face with the mystery of being. Anyone who has ever given himself over with a pure heart to contemplation of his inner self knows how impossible it is to detect the spiritual processes of the heart, because in its profundity the heart touches upon that state of being where there *are* no processes.[60]

---

## *NOTES*

[1] C. G. Jung, *C. G. Jung Speaking: Interviews and Encounters*, ed. William McGuire and R. F. C. Hull (Princeton, NJ: Princeton University Press, 1977), p. 97.

[2] Simone Weil, "Spiritual Autobiography," in *Simone Weil Reader*, ed. George Panichas (Wakefield, RI: Moyer Bell Limited, 1977), p. 24.

[3] Simone Weil, *Gravity and Grace*, trans. Emma Crawford and Mario von der Ruhr (New York: Routledge, 2002), p. 32.

[4] Simone Weil, *The Notebooks of Simone Weil*, trans. Arthur Wills, vol. 1 (London: Routledge, Chapman & Hall, 1959), p. 55.

[5] Weil, *Gravity*, p. 104.

[6] *Ibid.*, p. 105.

[7] *Ibid.*, pp. 32-33.

[8] Aniela Jaffé, *Was C. G. Jung A Mystic? and Other Essays* (Einsiedeln: Daimon Verlag, 1989), p. 69.

[9] Weil, *Gravity*, pp. 40-41.

[10] Marcus Aurelius, *Meditations* IV, 23, quoted in "Marcus Aurelius," Wikiquote, 2008, http://en.wikiquote.org/wiki/Marcus_Aurelius_Antoninus.

[11] Weil uses this term to mean "to make something created pass into the uncreated" and differentiates "decreation" from "destruction," which she defines as "to make something created pass into nothingness" (*Gravity*, p. 32).

[12] Weil, *Gravity*, p. 33.

[13] Catherine Soanes, ed., *The Compact Oxford English Dictionary of Current English* (Oxford: Oxford University Press, 2005).

[14] Weil, *Gravity*, p. 46.

[15] *Ibid.*, p. 12.

[16] Marian Baynes, "A Talk with Students at the Institute," in *C. G. Jung Speaking: Interviews and Encounters*, ed. William McGuire and R. F. C. Hull (Princeton, NJ: Princeton University Press, 1977), pp. 359ff.

[17] Weil, *Gravity*, pp. 6-7.

[18] Louise Hay, *Heal Your Body* (Carlsbad: Hay House, 2003), p. 39.

[19] *Ibid.*, p. 49.

[20] Weil, *Gravity*, p. 22.

[21] Thorwald Dethlefsen and Rüdiger Dahlke, *The Healing Power of Illness: The Meaning of Symptoms and How to Interpret Them*, trans. Peter Lemesurier (Rockport, MA: Element Books, 1990), p. 158.

[22] C. G. Jung, "Answer to Job," in *Psychology and Religion, The Collected Works of C. G. Jung*, trans. R. F. C. Hull, vol. 11 (London: Routledge & Kegan Paul, 1958), § 620.

[23] Henri F. Ellenberger, *The Discovery of the Unconscious: The History and Evolution of Dynamic Pyschiatry* (New York: Basic Books, 1970), pp. 672ff.

[24] Sonu Shamdasani, *Jung Stripped Bare by His Biographers, Even* (London: Karnac Books, 2005), p. 69.

[25] C. G. Jung, *Memories, Dreams, Reflections*, ed. Aniela Jaffé, trans. Richard and Clara Winston (London: Collins and Routledge & Kegan Paul, 1963), p. 171.

[26] Dr. Mario Jacoby, personal communication.

[27] Shamdasani, *Jung Stripped Bare*, pp. 10f.

[28] Jung, *Memories*, p. 181.

[29] *Ibid.*, p. 17l.

[30] *Ibid.*, p. 165.

[31] Aldo Carotenuto, *A Secret Symmetry: Sabina Spielrein between Jung and Freud*, trans. Arno Pomerans, John Shepley, and Krishna Winston (New York: Pantheon Books, 1982), p. 13.

[32] Jung, *Memories*, p. 178.

[33] *Ibid.*, p. 173.

[34] Shamdasani, *Jung Stripped Bare*, pp. 40f.

[35] Deirdre Bair, *Jung: A Biography* (London: Little, Brown & Co., 2004), p. 154.

[36] Liz Greene, *Saturn: A New Look at an Old Devil* (York Beach, ME: Samuel Weiser, 1986).

[37] It is a topic in itself to speculate about Jung's later effect upon psychoanalysis and vice versa. There are many vexing questions such as the effect of Jung's problematic relationship with Karl Abraham. Abraham had worked under Jung at the Burgholzli, and apparently published ideas about infantile sexuality that Jung claimed were *his*, formulated through his work with Spielrein, without crediting Jung—a cause for resentment on Jung's part. Abraham later became the analyst for Melanie Klein, well known for her theories about infantile sexuality. See Hannah Segal, *An Introduction to the Work of Melanie Klein* (New York: Basic Books, 1964). Or, consider the reciprocal influence of Klein's last analysand, Donald Meltzer, and the British Jungian, Michael Fordham, who wrote *Freud, Jung, Klein—The Fenceless Field* (London: Routledge, 1995), on each other.

[38] Jung, *Memories*, pp. 96ff.

[39] Shamdasani, *Jung Stripped Bare*, p. 3.

[40] Quoted in Sonu Shamdasani, *Jung and the Making of Modern Psychology: The Dream of a Science* (Cambridge, UK: Cambridge University Press, 2003), pp. 1-2.

[41] Jung, *Memories*, p. 173.

[42] *Ibid.*, p. 181.

[43] Bair, p. 152.

[44] Baynes, p. 359.

[45] Bair claims that Emma Jung seriously contemplated divorce at least three times in the course of her marriage to Jung (Bair, p. 157).

[46] Cf. Shamdasani, *Jung and the Making of Modern Psychology.*

[47] Jung, *Memories*, p. 168.

[48] Weil, *Gravity and Grace*, p. 11.

[49] Jung, *Memories*, p. 59.

[50] Toni Wolff, *The Structural Forms of the Feminine Psyche*, trans. Paul Watzlawick (Zurich: C. G. Jung-Institut Zürich, 1992). First published as "Strukturformen der weiblichen Psyche," in *Der Psychologie*, Heft 7/8, Band III, ed. G. H. Graber (Bern, 1951).

[51] Baynes, p. 360.

[52] *Ibid.*, p. 359.

[53] Jaffé, *Was C. G. Jung A Mystic?* p. 25.

[54] Aniela Jaffé, *From the Life and Work of C. G. Jung* (Einsiedeln: Daimon Verlag, 1989), p. 174.

[55] C. G. Jung, "Is Analytical Psychology a Religion?" in *Speaking*, p. 98. (Italics added.)

[56] Weil, *Gravity*, p.95.

[57] Baynes, p. 361.

[58] Cf. James Hillman, "Peaks and Vales," in *Puer Papers* (Dallas, TX: Spring Publications, 1979).

[59] Weil, *Gravity and Grace*, p. 32.

[60] Archimandrite Sophrony Sakharov, *St. Silouan the Athonite* (Crestwood, NY: St. Vladimir's Seminary Press, 1991), p. 10.

Dariane Pictet is a Swiss Jungian analyst in private practice in London. She trained at the C. G. Jung-Institut Zürich and lectures at ISAP. She is a Visiting Faculty member of Regents College and a senior analyst in GAPS. She is a member of the Marion Woodman Foundation and facilitates Body-Soul affiliated workshops. She is an Associate Member of IGAP and has edited two anthologies of poetry.

# 13

# Rumi: Poet of the Heart

*Dariane Pictet*

Even as the contemporary rise of Islamic fundamentalism is causing great concern in the West, a compensatory phenomenon is being manifested in the corresponding rise in popularity of the Sufi mystic and poet Mawlana Jalal-ad-Din Rumi. Not only is he the most-read poet in America today, but UNESCO named 2007 "The Year of Rumi." *The Mathnawi*, his major work, which some call the Koran of Sufism, consisting of 24,660 couplets in seven books, discusses metaphysics, religion, and ethics. When I first read Rumi, I recognized in him the same fierce passion with which Jung explored human complexity in the arcane recesses of psychology, mythology, and religion.

Last year was the 800th anniversary of Rumi's birth. He was born in 1207 in Balkh, now in Afghanistan but then a part of the Persian cultural empire. In fact, Balkh had been a center of Muslim culture since the 8th century. Rumi grew up the son of an eminent Sufi scholar; his father, Bahauddin, was a religious teacher in a community that basked in religious tolerance and cultural diversity. According to Rumi, "there are Sufis everywhere."[1] For him, Sufism transcends religious systems and frontiers; it describes a particular orientation to the divine.

> Not Christian or Jew or Muslim, not Hindu,
> Buddhist, sufi, or zen. Not any religion
>
> or cultural system. I am not from the East
> or the West, not out of the ocean or up

from the ground, not natural or ethereal, not
composed of elements at all. I do not exist,

am not an entity in this world or in the next,
did not descend from Adam and Eve or any

origin story. My place is placeless, a trace
of the traceless. Neither body or soul.

I belong to the beloved, have seen the two
worlds as one and that one call to and know,

first, last, outer, inner, only that
breath breathing human being.[2]

As Genghis Khan's armies were threatening the town of Balkh, Rumi's father decided it was time to leave (Balkh was subsequently destroyed by the Mongols), and the family began an extended period of wandering throughout the Middle East before settling down in Konya, Eastern Anatolia, where Rumi lived for the remainder of his life.

Listen to the story told by the reed,
of being separated.

"Since I was cut from the reedbed,
I have made this crying sound.

Anyone apart from someone he loves
understands what I say.

Anyone pulled from a source
longs to go back ...."[3]

Jung said that "the work of the poet comes to meet the spiritual need of the society in which he lives."[4] Rumi's poetry is characterized by longing and thus appeals to those of us who have loved and lost, who have known separation and exile, and/or embraced the metaphor of seekers in search of wholeness. As the reed longs for the river bed, so the exiled soul longs for the Beloved. Longing, if we engage with it, can bring us home to the place in us that is always whole. We don't dwell there; we move in and out of it.

At the age of thirty-seven, Rumi had an encounter that changed his life: he met a much older itinerant dervish by the name of Shamz of Tabriz. This crucial meeting, which some say caused Rumi to faint, marked the beginning of the dissolution of Rumi's persona as an established and revered religious leader and teacher in his community.

If anyone had once, even once, glimpsed Your Face of
 Lightning,
They'd spend every second stammering Your praise.
Each moment, like the angels, they'd offer their heart to
 Your Fire,
Each moment, like the angels, they'd be reborn in You.[5]

The meeting with Shamz marked the beginning of Rumi's process of inner change. What Rumi saw in Shamz sparked one of the most creative relationships in literary history. If the ego can never contain the immensity of Love, it can nevertheless relate to an object that reveals that immensity to it. Shamz was, for Rumi, the human face of divine love, and Rumi spent years deepening this relationship, expanding his own heart's capacity to contain the flow of love that was released by Shamz's presence.

Rumi reminds us of the gentle attention that lovers bestow on each other, the tenderness of the Beloved. In these exalted moments, the elusive divine befriends us and discloses the fullness and radiance of Being; we know that we are profoundly received and accepted and known.

The connection to the Friend
is secret and very fragile.

The image of that friendship
is in how *you* love, the grace

and delicacy, the subtle talking
together in full prostration,

outside of time. When you're
there, remember the fierce

courtesy of the one with you.[6]

Robert Johnson, who has explored the phenomenon of romantic love, notes that when we fall in love, we demand of our lover that he or she complete us, make us whole. Falling in love, which I am sure all of us have experienced at least once, opens in us a longing to dissolve in the other. Johnson suggests that we begin to recognize that the longing that fuels the experience of falling in love is invariably sourced in the divine. It is the transcendent that is manifested to the gaze of each lover. Unlike regressive longing, which enfolds us back into the womb of the Great Mother, this prospective longing propels us towards individuation. As Johnson puts it:

> This little ego-mind, surrounded by the vastness of the unconscious, has a high and noble task, a special destiny to live out. Its role in this evolution is to integrate more and more of the unconscious until the conscious mind truly reflects the wholeness of the self.[7]

This wholeness is what Rumi might call the Beloved. However, projections plague the unanalyzed shadow with its mirroring duplicity. We are not able to embrace the vastness of what is meant by love until we have polished our heart of all its impurities, our human frailties and character defects.

The Sufi path begins with a process that is paralleled in Jungian psychology by the exploration of the personal shadow. As Jung described it, we start by projecting the hidden part of ourselves, our animus or anima, with all its shadowy content, onto those we love. As we get to know ourselves better and free ourselves from some of our blindness, these projections begin to reflect the wider Self. The Sufi master Vaughan-Lee states that "[p]sychological work is a necessary preliminary stage on the path, in particular the work on the shadow …,"[8] which encompasses the realm of the seven deadly sins, such as greed and sloth and envy, and the entire spectrum of human failings. If this groundwork is not done, the spiritual energies could unbalance us; the bright light can damage an ego that has not been forged into a solid container.

In analysis, the process of the development of the ego-Self axis begins to take place when the person can relate to something greater than himself or herself, when the ego can begin to harness the wisdom of Nature. This dialogue with this wider perspective we call the individuation process. By virtue of analytical work, through transference and relationship to both the analyst and the inner world, the Self is constellated.

For Rumi, the heart is the center of all transformation, the seat of spirituality and compassion, and only a polished heart can reflect divine reality. This wider perspective is opened by the heart's longing for union; his poetry speaks directly to the soul and awakens its longing for union with the ground of reality. If we hear this call, our own longing is constellated and it becomes our guide to the Beloved.

> Those with mirrorlike hearts
> do not depend on fragrance and color:
> they behold Beauty in the moment.
> They've cracked open the shell of knowledge

and raised the banner
of the eye of certainty.
Thought is gone in a flash of light.[9]

The Beloved and the Self may not be exactly the same thing, but this is in part because of the limitations of language. The immensity of what is encompassed by these images cannot be fully grasped by the ego; it goes beyond intellect, it is a lived experience.

How can you ever hope to know the Beloved
Without becoming in every cell the Lover?
And when you are the Lover at last, you don't care.
Whatever you know, or don't—only Love is real.[10]

Rumi met in Shamz the Friend who mirrored the Beloved; his relationship to Shamz was that of one who is being guided or mentored. This relationship between mentor and mentored can be seen as a metaphor for the Self entering into a creative dialogue with the ego. Corbin says that what the Sufi prays for from the depth of his being is a messenger, a teacher of truth, a companion and spiritual guide, who points the way home.[11] Shamz of Tabriz was the spiritual guide who led Rumi to the burning pyre of transformation. This is a process of ego-purification, which involves silencing the voices of the collective, of the false self, so that we can engage with the world in a freer and more spontaneous way.

In Islam, the Khidr figure embodies the archetype of the psychopomp, the guide of souls: "My name is Khidr, ... I am sent by Him, whom we both venerate. Do you recognize me? I am also yourself, the best in you, your innermost desire—and I have come to lead you home."[12] In his discussion on the 18th Sura of the Koran, Jung says:

> Khidr may well be a symbol of the Self. His qualities symbolize him as such; He is the "Long-lived One" who continually renews himself, like Elijah. Like Osiris he is dismembered .... He is analogous to the second Adam ... he is a counsellor, a Paraclete, "Brother Khidr". Anyway, Moses looks up to him for instruction. Then follow these incomprehensible deeds which show how ego-consciousness reacts to the superior guidance of the Self through the twists and turns of fate. ... Khidr symbolizes not only the higher wisdom but also a way of acting which is in accord with this wisdom and transcends reason. Anyone hearing such a mystery tale will recognize himself in the questing Moses

> and forgetful Joshua, and the tale shows him how the immortality-bringing rebirth comes about ....[13]

The spiritual journey leads to an inner silence, which for Rumi is an essential stilling down of the mind's chatter (what the Hindus call monkey mind), the inner monologue with its endless meanderings through the valleys of doubt, insecurities, and desires.

> Inside this new love, die.
> Your way begins on the other side.
> Become the sky.
> Take an axe to the prison wall.
> Escape.
> Walk out like someone suddenly born into color.
> Do it now.
> You're covered with thick cloud.
> Slide out the side. Die,
> and be quiet. Quietness is the surest sign
> that you've died.
> Your old life was a frantic running
> from silence.
>
> The speechless full moon
> comes out now.[14]

Spiritual discipline is necessary for lifting the veil between the very small vision of ego-consciousness and the infinitely expanded dimension of the heart that is the Self. This point begins in analysis when, freed from the reductive minuteness of biographical work, its trajectory turns towards future possibilities. When the ego is dislodged from its inflated position, it begins to stretch and widen to integrate the new perspective and possibilities that the Self reveals to consciousness. And, crucially, it begins to admit that "it doesn't know," and this opens up a field of wonder at the mysterious unfolding of the landscape of existence. This state is characterized by a deepening compassion towards the human condition—its pain and suffering—mingled with joy for the richness and beauty that is increasingly being revealed.

> I am so small I can barely be seen.
> How can this great love be inside me?
>
> Look at your eyes. They are small,
> *But they see enormous things.*[15]
> (Italics in original.)

Rumi's family and community were suspicious and jealous of the intimacy between the scholar and the wandering dervish and forced Shamz into exile. Rumi's grief was intense and this initiated a period of disorientation that fired his individuation process.

> A certain person came to the Friend's door
> and knocked.
> "Who's there?"
> "It's me."
> The Friend answered, "Go away. There's no place
> for raw meat at this table."
>
> The individual went wandering for a year.
> Nothing but the fire of separation
> can change hypocrisy and ego. The person returned
> completely cooked,
> walked up and down in front of the Friend's house,
> gently knocked.
> "Who is it?"
> "You."
> "Please come in, my self,
> there's no place in this house for two."[16]

Duality must be dissolved for an experience of mystical rapture. When the ego "comes first" the Beloved cannot find a dwelling place—there is no room at the inn. To Jung, the Self is not only the center, but also the circumference that encloses consciousness and the unconscious, and it relates us to a timeless perspective. To Rumi, the Lover is the Love and the horizon and everything within.[17] Corbin also tells us that "the personal interior guide ... who rules the mystic's inner horizon, is the symbolon par excellence, the figure with whom one's most intimate personal being symbolises; it is the Self reached through self-knowledge."[18] What Jung refers to as "the passionate religious eros of Islamic mysticism"[19] is evident in Rumi's poetry (he often either ended or signed his poems with Shamz's name, which incidentally means "the Sun," the source of all life and light).

Eventually, Rumi begged his son Walad to find Shamz and bring him back. Walad traveled to Damascus and returned with Shamz. As the two locked themselves up again and engaged in conversations lasting days and nights, weeks and more, the resentment in the community returned, and one day Shamz disappeared forever, some say killed by Rumi's youngest son.

Following the disappearance of Shamz, Rumi experienced profound loss. In his sorrow, he began spinning around a pole, which, some say, gave rise to the practice of the whirling dervishes of the Medlelevi Sufi order that Rumi founded. The Sema is a sacred dance that embodies the experience of turning away from grief to Love and the transformational process of becoming the Lover—turning away from illusion, returning to the Beloved.

> Dance, when you're broken open.
> Dance, if you've torn the bandage off.
> Dance in the middle of the fighting.
> Dance in your blood.
> Dance, when you are perfectly free.[20]

Although Rumi's entourage began fearing for his sanity, this crucial period of disorientation gave birth to the mystic and poet we know today. Psychological dismemberment is part of deeper inner change and can constellate the "wounded healer" of the shamanistic tradition. Jung's separation from Freud initiated a period of emotional turmoil, which Jung himself referred to as his "confrontation with the unconscious"—and which gave rise to, among other things, his dialogues with Philemon, the *Red Book*, and the *Septem Sermones*. Jung described the period from 1912 to 1919, which he experienced as a *nekyia* (a Greek word that denotes a descent into the underworld), as the one from which all his creative work arose.[21] Near the end of his life, Jung wrote:

> It has taken me virtually forty-five years to distil within the vessel of my scientific work the things I experienced and wrote down at that time. …
>
> The years when I was pursuing my inner images were the most important in my life—in them everything essential was decided. It all began then; the later details are only supplements and clarifications of the material that burst forth from the unconscious, and at first swamped me. It was the *prima materia* for a lifetime's work.[22]

Rumi described his own journey of spiritual transformation as: "first I was raw, then I was cooked, and then I burned."[23]

Some of you may be familiar with the work of the Swiss theologian Lytta Basset. A few years ago her son committed suicide. She kept a diary in which she describes with almost unbearable honesty the chaos she was thrown into by this tragedy. Yet through the suffering—

which she faced with astonishing courage—little by little, out of her broken heart, healing images emerged spontaneously in her dreams.

The shock of her experience opened up what Corbin refers to as the *mundus imaginalis*, the realm between the intellect and the senses; described as the dimension where "the spiritual takes body and the body becomes spiritual."[24] This point of transformation between body and thought is what Jung calls the psychoid realm. It is there that soma becomes psyche and vice versa. It is from this spiritual corporeality (or corporeal spirituality) that healing symbols emerge in dreams or in active imagination. These images are not accessed through the will, but erupt spontaneously from the depths and serve to point consciousness in the direction of an experience of oneness and a resolution of the tension of the opposites.

In the openness of her grief, Lytta Basset could suspend disbelief and engage with the images spontaneously rising in her heart. Synchronistic events, meaningful coincidences, abounded in her daily reality, awakening in her the felt-sense of a loving attendance. Her son began appearing in her dreams, at first in a state of sleep. Her reaction, as recorded in her diary, was:

> If he doesn't wake up, if he doesn't find his place in my terrestrial relational space, then what use is Jesus' resurrection to me? ... [I]f the dead don't awaken, then Christ is not awake either.[25] (My translation.)

She goes on to describe the imaginal process through which her son awakens from his sleeping state in her dreams, and the corresponding awakening of a Living Presence in her heart. Jung touched upon this sense of a Living Presence when he was asked if he believed in God; he paused and said, "I do not believe, I know." He described this "knowing" as a living relationship between ego and Self. And, because it is oriented to the Beloved, it enriches everyday reality and brings joy to the heart of darkness.

> When your chest is free of your limiting ego,
> Then you will see the ageless Beloved.
> You can not see yourself without a mirror;
> Look at the Beloved. He is the brightest mirror.[26]

Rumi says, "I would die into the love I have for you."[27] Dying into love is completely different from dying for love; one cannot physically die to resurrect another. But, as Lytta Basset surrendered to the experience, as she made space for the Other, the Beloved appeared in the polished mirror of her heart. She describes witnessing the parallel process of seeing her son awaken in her heart's eye and the felt-sense of the "Awakened One" taking up residence in her. The Beloved stood between them, protecting her from the engulfing longing to merge with her son, an overwhelming force pulling her towards death. This kind of experience dissolves the dualities of living and dead, inner and outer.

> I have lived on the lip of insanity,
> wanting to know reasons,
> knocking on a door.
> It opens.
> I've been knocking from the inside![28]

One can characterize the *unio mystica* between the Lover and the Beloved as a union that leads beyond the confines of conventional morality. The death of ego attachments is an alchemical process that must precede rebirth into the Beloved. The Heart is the arena of nonduality, where Lover and Beloved dissolve into oneness. When we operate from the heart, we feel compassion, we forgive, we respond with spontaneity and conscience.

> Out beyond ideas of wrongdoing and rightdoing,
> there is a field. I'll meet you there.[29]

To be an individual means to be able to opt out of conformity, to see the world in a completely new way. It asks that we trust the images and the feelings that arise in us and allow ourselves to "know" that they are real. Corbin points out that "the vast world of Imagination, the world of Soul proper, falls into disgrace ... [when] it is identified with the imaginary, with the unreal."[30] Lytta Basset seems to have accepted the challenge that her inner vision posed to rationality. This demands a sense of reverence for the mystery of existence that lies beyond any rational understanding.

> This being human is a guest house.
> Every morning a new arrival.
>
> A joy, a depression, a meanness,
> some momentary awareness comes
> as an unexpected visitor.
>
> Welcome and entertain them all!
> Even if they're a crowd of sorrows,
> who violently sweep your house
> empty of its furniture,

still, treat each guest honorably.
He may be clearing you out
for some new delight.

The dark thought, the shame, the malice,
meet them at the door laughing,
and invite them in.

Be grateful for whoever comes,
because each has been sent
as a guide from beyond.[31]

Rumi, like Jung, honored all aspects of human experience, for he knew them to be pregnant with meaning. In this poem, Rumi is telling us that our moods—our visitors—are teleological; they are not diseases to be healed, or neuroses to be cured, but purposeful encounters on the individuation path. If we can envisage life in this way, then everything that happens to us is significant and presents an opportunity for transformation. The inner journey is an opening to a deeper presence, which relieves terror with trust.

There is a way between voice and presence
where information flows.

In disciplined silence it opens.
With wandering talk it closes.[32]

The mystical path is not for everyone; it takes strenuous discipline and a solid container not to fly away on the wings of spirit. It demands the sacrifice of ideal and ambition. Rapture is forged by humbling prayer and service.

Every thirst gets satisfied except
that of these fish, the mystics,

who swim a vast ocean of grace
still somehow longing for it!

No one lives in that without
being nourished every day.

But if someone doesn't want to hear the
song of the reed flute,

it's best to cut conversation
short, say good-bye, and leave.[33]

Rumi's poetry offers burning beauty and joy if we allow it to penetrate and seed us with its longing. Rumi's call to passion urges us to awaken from our sleep, to reach beyond our usual words, into the silence of the depths; it calls us to listen for another melody, infinitely more beautiful, infinitely more nourishing than the trivial clatter that surrounds us. It calls us to love and compassion, insight and depth.

There is a saying that God chose to hide in the human heart, because it is in our search for the Beloved that we do our becoming. Rumi's poetry directs us back to our heart, where the Beloved awaits, hidden in the depth of our longing.

---

## *NOTES*

[1] Coleman Barks, *The Essential Rumi* (San Francisco: HarperOne, 2004), p. 34.

[2] *Ibid.*, p. 32.

[3] *Ibid.*, pp. 17-18.

[4] C. G. Jung, *Modern Man in Search of a Soul* (New York: Harcourt, Brace & World, 1961), pp. 168-171.

[5] Andrew Harvey, *Light upon Light: Inspirations from Rumi* (Berkeley, CA: North Atlantic Books, 1996), p. 39.

[6] Rumi, "Fierce Courtesy," in *The Glance: Songs of Soul-Meeting*, trans. Coleman Barks (New York: Penguin, 1999), p. 41.

[7] Robert A. Johnson, *We: Understanding the Psychology of Romantic Love* (New York: HarperOne, 1985), p. 4.

[8] Llewellyn Vaughan-Lee, *Catching the Thread: Sufism, Dreamwork, and Jungian Psychology* (Inverness, CA: The Golden Sufi Center, 1998), p. xiv.

[9] Rumi, "The Six-Faced Mirror," Mathnawi I, 3492-3494, trans. Kabir Helminski and Camille Helminski, in *The Rumi Collection*, ed. Kabir Helminski (Boston, MA: Shambhala Publications, 1998), p. 83.

[10] Harvey, p. 17.

[11] Henry Corbin, "Mystic Ethos and Prophetology," in *The Dream and Human Societies: The Visionary Dream of Islamic Spirituality*, ed. Gustave E. von Grunebaum and Roger Caillois (Berkeley, CA: University of California Press, 1966), p. 383.

[12] Nizami Ganjavi, *The Story of the Seven Princesses* (London: Cassirer, 1976), p. 123.

[13] C. G. Jung, "Concerning Rebirth," in *The Archetypes and the Collective Unconscious, The Collected Works of C. G. Jung*, trans. R. F.

C. Hull (Princeton, NJ: Princeton University Press, 1950/1977), vol. 9i, § 248 (all future references to Jung's *Collected Works*, abbreviated to *CW*, will be with chapter titles followed by volume and paragraph numbers).

[14] Barks *Essential Rumi*, p. 22.

[15] *Ibid.*, p. 279.

[16] *Ibid.*, p. 87.

[17] Coleman Barks, trans., *Rumi: Voice of Longing*, audio recording, Sounds True, W492D.

[18] Henry Corbin, "The Safeguard of the Mystic," *Parabola* 12, no. 4 (1987): 38.

[19] Jung, "Concerning Rebirth," *CW* 9i, § 258.

[20] Coleman Barks, *A Year with Rumi: Daily Readings* (New York: HarperCollins, 2006), p. 289.

[21] C. G. Jung, *Memories, Dreams, Reflections*, ed. Aniela Jaffé, trans. Richard and Clara Winston (New York: Vintage, 1965), p. 192.

[22] *Ibid.*, p. 199.

[23] Barks, *Voice of Longing*.

[24] Henry Corbin, *Alone with the Alone: Creative Imagination in the Sufism of Ibn 'Arabi* (Princeton, NJ: Princeton University Press, 1998), p. 4.

[25] Lytta Basset, *Ce lien qui ne meurt jamais* (Paris: Albin Michel, 2007), p. 136.

[26] Shahram Shiva, "When Your Chest is Free," in *Rumi: Thief of Sleep* (Prescott, AZ: Hohm Press, 2000), p. 77. For more on Rumi, go to www.rumi.net.

[27] Barks, *Voice of Longing*.

[28] Barks, *Essential Rumi*, p. 281.

[29] *Ibid.*, p. 36.

[30] Corbin, "Safeguard," p. 34.

[31] *Ibid.*, p. 109.

[32] *Ibid.*, p. 32.

[33] *Ibid.*, p. 19.

Bernard Sartorius, Lic. theol., received his degree in theology from the University of Geneva in 1965 and worked for several years as a Protestant minister, first in a parish and then in youth work. He received his training as an analyst at the C. G. Jung-Institut Zürich, getting his diploma in 1974. Since then, he has maintaind a private analytic practice, initially in Geneva, and, since 1997, in Lucerne and Zürich. He is a training analyst at ISAPZURICH. His publications include a book about the Orthodox Church, and several papers (published in the journal *La Vouivre*, Lausanne) on various subjects of interest to him, including an article entitled "A Pilgrimage to Mecca."

14

# A Glance at Ibn 'Arabi's *Tarjuman al-Ashwaq* (*The Interpreter of Desires*)

*Bernard Sartorius*

That I had to preface this lecture with Arabic Sufi music indicates from the very outset how difficult it is to speak intellectually on this topic and how necessary it is, therefore, to consider it in a spiritual atmosphere. A non-rationalistic spirit is a precondition for understanding (in the deep sense, understanding with the heart) even the merest skimming of the surface of the *Tarjuman al-Ashwaq* (in English, *The Interpreter of Desires*), one of the numerous writings by Ibn 'Arabi, the *Sheikh al-Akbar*, the Greatest Sheikh, as he is still called in the Muslim world.

Just a very brief sketch of Ibn 'Arabi's life and work:

- 1165: Born in Murcia, Spain; youth spent in Seville.
- 1190: First vision "of all the prophets" in Cordoba.
- 1193: First trip to the Maghreb—Tunis.
- 1194: Back in Seville, first major book, *Book of the Contemplation*.
- 1195-1196: With his sister in Fez, Morocco; writes *Night Journey* and *Setting of the Stars*.
- 1201: Last visit to Tunis; takes final leave of Spain and moves eastward.
- 1202: In Mecca; receives and starts writing his major work, the *Futuhat al-Makkia* (*Meccan Revelations*), then spends time in Cairo and Damascus.
- 1214: In Mecca; writes the *Tarjuman al-Ashwaq*.

- 1216-1223: Long stay in Anatolia; meets—maybe even marries—the widow of the Sufi Mawlana Jalal ad-Din Muhammad Rumi.
- 1223: Settles in Syria, first in Aleppo, then, till the end of his life, in Damascus; has vision of the Prophet (Muhammad), which inspires the book *Fusus al-Hikam* (*Wisdom of the Prophets*); completes *Futuhst al-Maqqia* (*Revelation in Mecca*)—around 14,000 pages.
- 1240: Dies in Damascus, possibly as a result of injuries received from an attack by a fundamentalist of his time.
- His tomb in Damascus: a Presence.
- Private life: Two or three wives; at least three children.

This biographical sketch reveals two important features of Ibn 'Arabi's life that illustrate his perception of reality, including the reality of the heart: (1) a continual moving from one location to another (life is in its very essence movement and not fixity); and (2) a persistence of visions throughout his life (in his youth, later in Mecca, and then, towards the end, in Syria) indicating—whether one believes that the visions came from the Beyond or not—that for Ibn 'Arabi life receives its ultimate content from a reality other than the one accessible to normal consciousness, and this gives us another angle from which to envisage reality than the usual ego perspective. We will bear in mind these two basic presuppositions about life—that it is essentially fluid and that it receives its reality from a Reality beyond everyday reality—when looking, as we shall now try to do, at the *Tarjuman al-Aswhaq* and its bearing on our main topic here in Beatenberg, *Intimacy: Venturing the Uncertainties of the Heart.*

*Tarjuman al-Ashwaq*, which consists of 61 poems and commentaries on the poems (written later), has Love, indeed, as its theme—real passionate love for a real young woman who happened to cross Ibn 'Arabi's path. *Al-tarjuman* in Arabic means "translator, interpreter (between two languages)," but it can also mean "biographer," someone who understands and "interprets" the life of somebody, the verb *tarjama* meaning both "to translate" as well as "to produce a biography." This is to say that the word "interpreter" in the title cannot be taken merely in the literal sense of someone who finds equivalences for words from one language in another language, but rather, must be understood in terms of what makes a good biographer: empathy, or erotic relatedness to the life being described. Thus, the *Tarjuman* is a description of the *life* of *ashwaq*, usually translated "desire." The Arabic word *ashwaq* implies loving passionately, or falling passionately in love; in another verbal form with an active sense, it means "to fit something together tightly," as, for instance, in carpentry, when dovetailing two pieces of wood. In other words, the topic of the *Tarjuman al-Ashwaq* is the deep understanding, the empathic translation into language of what is in the deepest possible sense the living and lived experience of being passionately—we could say "madly"—in love. The usual translation, "The Interpreter of Desires,"—a translation we owe to Reynold A. Nicholson,[1] who, in 1911, was still influenced by the Victorian Era—does not adequately convey the intensity, the overflowing eroticism expressed in the poems.

Ibn 'Arabi had indeed fallen passionately in love, in 1202, with a girl named *Nizam* ("harmony"), daughter of Sheikh Abu Shuja Zahir bin Rustem, one of his teachers, who had made him the precious gift of a collection of *hadiths* ("sayings of the Prophet") that were for him as yet unknown. Ibn 'Arabi's first meeting with her establishes right from the start the main message of the *Tarjuman*, on which we will try to expand, namely, that erotic life *is* spiritual life. He describes this first meeting with her in Mecca one day:

> … [A]s I was circumambulating the Ka'aba [the black structure, containing a black stone, in the center of the Great Mosque] suddenly a few lines [of verse] came to my mind and I recited them loudly:
>
> "I would that I were aware whether they knew what heart they possessed!
>
> And I would that my heart knew what mountain-pass they threaded!
>
> Do you deem them safe or do you deem them dead?
>
> Lovers lose their way in love and become entangled."
>
> No sooner had I recited these verses than I felt on my shoulder the touch of a hand softer than silk. I turned around and found myself in the presence of a young girl, a princess among the daughters of the Greeks. Never had I seen a woman more beautiful of face and body, softer of speech, more tender of heart, more spiritual in her ideas, more subtle in her symbolic allusions. … She said: "How, my lord, can you say, 'I would that I were aware whether they knew what heart they possessed?' I am amazed to hear such a thing from you, you who are the wise man of our time! Is not everything that is possessed already known? How can one speak of possession except after knowledge?"[2] (Explanatory comments added.)

And later, they meet again at Nizam's father's house, and Ibn 'Arabi recalls this meeting as follows:

> The sheikh had a daughter, a soft and slender girl of virginal purity, who captivated the gaze of all who saw her, whose presence was an ornament to our gatherings, giving pleasure to all present, bewildering all who contemplated her.[3]

We see that the first meeting, which led to real passion, also brought spiritual insight in the form of the girl's reply to Al 'Arabi's spontaneous utterances. She says, "Is not everything that is possessed already known?" With this, she is telling him that possession, this existential, real life-experience, *is* knowledge. In other words, real knowledge of life is not some kind of second step, the first one being simply to exist. This insight is the main feature of Ibn 'Arabi's evocation in the *Tarjuman* of his falling in love; it means—and we shall see this now more precisely by examining one poem—that the very *experience* of love implies *full* knowledge of it. And what this *full* knowledge implies, we shall see as well. So much we can already say here about Ibn 'Arabi's contribution to the general topic: the very phrase "uncertainties of the heart" implies a nostalgia for some certainty—a quest that could well be the motivation behind clinical psychological discourse and its hope to be scientific, a quest to which Ibn 'Arabi will react with the insight given to him by Nizam: Those uncertainties are in themselves the answer to your quest for certainty. There is no firmer ground beyond the uncertainties than the uncertainties themselves.

Why is it so? We will try to venture an answer by looking briefly at one of the poems of the *Tarjuman*. Before we do that, however, I want to emphasize that *all* of the poems—written some ten years after the first meeting—are love-poems expressing Ibn 'Arabi's passion for the girl. He writes:

> ... I have put into verse for her sake some of the longing thoughts suggested by those precious memories [of meeting her], and I have uttered the sentiments of a yearning soul ..., fixing my mind on the bygone days and those scenes which her society has endeared to me. ... Whenever I mention a name in this book I always allude to her, and whenever I mourn over an abode I mean her abode.[4]

Ibn 'Arabi himself designates the style of the poems: *erotic*. The Arabic word for this poetic form, *ghazal*, is derived from the verb *ghazala*, which means "to court, to make love," but whose basic meaning is "to spin." That is to say, Ibn 'Arabi experienced in his love for Nizam the very entanglement of being caught in the psychic and concrete web of being in love. Thus, while Ibn 'Arabi comments on the poems in highly spiritual terms, he actually poured out—and this is THE point—his heart and guts when he was writing them.

Yes, after the first publication of the poems, Ibn 'Arabi was forced to write a commentary on each one. The fact is that the poems initially raised questions among some scholars (in Aleppo) regarding whether those verses were the fruit of divine secrets. In answer, he wrote a commentary, in which—as it had appeared already in the meaningful exchange he had had with Nizam at their first meeting—he was inspired by "... divine knowledge and spiritual mysteries and intellectual sciences and religious exhortations."[5] He explained, "I have used the erotic style and form of expression because men's souls are enamoured of it ...."[6] In other words, it could be—and we will now try to substantiate this hypothesis—that according to Ibn 'Arabi the simple experience of being in love—or being touched, through poems for instance, by someone else's love-experience—is a way to spiritual knowledge, or, as we would say today, to higher levels of consciousness.

## Poem 11 of the *Tarjuman*

To be frank, I chose Poem 11 from among the 61 in the *Tarjuman* more or less at random, knowing that we would be able only to scratch the surface of such a complex and rich work—not to mention Ibn 'Arabi's experience of reality as a whole. I have translated Poem 11, based largely on the classic translation done by Nicholson in 1911, which I have modified slightly and into which I have incorporated parts of the French translation of 1996 by Maurice Gloton.[7] I will first read the whole poem and then we shall analyse it verse by verse.

1. O doves that haunt the arak and ban trees, have pity! Do not double my woes by your lamentation!
2. Have pity! Do not reveal, by wailing and weeping, my hidden desires and my secret sorrows!
3. I respond to her in the evening and in the morning with the plaintive cry of a longing man and the moan of an impassioned lover.
4. The spirits faced one another in the thicket of tamarisk trees and bent their branches towards me, and it (the bending) annihilated me;
5. And they [the spirits] brought me diverse sorts of tormenting desire and passion and untried affliction.
6. Who will give me sure promise of Jam' and al-Muhassab of Mina? Who of Dhat al-Athl? Who of Na'man?

7. These spirits encompass my heart moment after moment, for the sake of love and anguish, and kiss my pillars,
8. Even as the best of mankind [i.e., the Prophet] encompassed [i.e., circumambulated] the Ka'ba, which the evidence of Reason proclaims to be imperfect,
9. And kissed stones therein, although he was a prophet. And what is the rank of the Temple in comparison with the dignity of Man?
10. How often did they [feminine pronoun] vow and swear that they would not change, but one who is dyed with henna does not keep oaths.
11. And one of the most wonderful things is a veiled gazelle, who points with red fingertip and winks with eyelids,
12. A gazelle whose pasture is between the breast and the bowels. O marvel! a garden amidst fires!
13. My heart has become capable of every form: it is a pasture for gazelles and a monastery for Christian monks,
14. And a temple for idols and the pilgrim's Ka'ba and the tables of the Torah and the book of the Koran.
15. I follow the religion of Love: whatever way Love's camels take me, that is my religion and my faith.
16. We have examples in Bishr, the lover of Hind and her sister, and in Qays and Lubna and in Mayya and Ghaylan.[8]

Let us take this verse by verse. My commentary will be in the spirit of dream interpretation, employing free association in response to the text and the commentary on it by Ibn 'Arabi.

1. O doves that haunt the arak and ban trees, have pity! Do not double my woes by your lamentation!

Right away, the "doves" point to the spiritual experience that forms the core of passionate love, since they are images of "inspiration." They dwell in "arak and ban trees," "whereof the wood is used as a tooth-stick[.] ... 'The use of the tooth-stick purifies the mouth and pleases the Lord', i.e. The Divine Ideas are dwelling in the abode of purity."[9] "Do not double my woes" means that erotic passion is a spiritual event. It has an ego-transcending quality, which gives it an intensity that can become almost unbearable. To illustrate this, Ibn 'Arabi at this point quotes the following *hadith* (*hadiths* = "sayings of the Prophet"): "Says Allah: Towards the one who approaches me a hand's breadth, I shall come an arm's length nearer; towards the one who approaches me an arm's length, I shall come the length of two arms nearer; and toward the one who approaches me walking, I shall come running."[10] In other words, Allah is present in erotic passion and from Him comes its intensity.

> 2. Have pity! Do not reveal, by wailing and weeping, my
> hidden desires and my secret sorrows!

The fact that falling in love is one of the deepest possible inner experiences is shown here through the intimate connection made between emotion and not expressing it, between intense psychic life and silence. In his commentary, Ibn 'Arabi links this silence with the very silence of death by quoting this *hadith*: "I [Allah speaking] hate to displease him [the believer] but he will meet me [in death] unavoidably."[11] Passion is an experience of unfathomable spiritual abysses.

> 3. I respond to her in the evening and in the morning with
> the plaintive cry of a longing man, the moan of an
> impassioned lover.

In this helpless but passionate moaning appears the necessity to surrender to Allah. (The word "Islam" means "submission" and implies total surrender to God.) Ibn 'Arabi's comment on this verse:

> ... God said to the soul when He created her, "Who am I?" and she answered, "Who am I?" referring to her own qualities, whereupon God caused her to dwell for four thousand years in the sea of despair and indigence and abasement until she said to Him, "Thou art my Lord."

Here we see explicitly a main feature of Ibn 'Arabi's characterization of erotic passion: it is theophanic, an experience of the Divine, a surrender of ego-wishes made necessary and unavoidable by the fact that the intensity of passion in its very essence makes concrete fulfilment impossible. What one calls frustration in love—we as psychologists would see in it infantile desires—Ibn 'Arabi sees as a *necessary* feature, because it leads to surrender, to a softening of the intensity of the ego-wishes constellated in passion. And this giving up is for Ibn 'Arabi by itself a theological idea. Being in love is knowledge of God.

> 4. The spirits faced one another in the thicket of tamarisk
> trees and bent their branches towards me, and it (this
> bending) annihilated me.
> 5. And they brought me diverse sorts of tormenting desire
> and passion and untried affliction.

In these verses we see more precisely that it is indeed the erotic *fire* that is the *spiritual* reality: the "spirits" are among "tamarisk" trees, which in Arabic lyrics often evoke fire because they are highly flammable. Their "branches"—the concrete erotic burning—have an "annihilating" quality (for the lover's ego). Ibn 'Arabi comments, "[Love is] my disappearance so that He [Allah] may be by Himself and not with me, in such a way [note this!] that there remains in the soul [of the lover] only his Beloved One [Allah]."[12] In other words, erotic passion, rather than being spiritualized in the Western way (the *eros/agapé* split), is envisaged by Ibn 'Arabi as being an ego-transcending experience; its very fire is an opening to the Unknown. Conscious suffering in the form of "diverse sorts of tormenting desire and passion and untried affliction" (v. 5) is part of this experience. Keeping in mind that the Arabic word *hawa'* means both "passion," and "air," "space," we can understand why Ibn 'Arabi sees in these "diverse sorts of tormenting desire ..." an "opening up of the soul [to wider spaces]."[13]

> 6. Who will give me sure promise of Jam' and al-Muhassab
> of Mina? Who of Dhat al-Athl? Who of Na'man?

The place names mentioned here are associated with the Hajj, the pilgrimage to Mecca, which in Islam is a central symbol of life and death. For reasons too complicated to explain here, Ibn 'Arabi in his commentary on this verse associates *Jam'* with proximity, *al-Muhassab* with distance, *Dhat al-Athl* with structures and principles, and *Na'man* with divine gifts and blessings. So this verse about proximity, distance, principles, and blessings in love can be seen as a paraphrase of our general topic here in Beatenberg: *Venturing the Uncertainties of the Heart.* It expresses the *ontological* uncertainty—this verse is a series of questions!—of erotic relationships because such relationships are an inseparable mix of proximity, distance, and the given psychic structures of the partners involved. All of this is a blessing (of individuation?) in that it is *one* dialectical movement of and in between souls. It is an experience of the Divine, an opening to the unfathomable depths of one's psyche. The next verses will shed more light on this last point.

> 7. They [the spirits] encompass my heart moment after
> moment for the sake of love and anguish, and kiss
> my pillars,
> 8. As the best of mankind [the Prophet] encompassed the
> Ka'ba, which the evidence of Reason proclaims to be
> imperfect,

> 9. And kissed stones therein, although he was a prophet. And what is the status of the Temple in comparison with the dignity of Man?

The spiritual experience (cf.: "they," i.e., the spirits) that constitutes love and its *anguish* puts the lover in intimate touch ("kissing") with the *pillars,* which may well be an image of the basic structures of the lover's being. The reference to the *Ka'ba* (v. 8), a central symbol in Islam, would then indicate that those basic structures—the Self, Jung would have said—are an opening to and a reflection from the Beyond. *The Temple's* being of lesser "status" than "the dignity of Man" refers to the insight that any psychological, theological, or other structure is in a very radical way of secondary importance in comparison with the importance of Man. Here Ibn 'Arabi is alluding to what he elsewhere calls the "Great Man," (*insan kamil*) a term used to designate the mystery of the individuality of each person—again very close to Jung's Self.

That all this is no New-Age experience of peace and love but may involve loss and betrayal is illustrated in the following verses:

> 10. How often did they vow and swear that they would not change, but one who is dyed with henna does not keep oaths.
> 11. And one of the most wonderful things is a veiled gazelle [young woman], who points with red fingertip and winks with eyelids,
> 12. A gazelle whose pasture is between the breast and the bowels. O marvel! a garden amidst fires!

When love-passion is constellated with all its seductions ("henna," a plant dye used as a cosmetic, "points with red fingertip and winks with eyelids"), uncertainty, even outright betrayal ("does not keep oaths"), is a necessary aspect of the opening of the soul to its depths. As Ibn 'Arabi puts it in his commentary on this verse: "[The women using henna, etc.] are the psychic inspirations that reach the soul. At that very moment God asks her, 'Am I not your Lord?'"[14] How can Ibn 'Arabi associate unfaithfulness (not keeping oaths) with inspiration, with the recognition of the Mystery (God) in love? Because, as we have seen, the answer to the uncertainty of the heart—where betrayal has its roots—can come only from uncertainty itself, an uncertainty that reflects the unfathomable mystery of the divine. But in view of this totally unsatisfactory answer for the ego, "nobody can avoid," as Ibn 'Arabi points out, "an idolatric reaction [*shirq* 'to associate other realities' with

God] because everyone when being in love says to himself: 'I am experiencing this!'"

In other words, the ego-trip that characterizes the subjective experience of being in love is necessary and no sin, because it is the natural reaction to this unbearable uncertainty that belongs to the reality of love. Egoic reactions and their projections belong fully in the dialectics of love as a path of individuation. Hence the "veil" in the following verse: "One of the most wonderful things is a veiled gazelle who points with red fingertips and winks with eyelids." The "veil" is an image of this paradox: never do I feel more myself and less myself at the same time than when I am in love—a paradox that for Ibn 'Arabi points to the mystery of divine subtleties which cannot be explained.[15] All this takes place "between the breast and the bowels," i.e., in the heart, "a garden amidst fires!" That is to say, in the very "fire" of passion is a "garden," which for Ibn 'Arabi, as for Islamic spirituality more generally, is an image of being with God, but here in a very precise sense, as Ibn 'Arabi puts it, the fire of love cannot destroy knowledge (this includes knowledge of God) because it—the fire of love—produces this knowledge.[16] In other words, we have here another way of expressing what we have seen earlier as being the main beam of light with which Ibn 'Arabi illuminates our perception of love: the very fire of passion generates a knowing that we would call consciousness.

And thus we come naturally to these well-known verses, often quoted when one wishes to evoke Ibn 'Arabi's spirituality (a somewhat hollow concept when speaking of someone who has had visions); we come to them naturally, because when, as we have seen so far, the dialectical quality of erotic passion is experienced and acknowledged—between abandonment, absurdity, and fulfilment, between despair and joy, between cold and heat—we are led naturally to the quality of consciousness evoked in these verses:

> 13. My heart has become capable of every form: it is a pasture for the gazelles and a monastery for Christian monks,
> 14. And a Temple for idols and the pilgrim's Ka'ba and the tables of the Torah and the book of the Koran.

The heart (*khalb*), Ibn 'Arabi in his commentary quotes another writer as saying, get its name (in Arabic) from the fact that it is always changing (*khalaba*, i.e., to change, to turn things upside down). The heart, says Ibn 'Arabi, "varies according to the various influences by which it is affected ...; and [note this!] the variety of its feelings is due to the variety of the Divine manifestations that appear in its innermost interiority."[17] In other words, the "uncertainties of the heart" are characterized as being the natural psychic condition in love because ultimately they are an essential feature of the heart as organ reflecting the fluidity of the Divine. And so these verses evoke the paradoxical, surrealistic, unbearable (from the point of view of ego's need for stability and simplicity) and thus divine iridescent being of the heart ("a pasture for gazelles"), the field of all erotic moves and attractions ("a monastery"). What happens in the heart is a solitary (i.e., radically individual) way of experiencing love. There never were nor ever will be two identical love experiences. In erotic passion, one is enraptured by concrete realities, desires, and projections ("a temple for idols"). And now comes the good news: this loving heart, in its uniqueness and individuality—in its individual way crisscrossed by manifold desires and fears, obsessed with concrete commitments and/or concrete scoring—is ... the Ka'ba. This means that through all this, the heart is the organ of relating to Allah, of Allah relating to man. Ibn 'Arabi recalls here in his commentary the following verse from the Koran, "Those who turn to God when demons haunt them ... remember Him and wake up to Him."[18] Such is indeed the dialectical life of the heart: dissociation is fully part of the Ka'ba symbol of the One and His Unity as He mirrors Himself in the human heart. Thus the heart can also be the place of the Torah, i.e., of basic individual structuring of the psyche, and of the Koran, i.e., the place of revelatory experiences; when one is in love, a lot is revealed, new, dis-covered!

Verse 15, consistent with this dialectical quality of love, dialectical to the point of being an expression of the divine Fluidity itself, puts into explicit wording this permanent state of being on the trail, and the hardship this implies:

> 15. I follow the religion of Love: whatever way Love's
> camels take me, that is my religion and my faith.

The Arabic word *deen*, which is here translated as "religion" is thought to be a cognate of the word *dayn*, which means "debt," "liability," "obligation," "obedience," and even "death" (as the ultimate debt that everyone must pay). In other words, love as religion is for Ibn 'Arabi primarily a basic, structural, objective necessity—and not a moralistic stance involving some conscious act of the will (i.e., love as an ethical requirement). Often it is experienced as a burden ("love's camels"), whose path one cannot but follow. Love is also "faith" (*iman*)—let's not forget, we are still in the context of Ibn Arabi's passion for Nizam—and the use of this word in this verse calls to mind Islam's confession of faith, the *shahada*: There is no god but God and Muhammad is His Messenger. This is enough to indicate how much this verse emphasizes, as we have already noted, the fact that in Ibn 'Arabi's experience the spontaneous and powerful surge of love as it appears in erotic passion is an experience of (ego-)transcending Reality. Existentially this means that my perception of myself and of my place in life is shaken, transcended by my being in love. Ibn 'Arabi's commentary says: "No religion is more sublime than a religion based on love and longing for Him [Allah] whom I worship and in whom I have faith."[19] In commenting upon erotic love in such a theological way, he does not hesitate to see in erotic passion a way of experiencing the aspiration of the soul towards God.

And just so that the reader does not slip, after that, into some unerotic, spiritualistic interpretation of love, the last verse of the poem recalls some great lovers and love stories well known in the Arabic world of that time:

> 16. We have examples in Bishr, the lover of Hind and her sister, and in Qays and Lubna and in Mayya and Ghaylan.

You probably noticed that the lover Bishr referred to here is in love with two sisters—there is no normativity in matters of the heart.

## Conclusion

It is time to sum up the main impressions about love that we have received from this cursory reading of Poem 11 from the *Tarjuman*. For Ibn 'Arabi, passion for a literal beloved has by itself a spiritual quality, since the very experience of it puts ego-consciousness in touch with its inherent limitations, or, if you wish, affords us a glimpse of the Beyond. The state of being possessed by love, as Nizam told her lover (or as the anima says to the ego), is thus in itself knowledge, or if you like, consciousness. Regardless of whether in concrete terms the relationship is happy or not, the unfulfilled longing of love has a theological dimension in the sense that this longing entails the necessity of surrendering to the paradoxical essence of being in love. Thus, the ego of the lover is both annihilated and at the same time opened up by his or her passion, a dialectical quality of being alive, which, expressed more concretely, appears, as the poem illustrates, in the inner tension between despair and joy, absolute aloneness and total fusion, or even in confusion with the loved one—various extremes that cannot be integrated by the will. Any conscious effort in this field is for Ibn 'Arabi utterly impossible, because, as we saw, this dialectical, often painful fluidity, this "uncertainty of the heart," this possession—which is knowledge—is by itself an expression of the Divine. The perfect image of this surrender taking place in love as it points—whether the lover is conscious of it or not—beyond itself is, in Ibn Arabi's view, the Ka'ba, the central symbol of Islam (literally, "surrender")—central because all mosques are oriented to face in its direction and the lives of all Muslims are directed towards one overriding goal, the Hajj, that is, the pilgrimage to Mecca, the main feature of which is the circumambulation of the Ka'ba. The Ka'ba, a light provisional structure housing simply a black stone (possibly a meteorite), is the perfect image of what is ultimately simple in the extreme complexity of love-life: its pointing beyond itself, its opening up to the Unknown. This uncertainty and openness is of course unbearable for our ego, which needs clear references and thus has to associate other realities with the ultimate Beyond (i.e., Allah) when we are in love. Those other realities Ibn 'Arabi calls idols; we would call them projections. But for Ibn 'Arabi "idolatry" (projection) *is also* a reality, which, like all realities, is also a reflection of the Beyond—and hence ultimately not a sin. And, *summa summarum*, all that constitutes passion is absolutely individual in the forms it takes, hence it is fully respectable, and no value judgments are possible, regardless of the circumstances—even if they are psychopathological—because it reflects Allah, who is behind every being, and most particularly behind the individuality of each human and his or her specific personal way of relating.

Before coming to some implications for our work with the psyche (our job as analysts!) of what has been said so far, let me touch briefly upon how Ibn 'Arabi's perception of erotic love as an experience of the Beyond is consistent with his perception of reality as such. In Ibn 'Arabi's reality, desire for the concrete world is instilled by God—and this desire is purposefully sustained by the fascinations of *ouadjad* (emotions such as ardent love, ecstasy, and upheaval), and through *oualah* (confusion and pain). As the enlightened ones comprehend, all such passions *contain* God—therefore to live them is to live the quest for the divine and to enter into divine hope and contemplation.

Ibn 'Arabi is fully justified in assuming this intimate connection between erotic passion and what we would call a metaphysical perception of life because at least three times in his life he had visionary experiences of what Sufism calls the "Oneness of all Reality" (*wahdat al-wujud*). This expression sums up Ibn 'Arabi's—and I would say the underlying Islamic—perception of reality. The only "real" reality is God. *Allah hu akbar* means not only "God is the greatest," but at the same time, "God is the most real Reality." And all realities as we know them—ourselves included—are real only because of God's reality. So the expression "Oneness of all Reality" refers to that which constitutes, which gives substance, existence to all things. All realities—and thus, of course, also the realities of the heart—are the One Reality, Allah. Thus, as we have seen, the *Tarjuman* with its emphasis on passion as knowledge, even knowledge of God, is not the product of philosophical speculation, but grows out of mystical experience. It can be seen as a symbolic expression of Ibn 'Arabi's whole life-experience and of his hermeneutics, which is informed by an erotic rather than a rational-technological epistemology. Ibn 'Arabi's experience of the passion of love is in fact love for Allah, and, at the same time, a manifestation of God, since for Ibn 'Arabi, "all phenomena go back to the divine self-disclosures."[20]

In other words, for Ibn 'Arabi, "[t]he gnostics [we would say, "conscious people"] look with both eyes, and they perceive *wujud* [reality] as both absent, because it is none other than the Divine Essence, and present, because it is none other than God's self-disclosure as the selfhood of the knower."[21] To expand on this would take much more time than we have at our disposal, but we get a glimpse of the basic reason why for Ibn 'Arabi erotic life is in itself knowledge, without needing any other understanding added to it. As such it is a symbol (in Jung's sense of that which makes a living connection) of the One Reality, Allah, with whom no reality fantasized as really real can be associated, not even science.

Let us conclude with some questions that Ibn Arabi's perspective on love poses to our Western psychoanalytical thinking. I shall simply formulate the questions without daring to offer any answers.

a. Could it be that our Western psychologized love-relationship, based on the psychological needs of the individual (the need for less suffering and more self-development, happiness, meaningfulness, etc.), is blind to the objectivity of the erotic life that is revealed in those needs (but is not identical with them)—an objectivity that could shed light on the fundamental relativity of those needs?

b. What is the symbolic meaning of our criteria for determining what in loving is normal, pathological, and in between? Could it be that those criteria are expressions of anxiety in the face of the Unknown because to surrender to erotic life *as it really is, that is, in radically individual forms,* is felt to be dangerous? Could the importance given in psychology to these criteria overshadow the fact that all features of an individual psyche, including the so-called pathological ones, are *fully* part of this god-given individuality and its *specific* path to individuation?

c. For Ibn 'Arabi, as we have seen, the main insight that came from his meeting with Nizam is that the very experience of love, whatever its individual form, is knowledge, is an extension of individual consciousness, and that to live its reality—whatever the concrete shape of this experience—is an endless opening towards its unfathomable mystery. So my question is: Is the psychoanalytical mythologizing of a hidden unconscious that is distinct from consciousness not paradoxically a form of metaphysical thinking, looking for truths, real personality, etc. *behind* what is simply given by the reality of what is experienced?

d. Jung was aware of these questions, especially in the latter part of his life. He writes, for instance: "The real mystery of life is always hidden when there is love between two persons; this is the real Mystery that cannot be described in words nor exhausted through discussions."[22] But how can we interpret the dream that Jung had in Tunis in his younger days?[23] By his own admission, he was deeply impressed by the Islamic aura of the place. (You will recall from our biographical sketch at the beginning that Ibn 'Arabi spent some time in Tunis.) In the dream, Jung is pleased with himself for being able to subdue and compel a young Arab prince to read his (Jung's) "Manichean" book. Could it be that this Arab prince is an image of total surrender to the Reality of life and love? Was the "Manichean" (black-and-white) book that Jung forced upon the Arab an image of Jung's Western consciousness and its need for criteria and the value judgments they entail?

These are some questions to keep in mind as we "venture the uncertainties of the heart" in our analytic practice.

---

## *NOTES*

[1] Muhyi'ddin Ibn 'Arabi, *The Tarjuman al-Ashwaq: A Collection of Mystical Odes*, trans. Reynold A. Nicholson (London: Royal Asiatic Society, 1911), hereafter referred to as Nicholson.

[2] Stephen Hirtenstein, *The Unlimited Mercifier: The Spiritual Life and Thought of Ibn 'Arabi* (Oxford: Anqa Publishing, 1999), pp. 148-149.

[3] *Ibid.*

[4] Nicholson, pp. 3-4. When not otherwise noted, the translations of commentaries and "Poem 11" from here to the end are based on Nicholson, and freely incorporate my own translations from the origi-

nal Arabic. I also freely incorporate my translations of Gloton's French in *L'Interprête des Désirs*.

[5] Nicholson, Preface to the First Recension, p. 4.

[6] *Ibid.*

[7] Maurice Gloton, *L'Interprête des Désirs* (Paris: Albin Michel, 1996), pp. 118-127, my translation.

[8] Nicholson, pp. 66-67, translation modified.

[9] *Ibid.*, p. 60.

[10] Gloton, p. 25, my tranlation.

[11] *Ibid.*, p. 119, my translation.

[12] *Ibid.*, p. 120, my translation.

[13] *Ibid.*

[14] The Koran 7:172, quoted in Gloton, p. 122, my translation.

[15] My paraphrase of Ibn 'Arabi's commentary on verse 11.

[16] My paraphrase of Ibn 'Arabi's commentary on verse 12.

[17] Nicholson, p. 69, translation modified.

[18] The Koran 7:201, quoted in Gloton, p. 125, my translation.

[19] Nicholson, p. 69.

[20] William C. Chittick, *Ibn 'Arabi: Heir to the Prophets* (Oxford, UK: Oneworld Publications, 2005), p. 33.

[21] *Ibid.*, p. 37.

[22] C. G. Jung, "Letter to the Mother Prioress of the Contemplative Order, England, 12/8/1960," in *Briefe 3, 1956-1961* (Olten: Walter-Verlag, 1973), p. 328, my translation.

[23] C. G. Jung, *Memories, Dreams, Reflections*, ed. Aniela Jaffé, trans. Richard Winston & Clara Winston (New York: Vintage Books, 1989 [1961]), p. 242.

# Epilogue

*John Hill*

## An Archetypal Journey of the Soul

Odyssey, as we imagine it here, draws on the mythic image of Odysseus on his epic journey. It points to a voyage or quest that is undertaken in the wake of intense conflict—a war, if you will—and loss of home, a quest fraught with encounters with obstacles, dangers, and disorientation. In Jungian terms, we would speak of an archetypal journey of the soul, an individuation journey, in which one is confronted with the dangers and challenges, as well as the creative resources of the unconscious. Indeed, to attend the Jungian Odyssey may be to embark on such a journey, as many who have already done so well know. What many may not know is that the Jungian Odyssey itself is part of a larger odyssey, which was undertaken in the context of analytical training in Zürich.

Historically, training in Zürich had stood as a beacon throughout the world, and had thrived as such for several decades after Jung's death. The Zürich training program was in this sense the home of analytical psychology, and its flowering was well represented in the works of such analysts as Marie-Louise von Franz, Aniela Jaffé, Toni Frey, Jolanda Jacobi, and later, in the likes of James Hillman, Adolf Guggenbühl-Craig, Verena Kast, Kathrin Asper, Mario Jacoby, Helmut Barz, and Murray Stein. In the 1980s and early 90s, the Zürich training program experienced a boom, at one point serving nearly four hundred students.

However, by the mid-90s, clouds had begun to gather over this haven and storms were brewing. All around the world, long-term analysis came under fire for its alleged inefficiency, uneconomical procedures, and non-scientific basis—even its cultishness. By 1996, Swiss health authorities had jumped on the bandwagon, introducing revisions in the law that would have a potentially negative impact on traditional Jungian analysis, psychotherapy, and analytic training. Analysts were concerned that the interdisciplinary approach would be overshadowed as a result of the new requirement for both trainees and practitioners to hold an advanced degree in academic psychology. They further worried that soul life and its purposeful, creative suffering would be eclipsed by the focus on psychopathology, diagnosis, and the economical provision of treatment.

At first, the Zürich community weathered the storm with confidence. A research project—"The Practical Study of Long-Term Analytical Therapy" ("Praxisstudie Analytische Langzeittherapie"), or the PAL Study for short—was launched under the leadership of Dr. Guido Mattanza of the C. G. Jung Institute, Zürich, in conjunction with Professor Gerd Rudolf of the University of Heidelberg.[1] Using an empirical methodology, and enlisting the cooperation of several Jungian analysts, the PAL Study confirmed the effectiveness and efficacy of long-term Jungian psychotherapy. Early in 2003, Jungians and non-Jungians alike acclaimed the study at a festive event held at the Zürich University Psychiatric Clinic—otherwise known as "Burgholzli," where Jung achieved an international reputation at the beginning of the 20th century.

Despite this positive development, the turbulence persisted. Insurance companies had already begun to place severe restrictions on payments for psychotherapy. The government intervened continually to tighten the regulation of training and practice. This state of affairs led to internal tensions among colleagues in the training program and beyond. To go into the details here would exceed our present purpose. Suffice it to say that the old beacon of Zürich seemed to dim. Many analysts and students felt that their home was endangered. If the Zürich odyssey began with the many changes of the mid-90s, then the archetype was now in our midst and we felt the full impact of its disruptive force.

Bearing in mind the dangers of archetypal identification, let us turn to the old stories, in which we may detect parallels that stimulate closer contemplation of the situation from a mythic perspective. In the *Iliad*, the Greeks, robbed of their beautiful Helen, assemble as a band of jealous and vengeful captains. Under the leadership of Agamemnon, who has no compunctions about sacrificing his daughter, Iphigenia, they eventually set sail for Troy. Despite victory, the Greeks are subsequently subjected to continual humiliation. The gods force their will on Achilles in order that the Greek soul should appreciate the value of moderation; Agamemnon's cruelty is avenged; Poseidon, the earth-shaker, drives the artful Odysseus into exile, and, subjecting him to a variety of indignities, prevents his return home to Ithaca for ten years.

It is probably fair to say that such a mythic theme captures some of the dynamics and tensions of an uncertain future that were experienced by many, if not all, of the Jungians involved, irrespective of their affiliation. The myth suggests that division and loss of such great magnitude come with the equally powerful forces of shadow, suffering of soul, and winds of change. To feel overcome by such forces means to be subject to psychological death, and hopefully also to transformation. The search for Ithaca begins, whatever our Ithaca may finally turn out to be.

## Resetting the Course

Four years later, we all seem to have survived the archetypal processes and are all still sailing—even if on different courses, each of which suggests a continuation of the odyssey and the potential for the individuation of the collective. For its own existence, ISAPZURICH is indebted to the Association of Graduate Analytical Psychologists (AGAP), whose members worldwide had cast a safety net by approving the establishment of the school in 2004. Thus, AGAP became the mother ship under whose authority and compass ISAP conducts training. ISAP in turn embodies a spirit of renewal in one of the world's oldest professional Jungian societies—for AGAP, domiciled in Zürich, was founded in 1954 by Mary Briner, a first-generation graduate of the C. G. Jung Institute Zürich. AGAP itself is a founding member and the largest member society of the International Association for Analytical Psychology (IAAP), which in 1955 became the umbrella organization for professional Jungian societies throughout the world.

Now, ISAP's founding resulted largely from a collective and unrelenting need to regain, live, and safeguard the Jungian values that had once held the Zürich community together. Following the Homeric myth, it may well be said that those affiliated with ISAP are involved in a search for Ithaca, the original home. Whatever the goal, the idea of an odyssey implies a readiness for the unexpected as well as attunement to the dangers and the depth of meaning inherent in the process. In keeping with the myth, ISAP has faced the unexpected and will continue to do so.

## A New Point of Departure

The coming into being of the Jungian Odyssey itself is a further example of how a perilous voyage can give rise to creative impulse and renewal. At one of the first meetings of ISAP analysts, it was decided that a summer conference would be incorporated into the regular training program. This would serve not only to open ISAP's training to outsiders, but equally, to provide a point of departure for the intensive exploration of Jungian ideas. At the same time, we felt compelled to expand our horizons, to free ourselves from the assumptions and protocols that had, in the past, governed the nature of the summer intensive. It was John Hill who brought up the idea of a nomadic retreat. This would be a week-long, off-campus event, to take place each year in a different locale in Switzerland. Especially inspiring was the aim to link with nature and tap into the *genius loci*—the spirit of the place, or places—that vitally influenced Jung's thought and its development. In a short time, John's idea caught the attention of his colleagues; Cedrus Monte volunteered to steer the project, and the Jungian Odyssey was born.

Thanks to the good faith and enormous labor of ISAP's analysts, students, and staff—too many to name here—the Jungian Odyssey quickly evolved from a raw and risky project into an adventure from which there would be no return. The generally positive feedback suggests that participants from all around the world deeply value the Odyssey's rich program of lectures, seminars, and workshops, conducted in venues embedded in the awe-inspiring landscapes of Switzerland.

## Navigating the Ports: Jungian Odyssey 2006-08

If the initial idea of the Jungian Odyssey provided a new point of departure for exploring Jung, its evolution suggests a continuing journey from port to port. For the first Jungian Odyssey, in 2006, we traveled to Flueli-Ranft, a tiny village located in the very heart of Switzerland. With beginner's zeal (and confusion), we had programmed this event to cover two overarching and related themes: "Jungian Psychology Today: Tradition and Innovations" and "The Quest for Vision in a Troubled World: Exploring the Healing Dimensions of Religious Experience." These were inspired in part by Flueli-Ranft's vertical landscape (one can only look up or down!), which is possessed of extraordinary spirit and beauty.

Not least, we took our cue from Niklaus von Flue (1417-1487), otherwise known as Brother Klaus, Switzerland's patron saint. Both C. G.

Jung and Marie-Louise von Franz were moved to write about the life and visions of this extraordinary man. Brother Klaus left his wife and children to live, for twenty years, in a small hermitage in a deep gorge in Flueli-Ranft, near his family home. Brother Klaus was regarded as a living saint by his contemporaries, having performed many miracles and not eaten any food for twenty years. By a miraculous intervention, he pulled the young Swiss confederacy back from the brink of war. During the Odyssey, we descended to Brother Klaus's hermitage to partake in a world of silence, interrupted only by birdsong and the babbling of the nearby creek. This was one aspect of the overarching themes that developed to address the task of living in two worlds at the same time, the visible and the invisible, the world of discourse and the world of silence. Our two distinguished guests were David Tacey (Australia) and Mark Patrick Hederman (Ireland).

The venue for Odyssey 2007 was the Hotel Rotschuo in the village of Gersau, exquisitely situated on the shores of Lake Lucerne and surrounded by a lush, enchanting garden. Now less ambitious in our aims, we had decided on the theme, "Exploring the Other Side: The Reality of Soul in a World of Prescribed Meanings." This, again, was inspired by the place—first by the enormous, glimmering lake and distant shores—and then by a certain mountain meadow lying opposite Gersau, namely, the famous Rütli meadow. According to legend, it is here that Wilhelm Tell defied the foreign oppressors—and here was signed the 1291 pact that united the first three cantons and laid the foundations for the future Swiss Confederation.

It is little wonder that the region lured visionaries such as Friedrich Nietzsche, Richard Wagner, James Joyce—and C. G. Jung himself, who wrote of his transforming boyhood experience here. Developments of the theme included a focus on prescriptive rules, revolt, hidden meanings, and the discovery of private myth—all urging those present to explore alternate ways of being. James Hollis (U.S.A.), the keynote speaker, and Christopher Bamford (U.S.A.) joined us as special guests.

As we navigated each Jungian Odyssey, we were impressed by the high quality of the papers, which focused on themes that are of great concern for our times. Following the Odyssey in Beatenberg, we took a decision in favor of the scribes. It was time to collect the papers and make them available to those who could not participate in the form of a book. We hope this book will serve as an inspiration for your own personal odyssey. May it prove to be a helpful companion in all the trials and tribulations you face as you venture the uncertainties of the heart.

## *NOTES*

[1] Guido Mattanza, Isabelle Meier, and Mario Schlegel, eds., *Seele und Forschung: Ein Brückenschlag in der Psychotherapie* (Freiburg: Karger-Verlag, 2006).

# Spring Journal Books

The book publishing imprint of *Spring Journal*, the oldest Jungian psychology journal in the world

## STUDIES IN ARCHETYPAL PSYCHOLOGY SERIES

Series Editor: Greg Mogenson

*Collected English Papers*, Wolfgang Giegerich
- Vol. 1: *The Neurosis of Psychology: Primary Papers Towards a Critical Psychology*, ISBN 978-1-882670-42-6, 284 pp., $20.00
- Vol. 2: *Technology and the Soul: From the Nuclear Bomb to the World Wide Web*, ISBN 978-1-882670-43-4, 356 pp., $25.00
- Vol. 3: *Soul-Violence* ISBN 978-1-882670-44-4
- Vol. 4: *The Soul Always Thinks* ISBN 978-1-882670-45-0

*Dialectics & Analytical Psychology: The El Capitan Canyon Seminar*, Wolfgang Giegerich, David L. Miller, and Greg Mogenson, ISBN 978-1-882670-92-2, 136 pp., $20.00

*Northern Gnosis: Thor, Baldr, and the Volsungs in the Thought of Freud and Jung*, Greg Mogenson, ISBN 978-1-882670-90-6, 140 pp., $20.00

*Raids on the Unthinkable: Freudian and Jungian Psychoanalyses*, Paul Kugler, ISBN 978-1-882670-91-4, 160 pp., $20.00

*The Essentials of Style: A Handbook for Seeing and Being Seen*, Benjamin Sells, ISBN 978-1-882670-68-X, 141 pp., $21.95

*The Wounded Researcher: A Depth Psychological Approach to Research*, Robert Romanyshyn, ISBN 978-1-882670-47-5, 360 pp., $24.95

*The Sunken Quest, the Wasted Fisher, the Pregnant Fish: Postmodern Reflections on Depth Psychology*, Ronald Schenk, ISBN 978-1-882670-48-5, $20.00

*Fire in the Stone: The Alchemy of Desire*, Stanton Marlan, ed., ISBN 978-1-882670-49-9, 176 pp., $22.95

*After Prophecy: Imagination, Incarnation, and the Unity of the Prophetic Tradition*, Tom Cheetham, ISBN 978-1-882670-81-9, 183 pp., $22.95

*Archetypal Psychologies: Reflections in Honor of James Hillman*, Stanton Marlan, ed., ISBN 978-1-882670-54-3, 526 pp. $32.95

## HONORING DAVID L. MILLER

*Disturbances in the Field: Essays in Honor of David L. Miller,* Christine Downing, ed., ISBN 978-1-882670-37-X, 318 pp., $23.95

---

## THE DAVID L. MILLER TRILOGY

*Three Faces of God: Traces of the Trinity in Literature and Life,* David L. Miller, ISBN 978-1-882670-94-9, 197 pp., $20.00

*Christs: Meditations on Archetypal Images in Christian Theology,* David L. Miller, ISBN 978-1-882670-93-0, 249 pp., $20.00

*Hells and Holy Ghosts: A Theopoetics of Christian Belief,* David L. Miller, ISBN 978-1-882670-99-3, 238 pp., $20.00

---

## THE ELECTRA SERIES

*Electra: Tracing a Feminine Myth through the Western Imagination,* Nancy Cater, ISBN 978-1-882670-98-1, 137 pp., $20.00

*Fathers' Daughters: Breaking the Ties That Bind,* Maureen Murdock, ISBN 978-1-882670-31-0, 258 pp., $20.00

*Daughters of Saturn: From Father's Daughter to Creative Woman,* Patricia Reis, ISBN 978-1-882670-32-9, 361 pp., $23.95

*Women's Mysteries: Twoard a Poetics of Gender,* Christine Downing, ISBN 978-1-882670-99-XX, 237 pp., $20.00

*Gods in Our Midst: Mythological Images of the Masculine—A Woman's View,* Christine Downing, ISBN 978-1-882670-28-0, 152 pp., $20.00

*Journey through Menopause: A Personal Rite of Passage,* Christine Downing, ISBN 978-1-882670-33-7, 172 pp., $20.00

*Psyche's Sisters: Reimagining the Meaning of Sisterhood,* Christine Downing, ISBN 978-1-882670-74-1, 177 pp., $20.00

*Portrait of the Blue Lady: The Character of Melancholy,* Lyn Cowan, ISBN 978-1-882670-96-5, 314 pp., $23.95

---

## MORE SPRING JOURNAL BOOKS

*Field, Form, and Fate: Patterns in Mind, Nature, and Psyche,* Michael Conforti, ISBN 978-1-882670-40-X, 181 pp., $20.00

*Dark Voices: The Genesis of Roy Hart Theatre,* Noah Pikes, ISBN 978-1-882670-19-1, 155 pp., $20.00

*The World Turned Inside Out: Henry Corbin and Islamic Mysticism,* Tom Cheetham, ISBN 978-1-882670-24-8, 210 pp., $20.00

*Teachers of Myth: Interviews on Educational and Psychological Uses of Myth with Adolescents,* Maren Tonder Hansen, ISBN 978-1-882670-89-2, 73 pp., $15.95

*Following the Reindeer Woman: Path of Peace and Harmony,* Linda Schierse Leonard, ISBN 978-1-882670-95-7, 229 pp., $20.00

*An Oedipus—The Untold Story: A Ghostly Mythodrama in One Act,* Armando Nascimento Rosa, ISBN 978-1-882670-38-8, 103 pp., $20.00

*The Dreaming Way: Dreamwork and Art for Remembering and Recovery,* Patricia Reis and Susan Snow, ISBN 978-1-882670-46-9, 174 pp. $24.95

*Living with Jung: "Enterviews" with Jungian Analysts, Volume 1,* Robert and Janis Henderson, ISBN 978-1-882670-35-3, 225 pp., $21.95.

*Living with Jung: "Enterviews" with Jungian Analysts, Volume 2,* Robert and Janis Henderson, ISBN 978-1-882670-72-7, 261 pp., $23.95.

*Terraspychology: Re-engaging the Soul of Place,* Craig Chalquist, ISBN 978-1-882670-65-5, 162 pp., $21.95.

*Psyche and the Sacred: Spirituality beyond Religion,* Lionel Corbet, ISBN 978-1-882670-34-5, 288 pp., $23.95.

*Brothers and Sisters: Discovering the Psychology of Companionship*, Lara Newton, ISBN 978-1-882670-70-1, 214 pp., $23.95.

*Evocations of Absence: Multidisciplinary Perspectives on Void States,* Paul W. Ashton, ed., ISBN 978-1-882670-75-8, 214 pp., $22.95.

*Clio's Circle: Entering The Imaginal World of Historians,* Ruth Meyer, ISBN 978-1-882670-70-3, 325 pp., $23.95.

*Sexuality and the Religious Imagination,* Bradley A. TePaske, ISBN 978-1-882670-51-2, 299 pp., $ 27.95

*Mortally Wounded: Stories of Soul Pain, Death, and Healing,* Michael Kearney, ISBN 978-1-882670-79-6, 157 pp., $19.95.